# Intellectual Property Rights
## Basic Concepts

# Intellectual Property Rights
## Basic Concepts

M.M.S. Karki

ATLANTIC
PUBLISHERS & DISTRIBUTORS (P) LTD

ATLANTIC
PUBLISHERS & DISTRIBUTORS (P) LTD

7/22, Ansari Road, Darya Ganj, New Delhi
Tel.: +91-11-4077 5252, 2327 3880
E-mail: orders@atlanticbooks.com
Web: www.atlanticbooks.com

Reprint 2024, 2026

Published by Atlantic Publishers & Distributors (P) Ltd.



Printed & bound in India by Atlantic Print Services

# PREFACE

From specialized areas of law and policy-making the subject of intellectual property (IP) has come to the forefront of global economic policy. In the knowledge economy intellectual property rights (IPRs) have assumed great importance in every sphere of human activity. In fact, intellectual property has become a central element in economic and cultural policy in a world in which the source of wealth is increasingly becoming intellectual, as opposed to physical capital and in which markets are distributed across the globe. To ensure a better and more prosperous future for mankind, it is important to increase awareness of scientific knowledge as well as the creative power of country's youth. Critical to this effort is instilling respect for intellectual property and recognizing it as a valuable tool for scientific, cultural and social progress. The importance of intellectual property as a policy tool to promote development has been a key feature of Dr. Idris' vision as Director General of the World Intellectual Property Organization since 1997. He has campaigned extensively to enhance among global leaders, awareness and understanding of intellectual property and its strategic importance in promoting economic, social and cultural development. Books like the present one would contribute to the realization of the Director General's vision.

However, the subject of intellectual property is at a nascent stage in India. The books available in the market are by and large meant for legal professionals. With the help of available material, which is quite limited in scope, it is difficult to attract the student community and the public at large towards this subject. It needs an entirely new approach for developing a strong sense of creation in the students, who are future inventors, innovators, and creators, and who will constantly strive to produce tangible goods from scientific ideas and human creativity. Need of the hour is to make available a reference guide which could help in unlocking young adults' true potential and foster inventive spirit in them. With this object in mind the present book has been written, which could be particularly useful to students as well as those, who nurture an interest in intellectual property. At present, our graduates coming out of engineering and technology streams have no idea about IPRs, yet it is these young people who will have to generate and exploit the intellectual property. The industries they are going to serve in future are the ones that are going to be extraordinarily careful about IPR issues. We will have to introduce key elements of IPRs in their courses. Even our law graduates will have to learn more and more about these new areas. There will be enormous demand for professionals who are able to handle intellectual property; it is a very specialized job. As society progresses towards an innovation-based economy, there are numerous benefits of exposing all sectors of the public to intellectual property concepts. Once the public at large starts respecting the body of intellectual property law, even the concept of intellectual property itself, it will develop a concrete understanding of the nature of intellectual property, and recognize the key roles it plays in economic, social and cultural development.

Starting with creativity, intellectual creations, value of creativity, innovation, and importance of protecting creative works, the book comes to the theme of intellectual property. IP and IPRs are discussed up to some length. Basics of all the important forms of IPRs are discussed in a simple style and easy-to-understand language giving examples of inventions and their protection (patent), naming inventions (trademarks), and shapes of the inventions (industrial designs). A separate chapter is devoted to the IP on Internet, keeping in mind its growing importance. The book however, does not include the legal professional information and may be called to contain pre-professional information on IPRs. It aims at providing knowledge of IP and will be useful in intellectual property education programmes of various governments. The information contained in this book is not meant to be a substitute for professional legal advice. Its main purpose is limited to providing basic information about the subject.

Students are more interested in books, drawings, songs, poems, screenplays, dance, films, art, photographs, computer, Internet, etc. Therefore, role of IPRs in the development of these fields is discussed. Negative role of piracy and plagiarism in the whole process of creativity is described. A Glossary explaining certain frequently used IPR related terms has been given. A list of important information sources has also been provided, besides an exhaustive Index.

The book should form an essential reading for people from all walks of life in general and interested academics, scientists, technocrats, policy-makers, government officials, legal professionals, entrepreneurs, industrialists, small and medium enterprises, and corporate decision-makers in particular. It may also serve as a textbook for students of management, engineering, and those pursuing various courses in IPRs.

Writing this book has proved very enjoyable and I hope the readers will garner some practical benefits from it.

Both for text and illustrations, I have taken ideas from many published information sources and websites and I wish to record my appreciation for the creative works of all those authors.

I thank Atlantic Publishers & Distributors (P) Ltd. for supporting the idea of writing this book and for extending invaluable editorial help.

Finally, I would like to express my gratitude and love I feel for my family members, who encouraged me to complete this book even at the cost of my time with them.

**M.M.S. Karki**

# CONTENTS

# 1

# CREATIVITY: ESSENCE OF OUR DEVELOPMENT

There are many definitions of creativity, but there is no one that everyone can agree with. It is a mental process involving the generation of new ideas or concepts, or new associations between existing ideas or concepts. Creativity is capacity to have new thoughts and to create new things, new expressions. It is about new ways of looking at problems. Creativity is the ability to generate novel and useful ideas and solutions to everyday problems and challenges. Creativity researchers usually claim that being creative means being novel and appropriate. From a scientific point of view, the products of creative thought are usually considered to have both originality and appropriateness. Everyday conception of creativity is that it is simply the act of making something new. Perhaps the most widespread conception of creativity in the scholarly literature is that creativity is manifested in the production of a creative work (for example, a new work of art or a scientific hypothesis) that is both novel and useful. Colloquial definitions of creativity are typically descriptive of activity that results in producing or bringing about something partly or wholly new; in investing an existing object with new properties or characteristics; in imagining new possibilities that were not conceived of before; and in seeing or performing something in a manner different from what was thought possible or normal previously. A simple definition of creativity is the action of combining previously uncombined elements. It consists largely of re-arranging what we know in order to find out what we do not know.

Creativity is such a wonderful thing that people in low and high places with high intellect or with average intelligence wonder how the fine artist puts depth into a flat surface, and how the author concentrates through time to create meaningful yarns to feed the minds, how long it takes the musicologist to settle for a serious tune. The chain goes on. Creativity is with us since childhood. The childhood is a time when kid's imagination has no limits. Creative children view the world as endless possibilities and adventure and can imagine their life as a dream of their future with no boundaries applied. Each child is a genius. We can observe his ingenuity vividly. He makes up new words, invents the machine with odds and end, around the house. He creates the drawings of strange worlds. The songs he creates at the spur of the moment. These are the manifestations of child's natural genius.

Creativity is fundamental for humankind to go forward. It ensures a better and more prosperous future for mankind. Recognizing and developing this limitless resource, and exploiting it as an economic asset, is key to achieving prosperity in today's world. Creativity of artists, scientists and others can transform our culture and the way we look at the world. It is a basic element in many human endeavours, such as art, music, literature, and performance.

It is the essence of our development, our past and our future. Our societies are based on creativity, and it is very hard to imagine living without it today. Our existence is powered by creativity, as is everything else in the universe. The world is what it is today because people have been creative. Creative works not only enrich us, they also collectively make up our national cultural heritage, an essential part of each nation's identity. The strength of our economy, our communities and the future of our state depend on arts and creativity. A nation's cultural heritage can help attract visitors to a country, bringing tourists for music or theater festivals, art exhibitions, museum or library collections, or other activities deriving from the creative resources of the population. Tourism is a good example of an industry that can be boosted by a nation's creative activity.

## ENJOYING THE PRODUCTS OF HUMAN CREATIVITY

The creations of human mind are with us every day of our lives. Our place of work or home is a place built and filled with the products of human creativity. From a hand-woven carpet to a sofa, from a clay pitcher to a cut-glass carafe, from the objects and appliances we use for everyday life—the can-opener, the refrigerator, the telephone—to the music, the books, the paintings and family photographs that make us smile; everything with which we live is the product of human creativity. No matter what we do, the fruits of human creativity surround us. Creativity permeates our daily lives from the moment we wake up in the morning to the time we retire in the evening. In this modern society, the creativity follows us throughout our day as we make our way to work, during our shopping sprees, at the groceries, and in the evenings as we catch the latest blockbuster movie at our favourite cinema hall. All of these products of creativity that surround us, nourish us as human beings. We learn new things. We appreciate art, we learn about different cultures.

For children, comics and cartoons are best examples of human creativity. At times we take these products of creativity for granted; we are at other times amazed. However, with these the daily chores have become easier and the varieties of entertainment and pleasure have increased. Inventions are one of the important forms of creativity. Creativity can move to innovation; creativity can power innovation; creativity can result in innovation. Throughout history, inventions have helped people discover new worlds, build communities, develop resources, increase productivity, cure diseases, ease burdens, and enjoy life to the fullest. For example, the desktop computer is a powerful tool for working, creating, and communicating. Perhaps no invention in the recent times has revolutionized our way of living or working as much as computer. The development of personal computer brought the computers into our homes. And with the growth of Internet and World Wide Web (www), interlinking computers and people, we are witnessing yet another dramatic revolution in the area of communication. Our work place is connected to our homes. Homes are connected to utility services like bank or super markets. It has made possible things like Internet banking or phone banking. A day is not far off when all these places will be networked. This will all be possible due to the fruits of human inventions. This is how we are enjoying the products of human creativity, products of scientific creativity,

Geodesic Dome
(An architectural wonder)

Sculpture

Desktop Computer
(Invention)

Literary Works

Music

Mona Lisa by Da Vinci
(Painting)

*A few Products of Human Creativity*

which is an interesting thing. This is how scientists can be as creative as artists.

## DIFFERENT ASPECTS OF CREATIVITY

Ideas, inspiration, ingenuity are the seeds from which creations grow. Creativity has been considered in terms of process, product or person. It has been defined as the interpersonal and intrapersonal process by means of which original, high quality, and genuinely significant products are developed. At least three aspects of creativity have drawn much attention: (1) The creative process, receiving the most attention, focusses on the mechanisms and phases involved as one partakes in a creative act. (2) A second aspect of creativity is the creative person. Here, personality traits of creative people are central. The environmental atmosphere and influence are concerns of a second aspect—the creative situation. (3) Lastly, the criteria or characteristics of creative products have been sought. This area is of particular importance because it is the basis of any performance assessment of real world creativity.

We must keep in mind that creativity takes place unavoidably inside our own personal, social, and cultural boundaries. Creative activity may exhibit several dimensions including sensitivity to problems on the part of the creative agent; originality, ingenuity, unusualness, usefulness, and appropriateness in relation to the creative product; and intellectual leadership on the part of the creative agent.

Other related words to creativity are creativeness, formativeness, innovation, inventiveness, originality, productivity, craftsmanship, authorship, creatorship, etc.

Creativity is about new ways of looking at issues. Therefore, a creative idea is a new way to handle people, places and situations. Creativity is considered the ultimate human activity, a highly complex process, difficult to formalize and to control. Although there is a general agreement regarding the distinctive nature of the creative product (idea, painting, poem, and so on), there is a controversy over the nature of the creative process. Some researchers hold that the creative thinking process is qualitatively different from "ordinary" day-to-day thinking, and involves a leap that cannot be formulated, analyzed, or reconstructed—the creative spark. Others adopt a reductionist view that creative products are the outcome of ordinary thinking, only quantitatively different from everyday thinking.

Normally, different ways exist whereby something creative can happen: (1) Generating something wholly new, (2) Combining ideas in a new way, (3) Finding new uses for existing ideas, (4) Taking existing ideas to new (different) people, and (5) Combinations of the above. The first of these occurs comparatively rarely.

There are barriers to creativity. Some of the well-known barriers to creativity are: (1) Fear of failure—fear of looking foolish or being laughed at. (2) Excessive stress—the over-stressed person finds it difficult to think objectively at all. Unwanted stress reduces the quality of all mental processes. (3) Not having time to think creatively. (4) A tendency to conform to accepted patterns of belief or thought. (5) The rules and limitations of the status quo hampers creative breakthrough. (6) The biggest barrier however is the belief you are not creative.

There is a myth that creativity cannot be controlled, managed or pushed. In reality, in many situations a deadline can be imposed for reaching a creative solution to a problem. Another popular notion, with no base in actuality, is that all creative ideas are complex and technical. In reality, most useful ideas are magnificently simple.

Being creative is seeing the same thing as everybody else but thinking of something different. Creativity involves the translation of our unique gifts, talents and vision into an external reality that is new and useful. Creativity involves adaptability and flexibility of thought. Creativity is more than being able to draw; it is knowing how the problem is solved in the workplace and at home. Creativity is essentially a form of problem-solving. But it is a special type of problem-solving—one that involves problems for which there are no easy answers: that is, problems for which popular or conventional responses do not work.

Creativity goes beyond possession and use of artistic or musical talent. In this context, talent refers to the possession of a high degree of technical skill in a specialized area. Thus, an artist may have wonderful technical skills, but may not succeed in evoking the emotional response that makes the viewer feel that a painting, for example, is unique. Many people incorrectly assume that creative thinking is a special gift, bestowed on only a few. While it is true that we rarely see the extraordinary creativity of Edison or Einstein, modern research from the fields of the cognitive sciences indicates that the ability to generate innovative ideas for change in our work is a common "gift" that we all possess.

Instinctively, we all know that creativity at work is important. If creativity sees the commercial light of day, if it actually happens, that is innovation—and to most of us innovation means growth. To some extent then, all our business futures depend on our ability to be more creative.

## CREATIVITY IN VARIOUS CONTEXTS

Creativity is a basic element in many human activities. Creativity and aesthetics are most often associated with intellectual creations and activities such as art, music, painting, performing, or writing, etc. These things are creations of the human mind. Human creativity drives advances in science, business, technology, and the arts—in all human endeavours. Creative thinking is crucial in the sciences as scientific inventions are one of the most important forms of human creativity. Humankind's creative output spans a huge range of field each with their own great developments and innovations during the last millennium.

Creativity has been studied from a variety of perspectives and is important in numerous contexts. Most of these approaches are undisciplinary, and it is therefore difficult to form a coherent overall view. Most people associate creativity with the fields of art and literature. In these fields, originality is considered to be a sufficient condition for creativity, unlike other fields where both originality and appropriateness are necessary.

Creativity is also seen as being increasingly important in a variety of other professions. Although popularly associated with art and literature, it is also an essential part of innovation and invention and is important in professions such as business, economics, architecture, industrial design, science and engineering. Architecture and industrial design are the fields most often associated with creativity, and more generally the fields of design and design research. These fields explicitly value creativity. Fields such as science and engineering have, by contrast, experienced a less explicit but arguably no less important relation to creativity. Some of the major scientific advances of the 20th century can be attributed to the creativity of scientists. This ability will also be seen as increasingly important for engineers in years to come. Accounting has also been associated with creativity, especially with creative accounting. Despite, or perhaps because of, the ambiguity and multi-dimensional nature of creativity, entire industries have been spawned from the pursuit of creative ideas and the development of creativity techniques.

Creativity is critical not only in the so-called creative industries but almost everywhere—town planning, urban transport, hotel management, and all sorts of things. It comes down to the recognition of the extraordinary talent within individuals and enabling them how to develop their talent in a corporate form. Today, creativity forms the core activity of a growing section of the global economy—the so-called "creative industries"—capitalistically generating (generally non-tangible) wealth through the creation and exploitation of intellectual property or through the provision of creative services. It is important to keep in mind that creativity is evidenced not only in music, art, or writing, but also throughout the curriculum, in science, social studies and other areas. There is a myth about creativity that it can be exercised only in a limited number of fields, such as arts, advertising, etc. This is totally untrue. There have been many creative engineers, scientists, financiers, entrepreneurs, etc., who have not been artists.

Creativity cannot be labeled as artistic or scientific creativity. In reality, creative problem-solving can be exercised in almost any field. One can engage in creative problem-solving in such diverse setting as manufacturing, office work, administrative work; gardening, kitchen and home repairs. In fact, the great new ideas have always happened in different fields, they will continue to happen time to time. Creative business, from museums to web designs firms, demand innovative people as well. The creative products of mechanical and computer engineering, literature, entertainment, art, etc., fall under the purview of intellectual property.

## WAYS TO FOSTER CREATIVITY

Creativity has been attributed variously to divine intervention, cognitive processes, the social environment, personality traits, and chance ("accident," "serendipity"). It requires not only talented individuals, but also a culture and field of experts that can foster and validate such work. Some say it is a trait we are born with; others say it can be taught with the application of simple techniques. In this age of change and adaptation, it is more important than ever that we learn to be creative and innovative.

Our greatest resource is the creativity of the people with whom we live and work. We can no longer rely on the creativity of a few individuals, but must find ways of cultivating creativity at all levels in our communities. Creativity feeds on itself, and as more people enhance their own creativity they in turn will influence a greater number of people. This enhances both individuals and communities.

One is never too old to enjoy that childlike creativity within him. One is never too old to stop learning new things. One is never too old to express those silly, spontaneous urges lurking inside him waiting to get out. The common notions that one has to be a child, an artist, or full of innovative ideas to enjoy his or her creativity are wrong. True creativity should be fun and uninhibited. It does not impose ridiculous restrictions such as staying 'within the lines' or producing perfect works of art. Creativity should be fun and exploratory; messy, and when necessary, left unfinished. The bottom line is: creativity should be enjoyed. The goal should be to help all to harness the creative energy within them to distress, inspire new ideas, and simply have fun. One need not be "good" at anything to enjoy, just be creative. Throughout the ages artists and authors have adapted to new technologies—beginning with simple paint and ink, then the printing press, cinema and television, and now via computers and the Internet—to better express their ideas.

The creator himself when he undertakes a piece of work does not know where it will take him. But sometimes, certain elements help him achieve something, and it can take just a second, then it goes away just as quickly. That is why creation is such a difficult and stringent process. When we create a functional object, we do not know whether people will appreciate it for its beauty or for its usefulness. Creators have sometimes to wait till the circumstances are favourable. They have to think about certain things, write, make drawings, even go back to some of their old ideas, or conceive a technique and develop it.

It means learning to see us and to see others, learning to see things, which others cannot see. It is always with us, provided we grab its hand and take good care of it. Creativity is like height, intelligence, or strength. People vary considerably in these dimensions, but as everyone has some height, some intelligence and some strength; they also have some creativity in them.

In fact, we are born with creativity; we just have to find it. However, creation cannot start from nothing. Everyone has to work using existing matter, things from their heritage, traditional forms—even though we evolve in a contemporary world. Sometimes, a creator's ambition is to achieve what nobody else has ever achieved. His contemporary world is not enough, which is why his imagination pushes him towards what is yet to come.

## TIPS ON CREATIVITY

The world we live in faces many challenges: environmental, social, economical, and political. These problems can seem so huge and insurmountable that we often give up on them before we even try to tackle them. But the mind is designed to meet creative challenges. The way to unleash its creative power is through responsibility and decision. When we decide that it is up to us, that we are going to do it, then our mind gets into gear and starts working at a higher level. We are purpose driven beings. And in each and every one of us there is a core desire to be of use. We all want to help make the world a better place. We all want to make a significant contribution. We all want to demonstrate to ourselves (and others) that our lives have meaning, that we are important. Our enormous personal creative power is unleashed by the thought: What can I do? How can I help? How can I make this world a better place? How can I help humanity have a better life and a better future?

Our creativity depends on our ability to discern between what is "real" and what is "not real". We need to find out how this is done. We cannot and will not be creative all the time. Creativity has its own internal rhythms. We need to learn to listen to ours. We should not underestimate the tremendous emotional and psychic risks the journey demands. We have to learn to push ahead even when we are afraid. We should learn to love the risk. Every successful creator has failed hundreds of times. Failure is an integral part of creativity. It does not mean we are wrong or stupid. It only means we have uncovered a path or technique that does not work. We should give our work time to percolate. We should open to the dance; listen to music that makes us feel like flying. We may go for a walk; laugh with a friend, child or lover. A change of atmosphere is good for us and gentle exercise helps shake up the brain cells. We should read as much as we can about everything possible. Books exercise our brain, provide inspiration and fill us with information that allows us to make creative connections easily. Brains, like bodies, need exercise to keep fit. If we do not exercise our brain, it will get flabby and useless. We should exercise our brain by reading a lot, talking to clever people and disagreeing with people—arguing can be a terrific way to give our brain cells a workout. Creativity is about feeling. Creativity is passion. Passion is always creative. The more we create, the better we will get. We should discipline ourselves. Successful creators are disciplined creators. So here is a chance to give our creative juices a blast by putting on our thinking cap. The code here is to work on developing all of our multiple intelligences so that we can become a fully rounded individual capable of fulfilling our creative potential. Genius may be 99% sweat, and only 1% inspiration but before we can sweat, we need that spark of inspiration that only creative thinking can give us.

The way to increase the power and force of anything is to compress and focus its energy to a point. The same principle applies when we are working with creative mind power. This can help us access that immense power of creative energy and talent that lies within us. Ideas are just ghosts until given flesh and blood through action. As a creator we should know that the initial idea is raw and needs refining through increased knowledge. And the only way to increase knowledge is through experience. And experience is gained through experiment. We need to toughen up, knuckle down and prepare to slug it out. Our best creativity will often come at the end of our tether. We need to make sure we see our best ideas right the way through to their fruition. If we quit too soon, we may leave our best ideas hidden in the recesses of unexplored minds.

We should get started by determining to set aside at least 20 minutes a day to concentrate possibility thinking and contemplation in the area of our particular interests. In the field of writing, for example, the best way to develop our vocabulary is to get a really good dictionary and pick 5 or 10 new words a day and learn what they mean, the different contexts in which they can be used, and what fields they would most likely be used in.

Creative thinking is a vitally important skill that one can learn easily. We have tremendous powers for creativity and our brain is already actively working in a creative thinking mode, but we may not have realized or recognized it. We tend to think of genius as belonging to special people, who live in a completely different way than we do. But that is just not the case. The truth is our brain dips in and out of states of genius all day long. We now have the opportunity to harness that genius and put it to work for us in more consistent ways.

Creative thought can be divided into divergent and convergent reasoning. Divergent thinking is the intellectual ability to think of many original, diverse, and elaborate ideas. Convergent thinking is the intellectual ability to logically evaluate, critique and choose the best idea from a selection of ideas. Both abilities are required for creative output. Divergent thinking is essential to the novelty of creative products whereas convergent thinking is fundamental to the appropriateness.

Because creative ideas are different from those that normally arise, people often believe that such ideas require conditions dramatically different from the usual. The notion goes that, in order to overcome mental barriers and reach creative ideas, total freedom is necessary—no directional guidance, constraints, criticism, or thinking within bounded scope. Then ideas can be drawn and contemplated from an infinite space during the creativity process. This view prompted the emergence of various idea-generating methods: brainstorming, synectics, lateral thinking, random stimulation, and so on, all of which consist of withholding judgement and relying on analogies from other members in the group or on randomly selected analogies. This family of methods relies on the assumption that enhancing randomness, breaking rules and paradigms, and generating anarchy of thought increase the probability of creative idea emergence. A related version of this says that new ideas happen by evolution and that this cannot be speeded up. New ideas will continue to happen from time to time, but we can also seek to get ideas in a more direct way through the use of deliberate creativity. One does not exclude the other.

Puzzles enhance creativity. There are many different kinds of puzzles. Some exercise the left-brain and others exercise the right-brain. One needs to find out why doing puzzles increases creative potential. By doing certain puzzles we will be calling on different properties of mind, *i.e.*, logical sequential processes or, conversely, pattern recognition. Logical sequential thinking processes are generally thought to tap the resources of the left-brain. These require following a definite sequence of logical steps that will eventually lead to the solution. Word puzzles also tap the left-brain since language is thought to be dominant here. Words are sequential symbols that describe concepts.

In the world of imagination, anything can happen. It is as fragile as a budding flower. Imagination has a vital role in creativity. It is the beginning of creation. The man who has no imagination has no wings. Using imagination we may do many fun things. We do not need any special kind of training to do this magic sort of entertaining. All we need is a simple inclination toward using our imagination. In fact, all big corporations started with an idea. We have to cultivate creative imagination. Everything created was given birth through imagination. "Imagination is more important than knowledge," said Albert Einstein.

Every form is the outcropping of mind. Before anything becomes formed it was conceived in someone's mind first through the power of his or her imagination. The ability to imagine is universal. The power to imagine is not limited by gender, culture, education or intelligence. If more people understood this power they could transform their life accordingly. The power of imagination is the ultimate creative power. The most important attribute we can have is creative imagination—the ability to be first to figure out how all the enabling tools can be put together in new existing ways to create products, opportunities and profits. It is seeing things that others do not see and coming up with new ideas. As reported, this has always been America's strength, because America was, and for now still is, the world's greatest dream machine.

Creative memory plays an important role in creative imagination. Memory is the cabinet of imagination. Creative thought could not exist without memory. Though creativity is usually thought of as a spontaneous original response, the ability to remember one's past experience and use it as a springboard for new potentials is necessary. Without a clear understanding of what is already known, how could we know that we had discovered something unknown? This is especially the case in problem-solving. Creative artistic inspiration draws more on aesthetic considerations. Yet both are dependent upon the remembrance of known experience as a platform for new creations.

Creative dreaming is also an act of imagination. We spend one third of our lives asleep. Learning to use the dream state to enhance our creative mind is a potent tool. There are many ways to learn, to become lucid in the dream state and to utilize the language of the psyche to benefit our waking life. Dreaming is the language of the mind during our nightly sojourns. It stands to simple reason that this time could be used wisely. Personal creativity is greatly increased by utilizing the information gleaned from the sub-conscious mind in dreams. It is also possible to learn to control our dreams, adding a whole new dimension to the sleeping experience. Kekule found the structure formula of benzene in his dream.

The ability to direct our focus is an art. All creative work is the result of clarity and the expansion of focussed intent. There are two kinds of focus, hard and soft. Every problem or creative project needs to use both kinds of focus to be successful. We have to learn the difference. Hard focus is the willful concentration of attention on a single point or idea to the exclusion of all else. Soft focus is the purposeful expansion of awareness to include the whole environment, without singling out any one part, and being aware that we are aware.

Here and there in the ancient literature we encounter legends of wise and mysterious games that were conceived and played by scholars, monks, or the courtiers of cultured princes. For the creative mind, chess is more than a game of conquest, conflict, and competitive skill. Chess is a reflection of life creatively engaged. Chess is more than just another board game for the competitive spirit. Each piece has a unique mobility upon a deliberate landscape of opportunities. Once we understand the relationships and harmonies between each piece as they relate to the rules of the game, we can play with new insight. Chess will teach us a lot about ourselves, and may help us to correct some attitudes that are keeping us from being who we want to be.

Intuition is more powerful than linear thought in arriving at new and unique solutions to problems. Our sub-conscious mind is a powerhouse of ideas that have yet to surface, or never get to the frontal lobe. There are definite ways we can learn to increase our intuitive abilities. At those times when we need an immediate solution to an imposing problem, this technique will save the day.

Creativity and the ability to remote view are intimately connected. Much of what is gleaned as creative vision or an intuited idea is accessed through the same channels that psychic information is obtained. To be truly creative we need to use all of our mental, emotional and spiritual potential. If we exclude anyone of these areas of perception, we have limited our creative potential accordingly.

Humour is the magic elixir of life. When we have learned to cultivate our own sense of humour we have harnessed one of the most valuable tools of the mind and heart. Humour allows for detachment and detachment allows for humour. We need to learn this technique for creating humour in our life and see how our creativity grows as a result. Humour is an essential creative attitude. Creativity is the best performed in a light-hearted environment. Learning to generate humour in any situation will greatly enhance creative options and resolutions to life's challenges. An excellent method for generating humour in any circumstance is personal detachment.

If one really wants to appreciate a creative work, there is no substitute for seeing it in person. Seeing masterpieces may enrich or even change our life. As far as possible, budding creators must visit art museums, galleries and exhibitions of innovations and other creative works.

## TOOLS AND TECHNIQUES

The creative process is an ongoing exercise. Everything we do that is not habit is creative. Harnessing this creative power and directing it toward new ideas and solving problem most people need help. "You cannot teach a man anything; you can only help him to find it within himself" said Galileo.

There are many models and techniques that aim to help people come up with creative ideas. We may use these great creativity techniques to stimulate our creative thinking. However, some believe that any development of systematic tools and techniques will be contrary to the very nature of creativity, which must be 'free'.

Creativity techniques generate brilliant ideas, innovations and great creative thinking's. Following are a few tools and techniques available in the literature. These are tools that prepare the mind for creative thought; tools that stimulate the imagination for new ideas. They may help unleash our creativity. However, many more simple, practical and user-friendly techniques have been used and recommended by the luminaries of art, science, literature and philosophy. So who better to learn creative thinking from than this Genius of Geniuses? For creative thinkers everywhere, Da Vinci is a hero and awe-inspiring role model. To unleash our creative intelligence and start thinking like Leonardo da Vinci, we can emulate some of the things he did to be more creative. So we should definitely make it a practice to think of ways that different things relate to each other, and how different things could be combined to make something completely different. We may also emulate the creative techniques used by other great creators.

The ability to create is a gift. But every gift must be developed. In fact, creativity needs to be cultivated not only in traditionally creative fields like sciences and arts, but also in business, government and education. It is true that some people have a natural curiosity; some have an active imagination and other are some, always trying to change things. But all these effects can also be obtained through formal creativity enhancing techniques. Creative problem-solving depends on using the right tools, tricks, procedures or methods of analysis. In some cases new tools and methods of analysis must be developed from scratch by the inventor before a problem can be solved and in other cases special tools and procedures must be developed to take the final critical step of enabling successful commercial applications.

**Brainstorming**

Alex Osborn as a technique to stimulate creative thinking amongst advertising copywriters invented brainstorming. Since then it has been widely adopted the world over as a brilliant tried-and-tested creative thinking technique that we will benefit from. Brainstorming remains one of the most effective creative thinking techniques in use today. With its policy of non-judgement and rapid fire spitting out of ideas that spark off one another, it is a real firecracker way to generate quality, new insights, breakthroughs and innovations. A fire is started with a spark. Our 'spark' to unleash a brainstorming inferno is our set-up, the creative challenge we lay before the participants or ourselves. We may think of various different ways of structuring the description of our creative challenge. The mindset with which we approach a problem will determine the direction that we set off in pursuit of an answer. By asking the question in a variety of different ways, we reframe the problem and affect the answers we get from brainstorming. By looking at the challenge from as many different perspectives as possible, we move the target scope across the landscape of our creativity. And we will hit a lot more unique ideas. If properly carried out, brainstorming can help us not only come up with sacks full of new ideas, but can help us decide which is the best.

### Image Streaming

Image streaming is one of the great modern techniques for accessing our highest powers of creative thinking. Image streaming unleashes the powers of our unconscious mind power for unrivalled creative thinking excellence. Win Wenger invented image streaming and its effectiveness as a process for accessing higher mind insights and creative bolts from the blue has been established by the thousands of people, he has trained in this creativity technique.

### Dream Incubation

Dream incubation is a phenomenal way to access our deep inner creative resources to make amazing creative breakthroughs while asleep and dreaming. We may learn how to use this brilliant creative thinking technique to launch our dreaming mind on an odyssey of innovative thinking, idea generation and self-discovery. Incubating creative ideas through our dreams stimulates extraordinary thinking, creativity, innovation and breakthrough idea generation. Dream incubation is a creative thinking technique that uses our dreams to come up with creative breakthroughs. Basically, we set the scene for our inner dreaming mind to do our creative thinking for us. This is really neat if we can summon enough discipline at the end of the day and first thing in the morning to do what we need to do to incubate dreams. It only takes a few minutes but like anything we are not used to, it is going to be awkward at first.

### Note Booking

Note booking is a really simple way to unleash our genius for creative thinking; a simple way to stimulate our creative thinking and capture our best ideas. We call it note booking because it involves getting a notebook and jotting down the thoughts and observations that meander through our mind during the day. This simple practice spurs our mind into greater creative thinking. The fact is that great ideas pass through our head all the time, and we entertain them without really being fully conscious of them. We just do not recognize the value of them and it is so easy to forget them and lose them forever. With our notebook we will capture these ideas. But our focus is also upon observation. By writing our ideas down, scribbling our observations and thoughts, we create a feedback loop with our mind that accelerates and accentuates our creative mind power. We may leave a legacy of our insight, creativity and observations on life, our special interests and everything that amuses us. It is an inescapable fact that all the great creative minds have been writers, note bookers who record their observations, thoughts and ideas. Writing down our thoughts with words and sketches gives massive encouragement and impetus to creative thinking and we should begin immediately to apply this most simple creative thinking technique. One should always carry a small notebook and a pen or pencil around him or her. That way, if one is struck by an idea, he or she can quickly note it down. Upon rereading our notes, we may discover about 90% of our ideas are draft. There is, however, no need to worry that is normal. What is important are the 10% that are brilliant. If one is stuck for an idea, he should open a dictionary, randomly select a word and then try to formulate ideas incorporating this word. He would be surprized how well this works. One should define the problem, grab a sheet of paper, electronic notebook, computer or whatever one uses to make notes, and define his problem in detail. One will probably find ideas positively spewing out once he has done this.

### Adopting Fake ID

Wearing a "mask" and adopting a fake identity (ID) can unleash a torrent of creative brilliance. To trigger a torrent of creative brilliance we might need to get away from us and try adopting a fake ID. We may do as writers do and adopt a *nom-de-plume*, a pen name, and we will give ourselves a whole different personality to think with. Taking on a new persona could be just the thing that gives us the freedom to be creatively expressive. We may therefore use fake IDs in our creative thinking, in our writing and for specific creative projects in different fields of creative endeavour. It will shake us up, shake us lose and give us a freedom to be a multi-faceted dazzling creative thinker.

Besides creative tools and techniques, there are books and consultants to help enhance one's creativity. Creative thinking books are hugely popular and likely to become even more so with the growing trends in creativity and the need for innovation. With China dominating the world in manufacturing, the West recognizes a need to focus on cutting-edge creativity and innovation. Fortunately, there are some phenomenally gifted teachers, experts and specialists everywhere in the field of creative thinking and maximizing the creative output.

Creativity consultants are a growing breed in an era when creative innovation is essential for businesses and individuals to thrive in an ever more competitive marketplace. With Asia expanding and challenging Western countries' traditional dominance in the marketplace, most are becoming aware that only constant re-invention, innovation and a commitment to never-ending improvement will give them any chance of competing.

## CREATIVE PEOPLE

Someone who writes a song that has words and a rhythm, a lyric, and a sound that we all like is creative. A film producer, a film director, an orchestra conductor, a designer can be creative.

For creative people creativity is life; it is passion. A world without creators would be monotonous, it would be dull, and it would be static. Various groups of creative people are writers, artists, performers, designers, musicians, inventors, entrepreneurs, etc. We all share in the fruits of their ideas, their imagination, their talent and hard work. A creator's dream is to devote every minute of his or her life to creation and creativity. The most important thing to a creator is end up creating a beautiful piece of work. Moreover, creators like musicians, writers, poets, singers—who have such influence—can lead the way in creating the better society. The creativity of artists, scientists and others can transform our culture and the way we look at the world. Some of the major scientific advances of the 20th century can be attributed to the creativity of individuals. Those individuals who create works are called authors. They may create literary works such as novels, poems and scientific texts, or artistic works such as paintings, musical compositions and films. Performing artists—singers, musicians and actors—perform works and are known as performers. All of us can take pride in our creators and artists, and in their successes at home and abroad. We conventionally expect some creative people (dancers, actors, orchestral members, etc.) to perform (interpret) while allowing others (writers, painters, composers, etc.) more freedom to express the new and the different.

Creative people use deliberate creativity techniques to stimulate their flights of creative thinking. Creative thinking with the great minds of history will unleash our own genius for creativity and innovation. We may use their special creative thinking techniques to stimulate our mind and it will help us get creative. With the simple techniques used and recommended by these luminaries of art, science, literature and philosophy, we will have a formidable armoury of practical, user-friendly techniques to access our creative thinking ability. We may take this gift from the world's most creative people, unwrap it and enjoy what we find within. We will never be the same again and the world and we will benefit from our new-found creative thinking abilities. Creativity techniques and creative strategies from or inspired by the great minds of history, the genius men and women, who have changed the world with their creative output and genius thinking we may harvest the fruits of our creativity. We will be able to deliberately expand our creative output and we will become convinced of our ability to be a creative genius in our own right.

Creative people are bright but need not be brilliant. They have a youthful curiosity throughout their lives. They are good at gathering alternative solutions to problems in a short period of time. They tend to have positive self-image. Our ability to change our images to correspond to a new reality is the crux of our creativity. A creative person is one whose images correspond most closely to reality, because then his actions will lead to the results, which he images.

It is believed that rebels are creative because rebels want to be different. The rebels always have the motivation to challenge and to be different. So the conformists can become creative but they have to want to. It is necessary for them to acquire creative skill.

### Leonardo Da Vinci

Leonardo Da Vinci, the genius of all geniuses, used specific creativity techniques to generate his brilliant creative thinking, insights, ideas and inventions. He was one of the greatest geniuses of the world has ever known. More than 500 years ago, he designed flying machines, robots, submarines and underwater breathing gear; laid much of the groundwork for the artificial heart valve; and created some of the greatest paintings in the history of art. With little formal education, his brilliance lay in his ability to master different subjects and fuse them together through observation, insight and inspiration. The machines and paintings feature the amazing interpretive insight into his character.

Leonardo Da Vinci was a scientist, engineer, artist, instrument inventor, anatomist, philosopher, composer, he was highly popular as a story-teller, joke-teller, riddler, and was famous for excelling at whatever he applied himself to. Leonardo was great at juggling too. The primary thing to remember with Da Vinci is his observation and belief that "everything connects". Making connections between disparate things is perhaps the number one creative thinking skill. Leonardo Da Vinci had specific techniques that he used to stimulate his intelligence and heightened creative thinking. He was ambidextrous and could write and paint with both hands at the same time. He made copious notes, which he wrote in mirror writing (backwards letters written from right to left). Leonardo Da Vinci left us a code of four principles to stimulate and encourage creative genius: (1) Study the science of art. (2) Study the art of science. (3) Develop all your senses especially your ability to see. (4) Study all the above in the light of the idea that everything connects, in some way, to everything else.

Leonardo da Vinci

**Thomas Alva Edison**

Thomas Edison's contribution to creative thinking is immense. Here are some powerful ideas from this great inventor. Thomas Edison knew that an idea before its time would founder on the rocks of outright rejection. So, he deliberately kept his mind trained on projects that were already being explored by other inventors and scientists. Thomas Edison was not only a creative genius; he was street smart and canny with it. He knew that a clever idea is no good unless you can sell people on it. He invested a lot of time and creative ingenuity in making sure that people (the paying public) understood and were duly impressed by his new inventions. Thomas Edison compiled over 3,500 notebooks detailing his ideas and experiments and poured his thoughts onto over four million pages of notes during his lifetime.

Thomas Alva Edison

Thomas Edison applied his creative thinking, putting it to the test through trial and experimentation. As an inventor, Edison knew that the initial idea was raw and needed refining through increased knowledge. And the only way to increase knowledge was through experience. And experience was gained through experiment. Edison is famously quoted as describing creative genius as "2% inspiration and 98% perspiration". He also declared "Many of life's failures are people who did not realize how close they were to success when they gave up." Thomas Edison bequeathed a wonderful motivational tool for attaining a great quantity of creative thinking output, and that his concept of an 'Idea Quota'. By the time of his death in 1931, Edison held 1,093 patents, a record for an individual. His phenomenal output was down to his personal idea quota, which demanded that he come up with a minor invention every 10 days and a major invention every 6 months. Thomas Edison slept little and topped up his batteries with what he referred to as powernaps. He would just climb up on a workbench and have a nap for twenty minutes. He soon noticed a funny thing though. Great flashes of insight on a particular problem seemed to come to him during these powernaps. He soon refined the process of realizing that his creative thinking went into overdrive in that space between being fully awake and fully asleep. Thomas Edison knew that when it came to creative thinking, two heads were better than one. He was a master at organizing and utilizing the creative abilities and talents of others in very much focussed creative pursuits and projects. Edison's dynamic and forceful character galvanized the enthusiastic young team of bright minds that he attracted to his Menlo Park "Invention Factory".

### Albert Einstein

Albert Einstein

The primary creative mindset of Albert Einstein is that of possibility thinking. Basically, this means giving us permission to think extraordinary things. Part of giving us permission to think in exceptional and creative ways is also giving us the opportunity to do so. Albert Einstein's thinking on the subject of quantum physics obviously demanded more of his thinking time than someone, who wants to think up a really creative idea for a birthday surprise. Albert Einstein is someone who asked questions and looked at things in ways that no one else had thought to do. Possibility thinking means exploring what is creatively possible, usually way beyond the boundaries of what you know. You need to keep pushing the envelope, testing and probing to breakthrough the boundaries of the tried and familiar. Einstein's classic thought experiment that helped him develop the Theory of Relativity was when he imagined what it would be like to ride on a beam of light. This was something that he could never do in reality but by imagining it his creative thinking was stimulated to the insights and understandings of how light and time functioned. From those imaginings came his world-famous theories in quantum physics. Albert Einstein once remarked that he thought in a stream of pictures. Visualization can be enhanced with practice until it is rich and vivid like an inner movie. Words are useful but clunky when it comes to making creative breakthroughs. The old Chinese saying, "A picture is worth a thousand words" is so apropos to the subject of creative thinking. When exploring a creative challenge, take a leaf out of Einstein's book and utilize the power of hard thinking followed by soft thinking. Hard thinking occurs in the time you deliberately set-aside to fully explore a creative challenge. For Einstein, he would pour over his calculations, covering everything he knew and he would conduct the thought experiments previously mentioned, and have deep discussions with his peers. All this involved hard creative effort. But Einstein appreciated the concept of soft thinking when we consciously set aside the problem and redirect our attention to something enjoyable and relaxing.

### Buckminster Fuller

R. Buckminster Fuller

Buckminster Fuller had extraordinary creative thinking and power to innovate. Buckminster Fuller and creative thinking go hand in hand. Those who knew him or his work revere this creative powerhouse as a genius. His extraordinary creativity drove him to become a philosopher, thinker, visionary, inventor, architect, engineer, mathematician, poet, cosmologist, and more. And the amazing thing is, all this creativity and effort was spurred on by one life-focussing thought. In his depressed mindset, Buckminster Fuller had been thinking about everything that was wrong with the world and all the awful challenges it faces. And the idea that struck him was so exciting to him that he resolved then and there to put it into practice and see where it led. In his own words, he embarked on "an experiment, to find what a single individual can contribute to changing the world and benefiting all humanity." Fuller's thought: What can I do? How can I help? How can I make this world a better place? How can I help humanity have a better life and a better future? One of Buckminster Fuller's innovative concepts was of the earth as a spaceship. This implied the idea of all people of all races being together on one finite vehicle. He invented the Dymaxion Map, which also showed how all the countries of the world are closely linked. All this pointed at our need to work together as a human team. That our long-term and best future would only come as a result of co-operation in meeting the challenges that face each and everyone of us collectively and individually. Our future on 'spaceship earth' will be determined by our ability to figure out the 'operating manual' and maintain the health and efficiency of the integral biosystems that combine to make the planet work. Fuller knew and accepted that most people would see this kind of thinking as pie-in-the-sky idealism. His motto though was dared to be naive. To be creative you have to be a little foolish.

### Yoshiro NakaMats

Dr. Yoshiro NakaMats is Japan's greatest inventor; in fact, he is the world's most prolific inventor with over 3,000 patents to his name. He is the guy that invented things like the floppy disk, the hard disk, and the digital watch. He is a living genius able to come up with so many brilliant, zany ideas. One of his best secrets for generating awesome creative ideas he describes humorously as: "swim till almost die!" It is called the Brain Bubbles technique because: (1) It is going to cause your brain to bubble with new ideas and high IQ thinking, and (2) It is all about forcing more and more oxygen into your brain so that you can think better.

### William Shakespeare

William Shakespeare was a truly awesome 17th century literary dude. He saw life as theatre and theatre as life. His works are phenomenal, ranging over the entire spectrum of human experience and emotion. And what is more, he left us plenty of clues to his genius. His techniques to build extremely powerful communication abilities are:

1. Develop a large vocabulary. The average person uses slightly more than 1,000 different words in general conversation, slightly less than 1,000 words when writing and can recognize approximately 5,000 words. Shakespeare used over 25,000 different words in his writings—that is more than any other English writer has ever used.
2. Play with words. We may get some poetry books and read them and savour the way the words are woven together. We may make our own poems, try and make connections between words, the more unlikely the better. Take two words

at random and try to think of all the ways they might connect.

3. Invent new words and phrases. Shakespeare is responsible for inventing so many words and phrases that are used today in popular parlance. It takes a wonderful twist of creativity to invent new words and phrases and we do it all the time. Our lives are littered with invaluable jargon and catch phrases.

**William Shakespeare**

4. Develop the common touch. Shakespeare had a phenomenal talent for giving the public what it wants: blood and guts; sex, lust and love; tragedy and triumph. He wrote about what matters to people—the things they experience and relate to in their own lives. Of course, he threaded that in amongst some of the most moving and powerful stories ever told.
5. Read great literature. Study the great orators, actors and the popular. Live with passion. Write, write, and write. Writing is the first and last tool of genius. We write to get ideas and we write to express and share the ideas we have already got. Needless to say, Shakespeare wrote prolifically in his short life.

## ENCOURAGING CREATIVITY

For the world to move forward, for things to be better than what they were the previous day, the previous minute, people are supposed to be creative. It is about time our nations should recognize that our economy thrives upon a creative and innovative work force and that we must foster creativity in our schools and in our students to compete in the global market place. Governments should incorporate in curriculum the arts, increase funding for arts programmes, and create a public-private partnership to promote creativity in our schools and communities. Education that spreads creativity, not rote learning.

The arts help all students learn to succeed in school and beyond. Students who participate in the arts are more likely to be recognized for academic achievements. Whatever students learn through the arts and curricula infused with creativity helps prepare them for the real life demands of today's economy. Creative programmes help students learn how to collaborate with others, enhance critical thinking skills, communicate clearly in a variety of media, produce results in real time and think outside box. Besides governments, it is imperative on the part of communities, civil societies, parents and teachers to encourage creativity in young adults. They should encourage students to recognize in themselves the essential qualities of curiosity, creativity and perseverance, which enable individuals to invent. Governments should provide incentives for people to produce scientific and creative works that benefit the society at large.

Creativity lies within us. And of course, it has got to be stimulated by the environment. We have to nurture an environment that inspires creativity. Coaching and training can alter any ability. It is the same with creativity. If we do nothing about it, then we can only depend on natural talent. But if we develop formal techniques and offer training in these techniques, then everyone will be much more creative than before. Some people will still be more creative than others, as with any acquired skills. One popular concept of creativity is that everyone is creative but inhibited. Therefore, people need to be encouraged to be playful and childlike to become creative. We have to develop techniques for getting out of established patterns.

Society needs to recognize that every child is a gifted child, one who has inalienable right to explore, seek information and use his or her imagination. It should provide support to the child's creative development and act as catalysts to help provide a conducive environment for growth and development of his creative power. Children are adept at finding unconventional solutions to problems. The challenge is to keep that natural creativity as they grow up. To do so, they must be encouraged, to feel that their ideas are valuable and useful.

While individuals can make their own opportunities, a supportive society offering resources and rewards can foster creativity. Parents, schools and the country as a whole should foster creativity. We believe that creativity takes root in childhood. For the child, life is a creative adventure. The most basic explorations of a child's world are creative exercises in problem-solving. They begin a lifelong process of inventing themselves. In this sense, every child reinvents language, walking, and love. Creativity flourishes when things are done for enjoyment. By letting a child explore a range of activities, budding talents are more likely to emerge. It is very much necessary to keep the minds ignited and the process intact. This will give a chance to show their creativity in designing the product, which can suit to people. Creators must know the ways to enhance one's own personal creativity. Adults can encourage creativity by emphasizing the generation and expression of ideas in a non-evaluative framework and by concentrating on both divergent and convergent thinking. Adults can also try to ensure that children have the opportunity and confidence to take risks, challenge assumptions, and see things in a new way. "Young people are our future," says WIPO Deputy Director Rita Hayes. "They are the creators—and the consumers—of tomorrow." For a proper understanding of children's creativity, one must distinguish creativity from intelligence. Everyone has a special gift of creativity. But, sometimes people need a little encouragement to discover their creative talents, especially children.

It is important to increase awareness of scientific knowledge as well as the creative power of children. Developing a strong sense of creation in the students, who are future inventors, innovators, and creators, and who will constantly strive to produce tangible goods from scientific ideas and human creativity. We should encourage the creators and innovators of tomorrow. The time has come to unleash the creative potential of our scientists and innovators at grass-root level. There are several ways of awareness building such as exhibitions of different kinds of creativity, film shows, hands-on training, and organizing inspiring lectures, talks, etc. Similarly, other options could be organizing concerts or other public performances centered on the "Encouraging Creativity" theme; arranging for performers to deliver messages encouraging respect for creators and creativity, conducting workshops aimed at various groups of creative people—artists, performers, designers, musicians, inventors, entrepreneurs, etc.—to explain the concrete benefits provided by the intellectual property system for these professions.

As a part of creating a broader awareness among the general public of the value of intellectual property and the role played by the intellectual property system in encouraging and rewarding creativity, the World Intellectual Property Organization (WIPO) is producing a series of short films for television called *Creative Planet*. The series explores, through portraits of musicians, artists, inventors, designers, and other creators, how the creative process works for them, how they view their own creative efforts, and how the intellectual property system has helped them achieve success. Besides, several pilot films have been produced in six-minute versions for broadcast on national and international television networks. The theme "Think Imagine Create," of the fifth World Intellectual Property Day was directed towards young people. Thinking, imagination and ideas have a vital role to play in creativity and inventiveness. Member States and non-governmental organizations the world over found different ways to realize the words of WIPO Director General Kamil Idris: "Our goal for World Intellectual Property Day and beyond should be to encourage young people everywhere to recognize the creator, the problem-solver, the artist within themselves." *Encouraging Creativity* was the theme chosen by WIPO for 2007 World Intellectual Property Day, celebrated on April 26, 2007. The power of creativity and innovation applied to artistic expression or the solving of practical problems is not the exclusive province of any country or people, but is a resource of limitless potential available to everyone. Harnessed in the form of intellectual property, it is a force that can be used to enrich the lives of individuals and the future of nations—materially, culturally and socially.

Museums, innovation and incubation centres, art galleries and theaters also play an important role in encouraging creativity. Similarly, strong national cultural policy, copyright law, copyright commissions, national commissions for galleries, film corporations, cultural centres, and national libraries play a facilitative role in encouraging creativity.

Innovation and creation have to be financed; like everyone else, the people innovating and creating have to make a living. Large amounts of time and money can be spent on researching and developing new technologies and products without any guarantee that these will be rewarded, as there is always a risk that a product will not be successful. If one really wants to appreciate a work of art and other forms of creativity and get inspired, there is no substitute for seeing it in person at places like art galleries, museums and exhibitions. Visit science centres, trade shows or online forums that focus on inventing. Seeing masterpieces may enrich or even change our life.

## PROTECTING CREATIVITY

We owe the inventions, designs and works of art that ease our workload, improve our living conditions and enrich and beautify our surroundings to a long line of men and women whose creativity and invention have led us from the inkwell to the Internet and from railways to rockets. We should pledge ourselves to ensuring that their works are put to good use for the common benefit of all countries. We must recognize the contribution of inventors and creators in making our world a better place. We all share in the fruits of their ideas, their imagination, their talent and hard work. We should recognize the dedication and perseverance of creators. We should respect these special individuals who power us forward and give us the opportunity to create a better future. They are an encouragement to all and should inspire us to work together—men and women, young and old, of every nation—towards a universal culture of creativity.

However, there are people out there that would rather steal the idea of creative people than come up with something original, on their own. The artistic empowerment, the brain strain, the complex and in fact inexplicable way that words get to the writer to put down as poems, dialogue, stories, texts need to be revered and therefore to be protected from thieves who take the products and sell them for their own gains, leaving the creator of the works in penury. This is discouraging and distractive to the creative mind. A number of people have discouraged their wards from developing their artistic talents, because it does not pay. Many artists have lost respect from their family members even from their children, for pushing and rightly too "a profession that does not yield good money", thereby robbing from nations of arts and entertainment. Many countries indeed endowed with so much talents in the artistic direction that it will be a great loss not only to those great countries but to the entire world, what with our dancers, sculptors writers, musicians, and the many performing artists, cooling in the doldrums. All creative work needs to be respected, protected and encouraged. If the law only allows for the copycats to copy artist's works for their own benefit will kill the artists and the arts. It needs reviewing the copyright laws and makes arts a respectable profession.

Therefore, if it is marketable idea, one should better know her or his rights and responsibilities, and the penalties for idea stealing. If one does not know, his loss could be enormous. Because, protecting creative works is the most difficult thing. Someone may steal his million-dollar idea out from under him. If the work is copied for purely materialistic and commercial reasons, then it is worrying, because this will lessen the vital resources and deprive the creator of the means, which enable him to keep creating.

Though, for many people, the connection between intellectual property and creativity is not obvious, it is the intellectual property system that sustains and nourishes the creators. The term intellectual property reflects the idea that this subject matter is the creation of the mind or the intellect. Intellectual property rights are the rights awarded by society to individuals or organizations principally over creative works: inventions, literary and artistic works, and symbols, names images, and designs used in commerce. They give the creator the right to prevent others from making unauthorized use of their property for a limited period. The intellectual property laws protect original creative works that have economic value. They also provide incentives for people to produce scientific and creative works that benefit the society at large. Creativity is as well protected internationally, international protection acts as a spur to human creativity, pushing forward the boundaries of science and technology and enriching the world of literature and the arts. For example, in most countries, certain classes of inventions are legally recognized and protected by their patent laws, and their use is temporarily restricted to the control of the inventor. Similarly, copyright law protects a variety of literary and artistic works, including paintings, sculpture, prose, poetry, plays, musical compositions, dances, photographs, motion pictures, radio and television programmes, sound recordings, and computer software programs. It is stimulus to creation. Copyright encourages the production of original artistic, literary and musical creations from books and paintings to movies, recordings and software. The copyright system rewards artistic expression by allowing the creator to benefit commercially from his work. Industrial design rights protect industrial and creative designs, including textile designs. An industrial design is the ornamental or aesthetic aspect of an Article. Without these intellectual property laws, it would be easy to duplicate original works and sell them for very low prices, leaving the original creators without any chance to secure economic rewards for their efforts. The legal system avoids this problem by making it against the law to reproduce various forms of intellectual property without the permission of the creator. Confidence in the intellectual property system is a powerful stimulus for intellectual creativity.

One purpose of the intellectual property rights system is to provide incentives to innovators to produce new inventions and creations. This in turn provides society with a steady stream of innovations that fuel economic, cultural and social progress, help to alleviate poverty and disease, and enrich our cultural heritage. Intellectual property rights enable people to benefit from their innovations and creative work, and to prevent others from copying or unfairly gaining from the inventor's creativity and investment. By according these rights, society provides an incentive for people and organizations to invest time, resources and original thinking to develop innovative products and technologies and expand knowledge and culture. This encourages the production of a wide range of quality goods and services, and helps maintain fair competition.

Once the creators decide to identify and claim ownership over their value-adding outputs through the operation of relevant legal tools of the intellectual property system of laws, it becomes possible to use and trade such assets in the market place. In the current era of vast amounts of information and knowledge, the importance of the intellectual property, embodied in these creative assets, has evolved to a point where practically all goods and services rely to varying degrees on the effective use of the tools of the intellectual property system for successful commercialization. As such creativity becomes private 'property,' which is recognized as being personal and/or owned. That is, while creativity in itself is universal, the exclusive proprietary rights over intellectual creations, which are inspired by people's creativity becomes the domain of binding legal norms and standards concerning property over intellectual creations.

One way to understand the value of intellectual property protection of creativity is to look at it from the perspective of the author or creator. These individuals devote their lives to the creation and dissemination of art, knowledge and culture. They write novels, they paint, they compose music or make films. They are talented individuals, who have something to say through the expression of ideas. That expression, protected by copyright, contributes in many ways to the well-being of our society. Many creators are freelancers, working from their homes or offices and at their own expense. Although they are artists, they have the same responsibilities as many other people. They have to pay for housing, send their children to school, and pay taxes. In order to meet these responsibilities, they must benefit financially from their work. Copyright provides the mechanism for this benefit. In many cases, creators entrust professional enterprises such as book publishers and record producers to bring their works to market. These enterprises make significant investments in the dissemination and marketing of works. As a result, consumers everywhere can enjoy cultural products and services in a wide variety of formats and media. Technologies and creations that have touched and changed millions of lives would probably not exist today without the incentives provided by intellectual property rights.

## CREATIVE ECONOMY

Creative economy is an economy where the major inputs and outputs are ideas. It is an economy where most of the people spend most of their time in having ideas. The creative economy consists of the transactions in creative products. Each transaction may have two complementary values: the value of the intangible, intellectual property and the value of the physical carrier or platform. In some industries, such as digital software, the intellectual property value is higher. In others, such as art, the unit cost of the physical object is higher. The term creative economy has become extraordinarily widespread throughout the world. Everybody wants to be creative, every country wants to be creative, and every city wants to be known as creative. The knowledge economy is being eclipsed by the creativity economy. Entrepreneurs in the creative economy (often called 'creative entrepreneurs') use creativity to unlock the wealth that lies within them. They believe that this creative wealth, if managed right, will engender more wealth.

Creative industries consists of advertising, architecture, art, crafts, design, fashion, publishing, film and video, TV and radio, interactive leisure software, music, performing arts, photography, software and computer services—which most countries have accepted and that are arts based. Now, science and other non-arts based industries are also being included in this list. The 'copyright industries' consist of all industries that create copyright or related works as their primary product. The 'patent industries' consist of all industries that produce or deal in patents. The 'trademark and design industries' are even more widespread, and their sheer size and diversity make them less distinctive. Together, these four industries constitute the 'creative industries'. In the cultural industries, or content industries or copyright-based industries, what is pivotal is that human endeavour and its resulting 'creations' begins with creativity. One's capacity to then exploit such creativity will be the key driver to a competitive and vibrant business community. Along with creativity, intellectual property will fuel modern creative economies.

The existence and function of such industry has enriched great nations like Italy, Japan, India, and the America to mention but a few. This industry needs structuring, funding, and heavy investment by the government. The governments by now know of other nation's gains from arts and entertainment. Entertainment can fetch so much for a nation. Oil has made a lot but can dry up whereas entertainment can make so much more and keep on forever. Arts can be used for the advancement of technology, and creativity through innovations and improvisation. Japan, India and Italy are examples of nations that have passed through the mills successfully to swell their national economy and thinned out their unemployment queues. It is possible for art to create mass employment because it is difficult for machines to replace the human factor in arts' productive processes. In fact, creativity knows no limits. Recognizing and developing this limitless resource, and exploiting it as an economic asset, is key to achieving prosperity in today's world. The creative industries require creative thinkers. Day-by-day the demand for creative thinkers is increasing. It is the demand of 21st century. Creative industries, such as publishing, music, film, software and arts, are a powerful generator of economic growth and employment in both the developed and developing world.

The World Intellectual Property Organization (WIPO) has recently established the Creative Industries Division. This has been done in response to the growing interest and needs of the Member States of WIPO to address the economic developmental impact that intellectual property policies and practices have on the creative industries. The objective of the Division is to provide a focal point for related policy and industry discourse. It aims to engage with the traditional and non-traditional intellectual property stakeholders in order to advance the conceptualization of the creative industries. Its activities will relate, among others, to developing tools and carrying out studies on the creative potential of nations, visualizing and quantifying the economic contribution of creative activities, developing practical tools, and assisting creators in benefiting from their intellectual property assets.

2

# IDEAS, INVENTIONS AND INNOVATIONS

An idea is a prescription for action. It is starting point of all intellectual creations, the seeds from which all innovations and creative works grow. In fact, intellectual property starts with idea. From the words, music and images, which move us, to the brands which attract us; from the bicycle to bio-fuel, from the microchip to mobile phone—it all starts with an idea. Ideas, inspiration, and ingenuity are the seeds from which grow the simplest ideas for problem-solving devices or the great scientific advances. From thoughts, which inspire the latest musical hits, to the genius which produces literary masterpieces grow from the seeds of ideas. In fact, entire innovation process starts from idea.

Ideas shape our world. They are the raw materials on which our future prosperity and heritage depend. Mankind's inexhaustible capacity for producing ideas makes us unique. Yet this extraordinary ability is often taken for granted. Everybody has ideas. Our sub-conscious mind is a powerhouse of ideas. We hardly notice the countless ideas we generate everyday, or how much of what we value is the fruit of others' ideas: labour-saving inventions, pleasing designs, and life-saving technologies. Many great ideas were not even recognized by their inventor. Most people can have a single great idea. But what separates great thinkers from the rest of us is a single great mind that springs many great ideas.

Ideas are more potent than facts, even though the ideas may be illusions. Every great achievement is a vision in the soul before it becomes a fact of history. Ideas control the world. They triumph over the blind forces. If we contemplate the stupendous movement across the pages of history, we witness the power of ideas. From Plato to Gandhi, Cicero to Lincoln, great ideas have been impressing on the minds and conscience of the people, setting a fire their imagination, motivating them to rise to new heights, to seek means of endeavour, to tread new paths towards reconstruction, greatness and accomplishment.

We need ideas to save lives, ideas to make wealth, ideas to uplift or entertain. It is man's inexhaustible capacity for new ideas, which provides the raw materials on which technological, economic and cultural development depends. However, the ideas, which lead to discoveries are not limited to certain regions, they are distributed throughout the whole world.

## GETTING GOOD IDEAS

It is important to provide environments in which innovative ideas are encouraged and rewarded. In order to overcome mental barriers and reach creative ideas, total freedom is necessary—no directional guidance, constraints, criticism, or thinking within bounded scope. Then ideas can be drawn and contemplated from an infinite space during the creativity process. Bringing a new idea to market requires experience and know-how. Most of us have had an idea for a new product only to dismiss or neglect it. Sometimes we later find that others had the same idea, but they did something with it and it is their product in the market, not ours. Idea generation consists of two steps: the creation of an idea and the commercial development of that idea. However, most ideas developed for maximum commercial value will need to be legally protected for encroachment and undesirable imitation. Possible sources of good ideas are our customers, our competitors, our peers, the literature, patents, and our own sub-conscious. Serendipity is a very effective process for coming up with useful new ideas, but requires us to keep our eyes open and imagination turned on. "Chance favours the prepared mind," said Louis Pasteur. We may find useful solutions by reviewing our backlog of problems while we browse at random in libraries, trade shows, and the real world. We should review our problems before we go to sleep at night and keep a notepad and audio recorder handy. We may meditate out under a tree or in an open field. We should play with combinations of ideas and concepts. We should think about analogies to the problem. We should work on ideas or themes that are being worked on by others. We may work with high performers in fields related to our own to identify and adopt their relevant methods, tools and "tricks of the trade". We may trade ideas with all.

New ideas take a while to catch on. Great enthusiasm is, however, needed to embrace the new idea. There are series of steps to have a useful idea: have idea, test it, note the result, tweak idea, and test tweaked idea, note result. According to necessity the process may continue. A marketeer may have a creative idea for a marketing campaign. He or she has to put it into action and do a test campaign to know whether it is as good an idea as is hoped. The results come back in. The idea will be tweaked to see whether the results can be improved on subsequent tests. Each test gives vital new information on the worth of this marketing idea. Depending on the results that are generated, the idea will be dismissed or put into wide spread use. Feedback is essential to the creative process of improving upon existing and new ideas. "A man with new idea is crank until the idea succeeds," Mark Twain.

If we expect to come up with a quantity of good ideas and we have an idea quota to meet. We should aim for a great idea a day, a brilliant idea a week. There is a saying, 'life brings idea, and idea brings life'. In his depressed mindset, Buckminster Fuller had been thinking about everything that was wrong with the world and all the awful challenges it faces. And the idea that struck him was so exciting to him that he resolved then and there to put it into practice and see where it led. In his own words, he embarked on "an experiment, to find what a single individual can contribute to changing the world and benefiting all humanity." This amazing idea could burst through the walls of suicidal depression and wrench Fuller back towards life. Similarly, Thomas Edison knew that an idea before its time would founder on the rocks of outright rejection. Ideas are just ghosts until given flesh and blood through action. As an inventor, Edison knew that the initial idea was raw and needed refining through increased knowledge. And the only way to increase knowledge was through experience. And experience was gained through experiment. We may generate brilliant ideas, innovations and great creative thinking with these creativity techniques used by geniuses in the past.

Creative ideas are necessary for sparking creativity and creative thinking. Incubating creative ideas through our dreams stimulates extraordinary thinking, creativity, innovation and breakthrough idea generation. Because creative ideas are different from those that normally arise, people often believe that such ideas require conditions dramatically different from the usual.

## INVENTIONS

Inventions are one of the most important forms of human creativity. They are creation of new devices, objects, ideas, or procedures useful in accomplishing human objectives. It is the process through which something is produced or constructed by original thought. In simple term, an invention is a product or process that provides a new way of doing something, or offers a new and inventive solution to a technical problem. It may relate to the creation of an entirely new device, product, method or process, or may simply be an incremental improvement to a known product or process. Merely finding something that already exists in nature generally does not qualify as an invention; an adequate amount of human ingenuity, creativity and inventiveness must be involved.

Ideas are relatively easy to come by; inventions are more difficult. It takes knowledge, time, money and effort to refine an idea into a workable invention, even on paper. While the most inventions nowadays are the result of considerable efforts and long-term investments in research and development (R&D), many simple and inexpensive technical improvements, of great market value, have yielded significant income and profits to their inventors or companies. In common usage the term invention is applied only to the production of new materials or operable devices, and the term inventor is applied to a person, who has produced a new device or material. Inventors can be anyone, male or female, old or young, rich or poor, college educated or high school drop-out, anyone who is motivated to design and market new products and ideas. The inventor uses his skill and inventive ingenuity to invent. Inventor makes things better by making better things. The product of his labour is the invention. Many inventors say they were motivated to become inventors by the opportunity to make a difference in the world. While some inventors are employed by companies to develop new products, most work independently. They not only come up with ideas for new products, but they must also sell these ideas to investors, manufacturers, or the public. Inventors also build prototypes, apply for patents and research market demand and production costs.

Many successful inventors have a background in product design and development. Others become inventors simply by inventing. One can be able to train him to think like an inventor by studying major inventions of the past and following the path from idea to market, visit science centres, trade shows or online forums that focus on inventing.

Inventions in the context of patents are successful solutions to technical problems. New inventions lead to new technologies, create new jobs, and improve our quality of life. This is different from a discovery, which is something that already existed but had not been found.

## DISCOVERY

An invention has been distinguished from discovery. A discovery relates to things which are already existing in the nature and should not belong to any particular individual where as invention is man-made. Just as inventions can lead to discoveries, discoveries can sometimes also lead to inventions. A discovery can be as simple as the observation of a previously unnoticed phenomenon while an invention is a human-devised machine, tool, or apparatus that did not previously exist. Discoveries can only come from the greatest mind. They do not seem to need any financial incentive. Further, on the basis of criteria of patentability, only invention is patentable discovery is not. However, the difference between invention and discovery is not as clear as one might think.

Thus, scientific principles are not patentable nor are mathematical formulae. They are concepts, something discovered but which existed all along. Einstein could not patent his celebrated energy equation $E = mc^2$ nor could Newton have patented the law of gravity, because these were discoveries. Discoveries lead men and women to uncharted areas of the mind. Scientific principles and mathematical formulae are cases of discoveries of fundamental nature.

## INNOVATIONS

Similarly, in simple terms innovation is nothing but the successful exploitation of new ideas. It is implementing the creative idea and benefiting from it. Implementation is the key to innovation. Generally put, an innovation is developing a new idea and putting it into practice. Appreciating the distinction between "invention" and "innovation" is important. Invention refers to a technical solution to a technical problem. It may be an innovative idea or may be in the form of a working model or prototype. Innovation refers to the translation of the invention into a marketable product or process. Innovation is not the same as invention. It is a process, which begins from the conception of an idea to the launching of a new or improved product/process in the market place. While innovations are concerned with the commercialization of new ideas; in contrast, an invention may not be directly associated with commercialization. As such, innovation may be seen as a process of interaction and feedback during the various stages of the new product development process. Innovation is a social process. It is much more to do with developing a new way, a new method, new methodology of doing something for the market, and taking it to the consumer.

An invention is considered as the generation of a new idea or knowledge, which aims to solve a specific technical problem. As not all inventions are commercialized, so it is clear that not all inventions result in innovations. Only commercially successful inventions become innovations that change the way people do things. Turning an invention into an innovation—a new product launched into, and accepted by, the marketplace—takes a lot of effort, not to mention a little luck. There are formidable tasks and substantial barriers in the path of those, who pursue innovation. Accomplishing these tasks and overcoming the barriers typically require much careful planning and input from others. A lot of new ideas are created or born but most die a lonely death, never seeing the light of commercial success. However, in the context of patent, the use of the terms 'innovation' and 'invention' are synonyms.

Innovation is the key for the production as well as processing of knowledge. Indeed a nation's ability to convert knowledge into wealth and social good through the process of innovation determines its future. Dr. A.P.J. Abdul Kalam once said, "when a nation recognizes the innovation, the nation gets intellectually elevated". Innovative approaches to unraveling the mysteries of nature and exploiting them for social benefits are well-documented.

Technological innovation may be classified in several ways: product vs. process, radical (basic or fundamental) vs. incremental (improvement), and disruptive vs. sustaining (sequential and/or complementary). Other important types of (non-technological) innovations that do not result from scientific and/or technological R&D but are often crucial for profitably marketing the products and services resulting from the investment made in R&D are: marketing innovation, institutional innovation, and complementary innovation. Innovation happens when a new invention changes a way of doing things.

Technological basic or fundamental innovations produce new markets and new industrial branches for a new product. Such an innovation is also described as a radical or disruptive innovation. An improvement innovation (also called an incremental, sustaining, sequential or complementary innovation) would lead to an improved product over its ancestor in terms of quality, reliability, ease of use, environmental protection, raw material use, labour cost, and so on. It may also include the application of new and better production processes or techniques that allow old or new products to be made more both reliably, of better quality, or simply in larger quantities. Innovation moves science, technology and mankind forward; this is the highest reward that an inventor can receive. Technological innovation as an interactive process made up of a number of distinct stages, beginning with the formulation of a novel idea/concept, followed by research and development (R&D), ending in the launch of a new or improved product in the marketplace.

Some of the main reasons why companies innovate include: to improve manufacturing processes in order to save costs and improve productivity; to introduce new products that meet customer needs; to remain ahead of the competition and/or expand market share; to ensure that technology is developed to meet actual and emerging needs of the business and its clients; and to prevent technological dependence on other companies' technology. In today's economy, managing innovation within a company requires a good knowledge of the patent system in order to ensure that the company draws maximum benefit from its own innovative and creative capacity, establishes profitable partnerships with other patent holders and avoids making unauthorized use of technology owned by others. Unlike the past, many innovations nowadays are complex and are based on a number of patented inventions, which may be owned by different patent owners.

Innovations build upon each other. Every layer of innovation gets built on the next. Therefore, every inventor and creator are indebted to those, who came before. "If I have seen farther it is by standing on the shoulders of giants," said Newton. Entire innovation process starts from idea, to intellectual property protection, to commercialization. Every new product—from software to widgets—goes through a cycle that begins with basic research, then applied research, then incubation, then development, then testing, then manufacturing, then deployment, then support, then continuation engineering in order to add improvements. Each of these phases is specialized and unique. This is a whole product cycle. Businesses often invest large amounts of money in research and development and in the advertising and marketing of their products. These investments will not be undertaken unless businesses are in a position to recoup their expenditures.

Innovation, creativity, and technological development all contribute to economic growth. Innovation has become one of the most important vectors of sustainable growth for businesses, and of economic prosperity for society as a whole. Businesses must constantly improve or renew their products and services if they wish to keep or capture market shares and remain competitive.

## ENJOYING THE PRODUCTS OF HUMAN INVENTIVENESS

Inventions improve our lives in many ways. They make our tasks easier, entertain us, improve our knowledge of the world, and even save lives. Inventions make our life easier, better or simply more fun, they are essential to our everyday life. Stone Age man brought us fire. The engineers of ancient Mesopotamia laboured to invent the wheel, but, in more recent times, inventors have concentrated on conceiving countless devices to make our everyday lives easier. We owe our modern way of life to all the inventors who came before us. In fact, we are always surrounded by inventions. When we get up in the morning and put on our glasses, switch on the radio, and grab the morning paper. Already we have directly benefited from three of the greatest inventions: the glass lens, wireless communications, and the printing press. Later, when we use a computer and make telephone calls, we come across two more important developments made possible by scientific breakthroughs. Today, thanks to a millennium of scientific discovery and innovation, people's lives have been transformed. They can view events as they may happen half a world away. They can pick up the phone and talk to a friend or relative in a foreign country in seconds. Motorized transportation, from cars to jets, allows people to travel long distances in short time periods. Electricity runs a vast array of labour-saving and entertainment devices. Newspapers and books are inexpensive and readily available. Life expectancy has greatly increased as medical science tracks down the causes and cures of more and more diseases. The desktop computer is a powerful tool for working, creating, and communicating. All of these inventions have had a profound impact on the course of human civilization and sparked great cultural development. Throughout history, inventions have helped people discover new worlds, build communities, develop resources, increase productivity, cure diseases, ease burdens, and enjoy life to the fullest.

In fact, someone invented in the past most of the things around us now. We have grown so used to these things, however, that we often do not think of them as inventions. The greatest inventions disappear from view because they become an integral part of the environment. We may think about the alphabet that we are using to communicate right now. The ink that writes and paper that these words are written on. The clothes we are wearing. The chair we are sitting on. All of these are inventions and there is a person, a human mind, behind each of them. Similarly, the house, the plough, our shoes, wheeled vehicles, fire igniters, ships, knife, hammer, money are such ancient inventions which are all still in use. Most people know very little about their origins. Some inventions from thousands of years ago are still in use today. For example, (*i*) the kite (the first kites were made more than 2000 years ago in China); (*ii*) wooden goggles (the ancestors of the Eskimos in Alaska invented wooden goggles around 2000 years ago); (*iii*) lighthouse (the first known lighthouse was built around 280 BC on the Pharos Island in the harbour of Alexandria, Egypt); and (*iv*) the wheel (the oldest wheel known to humans was found in a part of modern Iraq known as ancient Mesopotamia. This wheel is more than 5000 years old). Sometimes different ancient civilizations independently invented very similar items. For example, almost every ancient civilization invented mirrors.

Our present-day homes are veritable showplaces of 20th-century advancements. Modern labour-saving appliances and household items have changed all the drudgery and backbreaking work and significantly altered the way we live. The technologies that created these household devices owe a huge debt to electrification, which brought light and power into the home. Then two major engineering innovations—resistance heating and small, efficient motors—led to electric stoves and irons, vacuum cleaners, washers, dryers, and dishwashers. In the second half of the century advances in electronics yielded appliances that could be set on timers and even programmed, further reducing the domestic workload by allowing washing and cooking to go on without the presence of the human launderer or cook. Thus, new inventions are changing the nature of our homes. Slowly and gradually 'smart' appliances like washing machines and dishwashers are entering to our homes. A day is not far off when various inventions and everyday appliances will be linked together. Our future homes will be 'intelligent' homes full of smart tools. There are now Wi-Fi-enabled, remote operated homes where many sci-fi features are provided in terms of security, safety, information, communication, automation and entertainment. This will all be possible due to the fruits of human inventions.

Office technology has driven much of the innovation in communications, working styles, and even in the value placed on certain skill sets. Trends point to smaller and faster office machines that will be capable of carrying out more complex functions with minimal human input in the 21st century.

So many seminal new inventions are coming into right now. Inventions such as airplanes and the Internet have made our world smaller. It is now faster and easier for people and ideas to travel around the world. The diffusion of personal computers, fax machines, windows, and dial-up modems connected to a global telephone network all came together in late 1980s and early 1990s to create the basic platform that started the global information revolution. People found that they really liked doing all these things on a computer, and they really improved the productivity.

Almost every piece of equipment that stores, transmits, displays, or manipulates information has at its core silicon chips filled with electronic circuitry. These chips each house many thousands or even millions of transistors. Today these chips are not just a part of computers, they are also important in devices as diverse as video cameras, cellular phones, copy machines, jumbo jets, modern automobiles, manufacturing equipment, electronic scoreboards, and video games. Without the transistor there would be no Internet and no space travel. Transistors are deeply embedded in the fabric of modern technology.

The growth of Internet and World Wide Web (www) enabled people to connect with other people as never before. WWW is a system for creating, organizing, and linking documents so that they could be easily browsed—a concept created by the British computer scientist Tim Berners-Lee. With these innovations, today remarkable searches are going on via search engines like Google in so many different tongues. Google is now processing roughly one billion searches per day. Never before in the history of the planet have so many people had the ability to find so much information about so many things and about so many other people. Kids had universal access to the information in libraries all over the world. Internet has made easily available the world's knowledge in every language. Today the most profound thing is that children in Romania or India or Soviet Union or Vietnam have all the informations, all the tools, all the softwares easily available to apply knowledge however they want.

With Palm Pilot, cell phone, everyone, everywhere can carry around access to all the world's knowledge in his or her pockets. The data communication—the ability to access Internet, e-mail or business files—can take place any time anywhere by a cell phone, Palm Pilot, etc. With cell phone and wireless technology we are now more informed. It has shortened the distance and provided more access to information. It aims at making all the world's knowledge, or even just a chunk of it, available to anyone and everyone, every time, anywhere.

IPod has empowered us in another way with entertainment instead of knowledge. We may now download all the favourite songs into our iPods and carry it all over. Now TiVo can become our own TV editor. TiVo allows viewers to digitally record their favourite programmes and skip ads except things they want to see. We can watch whatever we want when we want.

VoIP (Voice over Internet Protocol) service allows us to make phone calls over the Internet by turning voices into data packets that are sent down Internet networks and converted back into voices on the other end. Internet and personal computer (PC) or laptop will make every business and personal phone call to anywhere in this world as cheap as local calls, *i.e.*, almost free. It is going to revolutionize the telecommunication industry.

Once the PC-windows revolution demonstrated to everyone the value of being able to digitize the information and manipulate it on computers and word processors, and once the browser brought the Internet alive and made Web pages sing and dance and display, everyone wanted everything digitized as much as possible as they could send it to someone else down the Internet pipes. Thus, began the digitization revolution. Digitization is that magic process by which words, music, data, films, and picture are turned into bits and bytes—combinations of 1s and 0s – that can be manipulated on the computer screen, stored on a microprocessor, or transmitted over satellites and fibre-optic lines. It used to be post office where we went to send our mail, but once the Internet came alive, we wanted our mail digitized so we could e-mail it. Photography used to be a cumbersome process involving film coated with silver dug up from mines half way across the world. We used to take some pictures with our cameras, and then bring the film to our photographer to be sent off to a big plant somewhere for processing. But once the Internet made it possible to send picture around the world, attached to or in e-mails, we did not want to use silver film any more. We wanted to take pictures in the digital format, which could be uploaded not developed. And we did not want to be confined to using a camera to take them. We wanted to be able to use our cell phones to do it. We used to have to go to book depots to buy and browse for books, but once the Internet came alive, we wanted to browse for books digitally on Amazon.com as well. We used to go to library to do research, but now we wanted to do digitally through Google or Yahoo, not just by roaming the stacks. We used to buy CD to listen to popular film or classical songs—CDs had already replaced albums as a form of digitized music—but once the Internet came alive, we wanted those music bits to be even more malleable and mobile. We wanted to be able to download them into an iPod. In recent years the digitization technology evolved so we could do just that. Thus, everything from photography to entertainment to communication to word processing to architectural design to management of our home lawn sprinkler systems are being digitized and therefore can be shaped, manipulated and transmitted over computers, the Internet, satellite or fibre-optic cables. This is done with very high speed with total ease. In the mid-1990s—the opening of

Windows, the digitization of content, and the spreading of Internet browsers seamlessly connected people with people as never before, it did not take long before all these people, who were connected, wanted to do more than just browse and send e-mail, instant messages, pictures, and music over this Internet platform. They wanted to shape things, design things, create things, sell things, buy things, keep track of inventories, do someone else's taxes, and read somebody else's X-ray from half a world away. They wanted to be able to do any of these things from anywhere and from any computer to any computer seamlessly. Suddenly more people from different places found that they could collaborate with more other people on more different kinds of work and share more different kinds of knowledge than ever before. We are not just communicating with each other more than ever. We are now able to collaborate—to build coalitions, projects, and product together—more than ever.

It is an era in which new inventions and advanced technology will literally transform every aspect of business, every aspect of life and every aspect of society. As bio-science becomes more computational and less about wet laboratories, and as all the genomic data becomes easily available on the Internet, at some point we will be able to design vaccines on our laptop. Now we are going to see the real human mosaic emerge—from all over the world, from left field and right field, from West and East and North and South—to drive the next generation of innovation. This is how we are enjoying the products of human inventiveness.

The last 1,000 years have produced an incredible number and variety of scientific and technological breakthroughs. Some of these inventions proved to be turning points in the way civilization proceeded forward. The inventions, which were considered most important, are the compass, the mechanical clock, the glass lens, the printing press, the steam engine, the telegraph, electric power, wireless communications, antibiotics, and the transistor. These inventions either provided radically new ways to do an important job, or they made possible tasks that were previously unimagined. Their impact was felt, if not right away then eventually, by a large portion of humanity. These developments have enabled significant new technological innovations and scientific discoveries. And finally, they have had an enduring effect on the world. It is also reported that the five key technological advances, *i.e.,* the gun, the computer, the jet engine, the telephone and the television, triggered scores of subsequent developments.

## POPULAR INVENTIONS

The most popular and consequential inventions listed in the literature are described below. Before the invention of the mechanical clock, time was inseparable from events, the main one being the Sun crossing the sky. Only local time existed, no universal river of time. Mechanical clocks came around with gears, springs, pendulums, etc. Gradually, as these clocks all came to be co-ordinated, they created public time, a thing in itself: one single, universal current flowing everywhere throughout the universe, always at the same pace. People could now communicate with each other by co-ordinating to this universal frame of reference. Thus, clocks made factories, offices, schools, meetings, and appointments possible. The first true mechanical clocks emerged in the 14th century in Europe. History gives no single person credit for the key invention that made these clocks possible.

In 1440, German inventor Johannes Gutenberg invented a printing press process that, with refinements and increased mechanization, remained the principal means of printing until the late 20th century. Gutenberg's press, with its moveable type, launched publishing. In the short term, this made the reformation possible by putting a Bible in the hands of anybody who wanted one. Bible still stands as a landmark of typographical elegance. In the longer term, publishing universalized literacy. What civilization gained from Gutenberg's invention is incalculable. The inventor's method of printing from moveable type, including the use of metal molds and alloys, a special press, and oil-based inks, allowed for the first time the mass production of printed books.

Three centuries ago, almost everyone died of infectious diseases. When the plague broke out in 1347, it killed nearly half of Europeans in about two years. When diseases such as

*Thomas Edison's Telephone (1911)*

*Thomas Edison and the Phonograph*

*Japanese Lantern Clock*

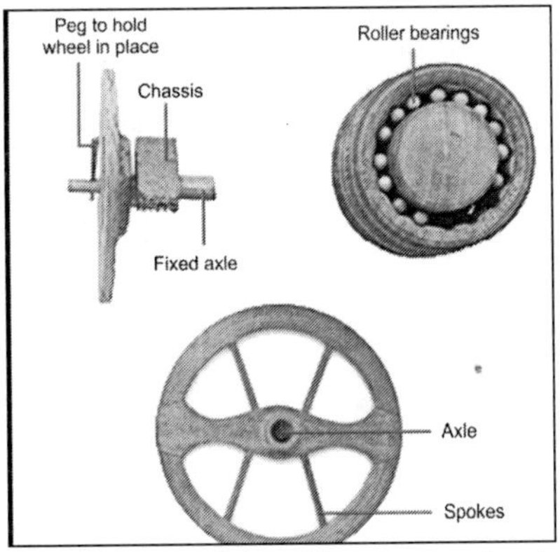


*Wheel (One of the oldest innovations)*

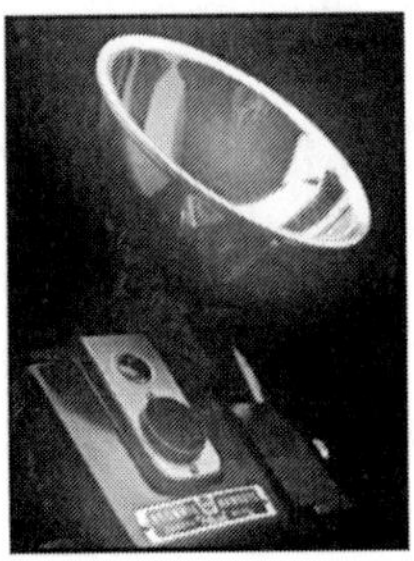

*Kodak Brownie Box Camera*

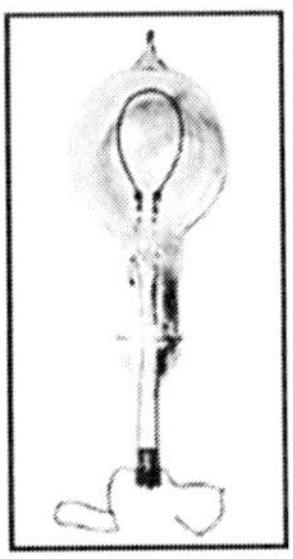

*Thomas Edison's First Light-bulb*

***A Few Early Inventions***

smallpox reached North America, they reduced the indigenous population by about 90 per cent within a century. As late as 1800, the leading cause of death in the West was tuberculosis. Today mainly because of immunization and antibiotics our life expectancy has increased. The development of penicillin and the huge range of antibiotics that followed may have had a more profound effect on the health of humanity than any other in medical history. Within the space of a few decades following World War II, whole classes of once-fatal or life-threatening diseases became treatable. The development of antibiotics gave people an enormously effective shield against the scourge of disease.

The invention of telephone made us talk to someone in another city without leaving home. However, once the device was invented, and businessmen had wrested it away from the inventors, the network began to form. That is the actual invention—the network. It enables anyone to talk to anyone anywhere at any given moment. Alexander Graham Bell came up with the telephone, a refinement that has become commonplace in modern society. More than a century of further improvements have brought high-speed communications of all types, including the Internet. But the telegraph shrank the world in one swoop in a way that no subsequent invention has matched. Wireless communication technologies have changed the world, bringing news and ideas to far-flung corners of the globe and influencing everything from fashion and language to the rise and fall of political systems. Probably no means of communication has revolutionized the daily lives of ordinary people more than the telephone.

The modern world is an electrified world. The light bulb, in particular, profoundly changed human existence by illuminating the night and making it hospitable to a wide range of human activity. Thomas Alva Edison invented the electric light in 1879. He was neither the first nor the only person trying to invent an incandescent light bulb.

Electricity existed all along, but the system of devices needed to generate this force and distribute it to individual buildings was an invention—Edison's masterpiece. Now, anyone in the

West and throughout most of the world can tap into the grid to power everything from light bulbs to computers.

The invention of the car or the airplane is among the most important inventions of the millennium. But these were merely evolutionary refinements of the steam engine—the first machine to convert burning fuel into mechanical energy on a large scale. Wood and later ones by coal powered the first steam engines.

The innovation that made electricity available in large quantities for human use was the dynamo, a machine that converted mechanical motion into electrical power. Access to cheap, reliable electric power at the flick of a switch has helped raise living standards around most of the world. Once cars were invented, roads were improved. Once roads were improved, cities sprouted suburbs, because people could now live in the country, yet work in the city. Wherever a television set is on, it absorbs attention like no other piece of furniture.

Carl von Linde, German engineer, whose invention of a continuous process of liquefying gases in large quantities formed a basis for the modern technology of refrigeration. Refrigeration is chiefly used to store foodstuffs at low temperatures, thus inhibiting the destructive action of bacteria, yeast, and mold.

Today, more and more people are having deepest, richest, most diverse, and rewarding relationship with their computers. Computer plays games with people, tells them jokes, and plays music to them. People have great conversations with computer, too. These conversations appear as e-mails.

The toilet and modern plumbing, the ability to remove sewage from and bring clean water into places of dense human habitation makes the modern city possible. Without it, we would still have cities, but not like the ones we know.

In more recent times, inventors have concentrated on conceiving countless devices to make our everyday lives easier. Here are a few such essential inventions: (1) The battery: Power is not enough for us; we want power wherever we go. We use millions of portable electrical devices everyday and most of them draw their power from the humble battery. Italian physicist Alessandro Volta, who named his creation the Voltaic Pile, invented it in 1800. Volta's breakthrough came when he generated an electric current by submerging copper and zinc strips in salt water. (2) The bar code: a system that would automatically collect product information. (3) The ballpoint pen. (4) The microwave oven. (5) The sticking plaster. (6) The parking meter.

Many inventions are the results of an accident. Many inventors find things that happen in their daily lives that cause them to think of some problem in a new way. The inventor of Velcro ®—fastener for clothes—thought of his invention while removing burrs from his pet's fur after walking in the woods. Eli Whitney watched a cat pull feathers through a cage. It was how he thought of the invention now known as the cotton gin.

Other inventions come about when their inventors try to think of uses for things. For example, vulcanized (heated) rubber for tires came about that way. Similarly, "yellow stickies" (PostIt ®) were the result of a "failed" adhesive experiment, which was too weak to market, until the chemist figured out that a weak adhesive had good uses too.

Many inventions have taken several centuries to develop into their modern forms and are rarely the product of a single inventor's efforts. A light bulb flashing over the head of a lone scientist is the universal symbol of invention, but Edison's electric light bulb, which was the product of a whole team of engineers working with ideas cribbed from other inventors, is the rule rather than the exception. Every breakthrough is a collective effort that combines and tweaks already existing ideas and technology in novel ways. Everyday objects seldom spring fully formed into the world. They evolve, sometimes slowly, over centuries. Therefore, a very important truth is, inventions are seldom the work of anyone mind. Each invention may be just one small step on the road to the ultimate goal. Every great invention is really either an aggregation of minor inventions, or the final step of a progression. It is not a creation, but a growth; several individuals frequently bring out the same invention in several countries, and simultaneously.

When we study the great inventions of the world, we find that they are either very simple, basic things like the wheel or very complex things like the computer. Some inventions were silly, some deadly serious, but even the inventions that were not successful were not all failures either. Each invention shed some light on the good intentions of the inventor and their quest to improve the quality of life. The economy of the present day world is driven by new products, new inventions.

Frequently an important invention is made before the world is ready to receive it, and the unhappy inventor is taught, by his failure, that it is as unfortunate to be in advance of his age as to be behind it. Inventions only become successful when they are not only needed, but when mankind is so far advanced in intelligence as to appreciate and to express the necessity for them, and to at once make use of them. Thomas Edison knew that an idea before its time would founder on the rocks of outright rejection. So, he deliberately kept his mind trained on projects that were already being explored by other inventors and scientists.

There is, however, a notable difference between the work environment of the older inventors and the present day inventor. Early inventors were usually isolated and unable to support themselves through their inventions. Today most modern inventions and discoveries take place in large research organizations supported by universities, government agencies, private industries, or privately endowed foundations. It is wonderful to have a world where single innovator can summon so many resources by him or her, assembles a team of partners from around the world, and make a real breakthrough with some product or service.

## BECOMING AN INVENTOR

The only traits that inventors have in common are creativity, curiosity and perseverance. Inventors are the ordinary genius next door. It is not surprising then that anyone can be an inventor regardless of age, gender, race or nationality. Young people are particularly well-suited to be inventors. For starters, young people can be just as talented and creative as adults. In addition, they often have more open minds and enthusiasm than older people. It is the young people of today who will improve our future world.

The first thing one needs to become an inventor is an idea, an inspiration for something new. He has to identify a need or problem. We should ask ourselves, do we need a better product than that which we can find on the market? Can we think of something that will make a task easier for us or for someone we know? We may think about something in an unexpected way. We may describe doing something in words for something entirely different. One should not be shy about asking for advice and guidance. So, the guiding principle for inventor is to carefully define a problem. He or she should focus on what he or she is trying to do in the first place—instead of simply how to do things. One should try changing the question—starting with a different word—who, what, where, when, why, how, etc. One should change his or her perspective on a problem—looking for something is not at all the same as finding it, and putting something away is very different from getting rid of it.

Many inventors find things that happen in their daily lives that cause them to think of some problem in a new way. Other inventions come about when their inventors try to think of uses for things. Many times inventors come up with a solution for a problem or find a problem that fits their solution by either "turning a problem around" or selecting two or more things at random and using them to "seed" new ideas. "Turning a problem around," means looking at it from a different angle or thinking about it in a new way. Einstein and his pupil, Leó Szilárd, motivated by the death of a family from toxic fumes from their gas refrigerator, patented new types of refrigerators. The patent rights sold to companies such as Electrolux in Sweden provided Einstein and Szilárd with a livelihood for a few years.

Once we have identified a need or problem and thought of a useful invention to solve it, it is time to start our research. We may find out everything we need to know about the science and technology related to our idea. Our textbooks may not contain all the information that we need for our research. We may find additional, more specific sources of information at our local library and the Internet.

Once we have done our research, we may start experimenting and adjust our invention until it works properly. We should remember to keep notes with descriptions and drawings of our experiments and of our final invention. At this point it is important to be patient and persistent. We should not despair if at first we do not succeed. We should remember that most inventors fail many times before they finally reach the result they want. We should remember also to keep an open mind at this stage. Experiments that go "wrong" can have excellent, unexpected uses. If our experiment fails, we should look at the result in a different way, you may find another use for this "failed" result.

In fact, in a country like USA, someone receives a patent grant every 3 minutes or registers a trademark every 5 minutes. Anybody may have done it. Anyone anywhere can be an inventor and file patent and trademark applications. It is just possible, at this very moment inventors all over the world are shaping their ideas into inventions that they will send to the patent and trademark offices as patent applications. Patent examiners examine those applications to see if they qualify to receive patents. Ultimately, those inventions, protected by patent grants, will be available in the marketplace. There, they may be sold under specific trademark names that have been registered at these offices. Someday, we might buy those products we recognize by their trademarks, and find that our lives have changed tremendously.

It is, therefore, very much necessary to keep the minds of our young adults ignited and the process intact. This will give a chance to show their creativity in designing the product, which can suit to people. The time has come to unleash the creative potential of our scientists and innovators at grassroots level.

## SOME OUTSTANDING INVENTORS

There are many great and often unrecognized pioneers in the field of invention and innovation. We owe our modern way of life to all the inventors, who came before us and yet most people cannot name more than one or two of them. Our world would have been different without Alexander Graham Bell's telephone, Garrett Morgan's traffic light, or An Wang's computer technology. Police officers and soldiers are safer today because of Stephanie Kwolek's development of Kevlar, the fibres used to make bulletproof vests. Looking around we would see many other famous inventions nearby that we know by their trademarks. American Thomas Alva Edison patented more than 1,000 inventions in his lifetime, including the electric light bulb, the phonograph, and a transmitter that made Alexander Bell's telephone a usable instrument on a wide scale. Edison conducted thousands of experiments before he finally improved the incandescent light bulb. He did this by using lower current, a smaller carbonized fibre and a better vacuum inside the bulb. In 1879, Edison showed his incandescent lamp to the world.

Kelvin was one of the most extraordinary figures of the nineteenth century—indeed of any century. He accumulated 69 patents from which he grew abundantly wealthy. Among much else, he suggested the method that led directly to the invention of refrigerator, devised the scale of absolute temperature that still bears his name, invented the boosting devices that allowed telegrams to be sent across oceans, and made innumerable improvements to shipping and navigation, from the invention of a popular marine compass to the creation of the first depth sounder.

Leonardo Da Vinci was a famous painter and sculptor but also a great inventor. He had an excellent understanding of how machines worked and invented many things during his lifetime. His inventions included parachutes, flying devices, diving gear and many other machines.

Einstein's outstanding contribution to science needs no further words. Less well known is that Einstein was himself an inventor with many patents to his name.

Melvin De Groote, with 925 patents to his credit, invented method to separate crude oil from water, process that adheres chocolate to vanilla ice cream.

Francis H. Richards invented Golf-ball-molding machine, air-cushion door spring, and high-speed envelope machine. He took 894 patents.

Elihu Thomson invented electrically operated pipe organ, cream separator, electric welding and obtained 696 patents.

*Rudolf Christian Karl Diesel*

With 554 patents Jerome Lemelson invented bar-code reader, computer-controlled tourniquet, audiocassette-drive mechanism, and magnetic-recording system.

Dr. Yoshiro NakaMats is Japan's greatest inventor; in fact, he is the World's most prolific inventor with over 3,000 patents to his name. He invented things like the floppy disk, the hard disk, and the digital watch. This living genius has been able to come up with so many brilliant, zany ideas.

*George Eastman*

Following inventors have also made human life more comfortable and enjoyable by their inventions. Prussian physicist Gabriel Fahrenheit invented the mercury thermometer in 1714. In 1800, Italian Count Alessandro Volta invented the first method of producing a steady flow of electric current. When photography was first invented in the early 1800s, materials were expensive and photography was complicated, limiting it to professionals. American photographer and manufacturer George Eastman, changed this by inventing the first dry, transparent and flexible roll film (patented in 1884) and the first camera specifically designed for roll film (patented in 1888). German engineer Rudolf Diesel invented diesel engines in 1892. French chemist Louis Pasteur invented pasteurization process in 1856.

## WOMEN INVENTORS

Women inventors in the 19th century as a group faced and often overcame significant hurdles to achieve their goals. Their one common bond is an innate curiosity that spurs them on to find something new, something better. Today, only about 10% of all patents are awarded to women. As we learn more and more about these creative women, their stories will inspire future generations of women inventors. Ada Augusta Lovelace laid some of the early conceptual and technical groundwork for high technology by helping develop an early computer. Marie Curie was the first female recipient of a Nobel Prize, for the discovery of radioactive elements. Mary Anderson was awarded a patent in 1903 for a window-cleaning device, a forerunner to the windshield wiper. Lizzie Magie invented a game called The Landlords Game a forerunner of the Monopoly game. Marion Donovan sold her disposable diaper invention for about $1 million in order to devote more time to developing other inventions.

Marie Curie

Grace Hopper was credited with devising the first compiler, a program that translates instructions for a computer from English to machine language. Ruth Handler invented an anatomically improbable molded plastic statuette named Barbie. Since its debut in 1959, the Barbie doll has become an American icon that functions as both a steady outlet for girls' dreams and an ever-changing reflection of American society. Stephanie Kwolek invented one of the modern world's most readily recognized and widely used materials: Kevlar. Her name appears on 16 patents; she is sole patent holder on seven.

Naomi Nakao, is a practicing gastroenterologist, founder of Granit Medical Innovations in 1989 and inventor of the Nakao Snare in 1991. She has 54 patents or patent pending in her name. Under Helen Greiner's leadership, iRobot Corporation is delivering robots into the industrial, consumer, academic, and military markets. In 2002, the ROOMBA robot vacuum was introduced to the consumer products marketplace.

Jennifer Tuttle submitted a short essay to the Live Your Dream contest. Tuttle created a game, Multiplication Madness. In February 2006 she was selected as the winner and won over $250,000 in cash, products and training for her effort.

## YOUNG INVENTORS

Following young inventors also deserve a mention here of their outstanding contribution. It covers both young inventors that became well-known and some lesser-known young inventors and their contributions. French engineer Sadi Carnot's was only 18 when he invented his famous Carnot Cycle. Van Hoff was only 17 when he won the Nobel Prize for chemistry. He discovered the tetrahedral structure of carbon. In 1850, at the age of 12, Margaret Knight witnessed a serious accident at a textile mill. Concerned for the safety of the mill's workers, she invented a stop-motion device to quickly stop the powered textile looms in case something went wrong. Her invention was put to use at many mills where it increased the safety of all mill workers. This was only the first of Margaret's many inventions. She was granted more than 25 patents in her lifetime, including one for a flat-bottomed paper bag still used in some stores today. In 1642, at the age of 19, Pascal invented a mechanical adding machine, which his father could use to calculate the taxes more quickly and accurately. Pascal's machine was called the Pascaline.

In 1721, Benjamin Franklin at the age of 15 was busily occupied in delivering newspapers by day and in composing articles for it at night. These articles, published anonymously, won wide notice and acclaim for their pithy observations on the current scene. When Louis Braille was 15 years old, he developed an ingenious system of reading and writing by means of raised dots. Today, in virtually every language throughout the world, Braille is the standard form of writing and reading used by blind people. At the age of 15, Cyrus Hall McCormick invented a lightweight cradle for carting harvested grain. Seven years later, in 1831 he invented the reaper, a horse drawn farm implement to cut small grain crops.

Henry Bessemer produced his first invention at the age of seventeen—embossed stamps for use on title deeds. At that time, the British government was losing thousands of pounds in revenue each year through the illegal reuse of title stamps. Bessemer's invention made the crime impossible and earned him his first job. When he was 15 years old, Thomas Alva Edison published a weekly newspaper, printing it in a freight car that also served as his laboratory. While working as a telegraph operator, he made his first important invention, a telegraphic repeating instrument. Since the age of 18, Alexander Graham Bell had been working on the idea of transmitting speech. While working on a multiple telegraph, he developed the basic ideas for the telephone.

George Westinghouse, at age 19, obtained his first patent, for a rotary steam engine. At age 17, Chester Greenwood applied for a patent. For the next 60 years, Greenwood's factory made earmuffs. Greenwood went on to create more than 100 other inventions.

Philo Farnsworth, a 14-year-old, had an idea while working on his father's Idaho farm. Philo realized an electron beam could scan a picture in horizontal lines, reproducing the image almost instantaneously. It would prove to be a critical breakthrough, towards electronic television.

At 16 years age, George Nissen finished high school and set out to develop a bouncing apparatus (trampoline). Working in his parents' garage using steel materials he found at a junkyard, he built a rectangular frame with a piece of canvas stretched across it. It was an instant hit. Nissen was sure he could commercialize it. As a 17-year-old high school junior, Robert Heft found himself in need of a class project. The teacher initially turned down his proposed 50-star American flag idea. He went ahead and finished his project, receiving a B minus for his efforts. Heft's teacher compromised and promised to deliver a better classroom grade if he could get the U.S. Congress to accept his flag. The rest is history. "I called it a Batball because I can store my baseballs inside the bat and I like it. It's really cool." says Jacob Dunnack age 8. Taylor Hernandez, age 10, invented "Magic Sponge Blocks," large building blocks made from sponge that can safely stack high without worry that they could fall and hurt a child.

## COMPANIES WHERE INNOVATIONS HAPPEN

The US is still the leading engine of innovation in the world. It was American innovators who started Google, Intel, HP, Dell, Microsoft and CISCO, and it matter, where innovation happens.

Following are the companies with most patents in 20th century. General Electric has 50,837 patents. Inventions in its credit are: electric fan (1902), X-ray tube (1913), first U.S. jet engine (1941), solid-state laser (1962), and computed tomography, a.k.a. CT scanner (1970). IBM with 32,498 patents has invented: integrated tabulator (1903), scanning tunneling microscope (1981), and deep blue parallel computing system (1995). Westinghouse Electric (28,005 patents) is known for its inventions like: full kitchen range (1917), commercial nuclear power plant (1957), and camera on the moon (1969). AT&T has 24,578 patents. Its well-known inventions are: coaxial cable (1929), quartz clock (1930), transistor (1947), solar cell (1954), Laser (1958), and Touch-Tone service (1963). General Motors has bagged 23,948 patents. Its popular inventions are: electric self-starter (1912), diesel-powered train (1934), automatic transmission (1940), and catalytic converter (1975).

## HISTORY OF HUMAN INVENTIVENESS

From the beginning of time, humans everywhere have been inventing. The earliest artifacts show evidence of human inventiveness. The names of the great archaeological ages—the Stone Age, the Bronze Age, and the Iron Age—are derived from the inventive use of stone and metal implements. Innovative approaches to unraveling the mysteries of nature and exploiting them for social benefits are well-documented in the archives. If we believe we are civilized today, it is only because our early ancestors were constantly struggling to improve things for themselves and future generations. There have been many significant inventions throughout the course of history. The latest evidence suggests that an ancestor of modern mankind, Homo erectus, was able to use fire around 500,000 B.C. Invention of the bow and arrow took place in 20,000 B.C. Domestication of animals began in 12,000 B.C. The ability to tame the land around us is at the core of civilized existence. The people of Mesopotamia were practising early forms of agriculture almost in 8,000 B.C. Pottery was invented in 7000 B.C. In 6000 B.C. weaving was invented. Irrigation systems were developed in the Middle East in 5000 B.C. First use of metals was reported in

4000 B.C. The earliest known examples of the wheel, dating from 3,500 B.C., are credited to the ingenious and industrious people of ancient Mesopotamia, situated in modern Iraq. Writing was invented in Sumeria 350 B.C. Around the same time Persian scientists had managed to extract copper from ore. The Chinese in 3000 B.C. invented abacus. In 2800 B.C. Egyptians devised the 12-month, 365-day calendar. Emperor Shen Nungin invented tea in China in 2737 B.C. In 100 B.C. Glassblowing was invented in Syria.

Ts'ai Lun in 105 A.D. invented paper in China. First description of Arabic numerals was found in 810. Windmills in Europe were found in 1180. In 1286 eyeglasses were invented in Europe. Spinning wheels were found in Europe in 1300. The earliest recorded mechanical clock is built in Italy in 1335. In 1440 Johannes Gutenberg invented printing press. Leonardo Da Vinci invented Mona Lisa Portrait in 1503. Blaise Pascal in 1642 invented adding machine. In early 18th century, Benjamin Franklin invented Franklin stove (1742), lightning rod (1752), and bifocal glasses (1760). Edward Jenner invented smallpox vaccine in 1796.

Some of the 19th century inventions are: electric battery invented by Alessandro Volta (1800); Alexander Bain invented fax machine in 1843; in the same year Charles Goodyear invented vulcanized rubber. Elais Howe invented sewing machine in 1846; Walter Hunt invented safety pin in 1849. Elisha Graves Otis invented elevator in 1852. Henry Bessemer invented Bessemer furnace in 1855. John Williamson Crary Sr invented brick making machine in 1858. Nathan Ames invented escalator in 1859. Daniel Hess invented vacuum cleaner in 1860. Alfred Nobel invented dynamite in 1866. Henri Nestlé invented baby formula in 1867. Sylvester Roper invented motorcycle in 1869. Nicholas Otto invented internal combustion engine in 1876. In the same year Carl Linde invented refrigerator. Alexander Graham Bell invented telephone in 1876. Thomas Alva Edison invented light bulb in 1879. George Eastman invented roll of film in 1884. William Stanley invented transformer in 1886. George Eastman invented camera, Kodak in 1888. In the same year Nikola Tesla invented electric power A.C. Karl Benz invented automobile in 1889.

Guglielmo Marconi invented wireless telegraph in 1895. Felix Hoffmann invented Aspirin in 1897.

A few 20th century innovations are: air conditioner invented by Willis Haviland Carrier (1902). Airplane invented by Wright Brothers (1903). Rocket, liquid-fueled invented by Robert Goddard (1912). Traffic light invented by William Potts (1920). Television invented by Philo T. Farnsworth (1927). Penicillin invented by Alexander Fleming (1928). Ballpoint pen invented by Ladislas & Georg Biro (1935). Nuclear reaction invented by Enrico Fermi (1942). Microwave oven invented by Percy LeBaron Spencer (1945). Instant photography invented by Edwin Land (1947). The transistor was invented in 1948 at Bell Telephone Laboratories by a team led by physicists John Bardeen, Walter Brattain, and William Shockley. Geodesic dome invented by R. Buckminster Fuller (1954). Integrated circuit invented by Jack Kilby and Robert Noyce (1958). In the same year Laser was invented by Arthur Schawlow & Charles Townes. Holography invented by Emmett Leith and Juris Upatnieks (1964). Hand-held calculator invented by Jack Kilby, J. VanTassel & J. Merryman (1966). Personal computer invented by Steve Jobs and Steve Wozniak (1976). Mobile phone invented by Richard Frenkiel and Joel Engel (1983).

IPod, invented by Tony Fadell in 2001, appears to be the significant innovation of 21st century. The machine age, which began with the Industrial Revolution and continues to this day, developed a group of inventions, of which the most important include the use of fossil fuels such as coal as sources of energy, the improvement of metallurgical processes (especially of steel and aluminum), the development of electricity and electronics, the invention of the internal-combustion engine, and the use of metal and cement in construction work.

## ENCOURAGING AND PROTECTING INVENTIONS

Inventions are so important to all of us that we should encourage potential and talented inventors to keep inventing. They should be given simple explanations of how top essential inventions (patents) work, why we need them, and how they contribute to scientific and technological progress. They should be exposed to the literature interspersed with the stories behind successful inventions. Inventor profiles may be drawn from around the world, and teachers are encouraged to supplement these by getting their students to research inventions from their home country. Scientific principles behind some of the featured inventions, such as the combination of concave and convex lenses in the telescope, or the laws of thermodynamics in cooling systems should be explained.

We should encourage students to recognize in themselves the essential qualities of curiosity, creativity and perseverance, which enable individuals to invent. They should be exposed to a roadmap for invention, taking students through the whole innovation process from idea, to intellectual property protection, to commercialization, a colourful journey through the world of inventions and patents.

When Russians landed Sputnik in 1957, US government became obsessed with educating young people to become scientists and engineers, a trend that was intensified by John F. Kennedy's commitment to a manned space programme. When Kennedy spoke about putting a man on the moon—his words inspired, assisted and launched many—into science, engineering and mathematics, and breakthrough and inventions they spawned went well beyond the space programme. The space race was really the science race.

University, public and private research laboratories do research, innovate and turn into products. In a way they are unique innovation-generating machines. They should be rewarded for risk-taking. USA has best regulated and most efficient capital markets in the world for taking new ideas and turning them into products and services. Risk capital is assigned to emerging ideas. Therefore, any country wanting to become technologically advanced needs the promotion of culture of innovation and entrepreneurship and pumping of more money in R&D. Top spenders on R&D in 2006 were USA ($330 billion), China ($136 billion) and Japan ($130 billion). China has beaten Japan to become the world's second biggest spender on research and development after United States. Fifteen of Europe's richest countries, including France, Germany and Britain, planned to spend a combined total of $230 billion on research in 2006.

One way to encourage inventors is by preventing people from stealing their inventions. We should build legal barriers to protect an inventor's intellectual property so that he or she can reap its financial benefits and plough those profits into a new invention. And from other side, we should keep walls low enough so that we encourage the sharing of intellectual property, which is required more and more to do cutting-edge innovation.

In the present day world a single innovator can summon so many resources by himself or herself, assemble a team of partners from around the world, and make a real breakthrough with some product or service. But someone else uses the same world platform and tools to clone and distribute the innovative engineer's wonderful new product. This happens in the world of software, music and pharmaceuticals everyday. And the technology is reaching a point now where we should assume that there is not anything that cannot be counterfeited quickly—from MS word to airplane parts.

In fact, the free software person in all of us wants no intellectual property laws. But the innovator in all of us wants global regime that protects against intellectual property piracy regime, we need a system of global governance. In the present world intellectual property protection is a great incentive to develop a new idea. Everybody wants his or her intellectual property protected. No country respects and protects intellectual property better than America, and as a result a lot of innovators want to come here to work and lodge their intellectual property. The quality of American intellectual property protection further enhances and encourages people to come up with new ideas. Moreover, US patents have the most rigorous procedures to prove novelty and utility, the prerequisites for granting patent to an invention. Any company believing that it has first-rate technology that can earn it global financial return will patent in USA, the world's most significant market. United States is a large, wealthy country whose market dynamics tend to attract cutting-edge innovations/technologies from around the world. It represents the most important single market for technological sales. It has been assumed that foreign US patent activity reflects innovative activity in the country where the patents originated. Japan files the highest number of patents in USA after USA itself. Craftsmanship was the best face that Japan had shown to the world. It took years to them to build up that reputation. Its engineers and innovators like the ones who invented the hand-held calculators and ink-jet printers help turn Japan into an industrial powerhouse.

As the invention is expected to alleviate some problems of society, the government is also anxious to see that the invention is worked to the maximum in the country to fulfill the needs of the public. However, unless the inventor is guaranteed protection from copying and unfair competition, he will not be inclined to disclose his invention. Inventors deserve a reward for the amount of time they spend developing their ideas. They also need the security of knowing that if they share the invention with the rest of the world, nobody will steal it, use it or copy it without their permission. The government therefore protects the inventor and, at the same time, ensures that the invention is disclosed to the public fully. This is where intellectual property rights play its role. Especially patent, one of the forms of intellectual property rights helps to achieve this. A bargain is struck between the government and the inventor. This bargain takes the form of the grant of patent for the invention to the inventor through the patent office. Intellectual property is a cluster of legally recognized rights associated with innovation and creativity—the works of the mind. Intellectual property protection fosters virtuous cycle of innovation and creation. It ensures that rewards flow to those, who improve upon previous works and inventions, and that others can use new ideas. This process lies at the heart of long-term economic growth.

So, if inventor's idea or invention receives a positive evaluation, the next step is to protect it. His concern probably would be making sure that he maintains ownership of his invention. Inventions could relate to products or processes. There are two basic strategies to protect any invention: trade secrecy and patent protection. By far the best way to protect one's invention is to obtain a patent covering it. A patent is a government granted monopoly, which allows the inventor to exclude anyone else from making, using or selling the invention claimed in the patent in the country that issued the patent. The government grants this monopoly to help encourage potential inventors to spend the time, money and effort to invent new things that help benefit others. But even though the government grants the patent, it is inventor's responsibility, not the government's, to enforce the patent.

Although the government grants this monopoly to allow the inventor to profit from his invention, it is important to know that when his patent expires, his invention will be in the "public domain". That means that anyone else can make, use or sell his invention without needing his permission or paying him anything. The government requires patents to expire because otherwise one person can control an entire industry if that person was the first to conceive of a type of product, to the detriment of the consuming public and the free enterprise system. A patent is a reward and an incentive for inventiveness. But the reward cannot be enjoyed indefinitely. Patent rights expire after a period, at which point any one can use the invention. This is done to achieve a balance between private good—inventor's reward for inventing useful product or process—and public good—society's need to have free access to useful inventions.

Modern patent laws protect the inventor for a specific period of time (usually 20 years) during which, in general, it is illegal for anyone else to copy, use, distribute or sell the invention without the approval of the inventor. In return for this protection, inventors reveal in their patent applications, the technical details of how their inventions work, so that other people can learn from them. If people copy, distribute or sell a patented invention without the patentee's permission, they commit a crime called patent infringement. The patentee can sue the patent infringer in a law court. When the patent protection expires, the invention enters the public domain.

In most countries, certain classes of inventions are legally recognized, and their use is temporarily restricted to the control of the inventor. For example, in the United States, any new and useful art, machine, manufacture, or material, or any new and useful improvement of these, may be protected by patent. The protection afforded by this legal recognition is limited; in many cases, if a person alters an invention and thereby improves or changes it, that person may be eligible for a new patent. Patent laws, however, do not provide coverage for all inventions. Moreover, many processes and ideas lacking clear-cut characteristics, such as psychological concepts useful in advertising, cannot be legally protected.

Key reasons for patenting inventions include: A patent gives its owner the exclusive right to prevent or stop others from commercially using the patented invention, thereby reducing uncertainty, risk and competition from free riders and imitators. If any company owns or obtains the permission to exploit a valuable patented invention it may be able to create a market entry barrier for competitors in respect of the same inventions. This will help it to become a pre-eminent player in the relevant market(s).

If the company has invested a significant amount of time and money in R&D, patent protection of the resulting inventions would help in recovering costs and obtaining higher returns on investments.

Companies can do one of the three things with an innovation. They can patent the widget they invent and sell it themselves; and they can patent it and license it to someone else to manufacture; and they can patent it and cross-license with several other companies so that they all have freedom of action to make a product—like a PC—that comes from melding many different patents.

As a patent owner one may license his rights over the invention to others in exchange for lump sum payments and/or royalties, in order to generate additional income for the company. Selling (or assigning) a patent implies transfer of ownership whereas licensing implies only permission to use the licensed invention under specified conditions.

If our company is interested in technology owned by others we may use our company's own patents to negotiate cross-licensing agreements, by which our company and the other party agree to authorize each other to use one or more of our respective patents under conditions specified in the agreement.

Licensing of patents (or even pending patent applications) to others may provide access to new markets, which are otherwise inaccessible. In order to do so, the invention must also be protected in the relevant foreign market(s).

Depending on the product or process in question, there may be other intellectual property rights that are suitable for protecting various features of an innovative product; these include: (1) Utility models (also known as short-term patents, petty patents or innovation patents). In many countries, some types of incremental inventions or small adaptations to existing products are protectable as utility models. Utility models/petty patents or patents are granted/registered under the relevant national/regional law by the relevant national or regional patent office. (2) Confidential business information may benefit from trade secret protection as long as: (*i*) it is not generally known to others dealing with that type of information; (*ii*) it has commercial value because it is secret; and (*iii*) reasonable steps have been taken by its owner to keep it secret (for example, restricting access to such information on a "need to know" basis, and entering into confidentiality or non-disclosure agreements). (3) Exclusivity over the ornamental or aesthetic features of a product may be obtained through the protection of industrial designs, in some countries referred to as "design patents." (4) Trademark protection provides exclusivity over distinctive signs used to distinguish the products of one company from those of others. (5) Original literary and artistic works may be protected by copyright and related rights. Copyright protection applies to a wide range of works, including computer programs. (6) In many countries, a breeder of a new plant variety, which fulfils the requirements of novelty, distinctness, uniformity and stability, and is designated with a suitable denomination, may obtain protection in the form of "plant breeder's rights". (7) One may be able to obtain protection for an original layout design (or topography) of an integrated circuit used in microchips and semiconductor chips. Such protection may extend also to the final product incorporating the layout design.

## IF INVENTION IS NOT PROTECTED

Inventions that are not patented can be copied, sold and distributed by anybody. This means that without a patent, inventors may miss out on the money they could have earned from their inventions. If the inventions are successful and many people want to buy them, there would be nothing to prevent copycat companies from selling the same inventions. Such competition would decrease the sales and profits that inventors could make from their own inventions. In addition, without a patent it is more difficult to license an invention to investors, manufacturers or distributors. This means that if inventors want to make money from their unlicensed inventions, they have to take care of all the investment, production, distribution and sales by themselves. This is not an easy task. It is also often the case that when inventors do not patent their inventions or share them with the public, at some point another inventor may think of the same invention and patent it. Once again, the original inventor would not receive any of the credit or financial rewards from the sale of this invention. Moreover, when inventors do not patent their inventions, the new knowledge or technological information, which led to those particular inventions sometimes, does not get shared more widely. In some cases this can slow down the advancement of science and technology by limiting the availability of important information that could be used by other scientists and inventors.

## IMPORTANCE OF INTELLECTUAL PROPERTY IN INNOVATION PROCESS

Intellectual property is a crucial instrument in the innovation process. However, exact role of intellectual property in relation to innovation needs to be ascertained. On the one hand, in theory, the intellectual property system is considered to be absolutely necessary to encourage creative intellectual endeavour in the public interest, and on the other, some observers believe that, in practice, the intellectual property system hinders competition to the extent that it is often seen to be playing a negative role in innovation. In the present discussion, former view prevails all through. Trade secrets, utility models/petty patents and patents are relevant for protecting, managing, exploiting and leveraging basic and improvement innovations.

As there are many players involved in facilitating the market success of an innovation, the effective use of the tools of intellectual property will play an important role in reducing risk for the players involved, who may then be able to reap acceptable returns for their participation in the process. Intellectual property plays an important role in facilitating the process of taking innovative technology to the market place. At the same time intellectual property plays a major role in enhancing competitiveness of technology-based enterprises, whether such enterprises are commercializing new or improved products or providing service on the basis of a new or improved technology. It is imperative that an innovative idea must be treated as a secret if an enterprise wishes to appropriate potential commercial benefits from the idea (*i.e.,* the information surrounding the creation of the idea must be protected carefully as a trade secret).

Since successful innovation includes taking a new product to market, other intellectual property tools become very relevant. Above all, trademarks and industrial designs play an important role in the marketing process. These enable consumers to identify a product/service of a particular company and enable them to distinguish the product from other similar product.

Technological innovation can also be supported well by a combination of patent, industrial design and trademark. A look at the invention and development of the vacuum cleaner provides a good example of strategic use of a combination of different types of intellectual property tools, namely, patents, industrial designs and trademark. In this case, one can see how the innovation is enhanced by the use of the three tools of intellectual property protection.

Trade secrets, patents, trademarks, industrial designs, and copyright may separately or jointly facilitate the acquisition of technology and its commercial use. Strategic use of a combination of intellectual property tools in the innovation process can significantly contribute to facilitating the appropriation of higher profits, maintenance of a premium market position, thus enabling technology-based, innovative enterprises to have a high return on investment.

Intellectual property rights can be used effectively to facilitate successful innovation. Innovative technologies stand a better chance of successfully reaching the marketplace if intellectual property is used strategically. Gauging the importance of intellectual property in innovation, by merely focussing on patents as input and/or output of innovation, does not do justice to the significant role that can be played by the other tools of intellectual property. A broader approach to the contribution of intellectual property in innovation is therefore needed.

Intellectual property also provides access to financing and technical facilities. In addition, intellectual property provides a strong negotiation position when it comes to entering into and maintaining business partnerships.

# 3

# HUMAN CREATIVITY AND INTELLECTUAL PROPERTY: AN INTRODUCTION

Though the connection between intellectual property and creativity does not seem obvious, it is the intellectual property system that sustains and nourishes the creators. In simple terms, intellectual property means the property in intellectual creations, which has some commercial potential and which is protectable by statute or legislation. Intellectual creations result from human ingenuity, creativity and inventiveness. It is a product of the intellect, which is owned by an individual or an organization that can then choose to share it freely or to control its use in certain ways. They cover inventions, literary and artistic works, and symbols, names, images, and designs used in commerce. "Property" means that protected intellectual creations can be used only with the consent of the inventor, author or other owner of the rights.

The rights, which protect intellectual creations through a system of national and international rules, are called intellectual property rights. Intellectual property rights aim at protecting the creative, insightful, unique and inventive creations of the human mind. It is important to understand that it is the rights that are the property, and not the intellectual work they apply to. In fact, intellectual property or IP refers to certain kinds of exclusive rights, which are collectively called intellectual property rights, a legal way of protecting all creations of human mind. Intellectual property rights are like any other property rights—they allow the creator, or owner to benefit from his or her own work or investment. The principal types of intellectual property are patents, copyrights, and trademarks.

People need to make money out of their ideas. So they need to be given some form of exclusive rights over their ideas. Therefore, we have copyright, patent, trademarks and other legal proprietary systems. Someone writes a song, writes a novel, has an idea, and develops a logo, a brand. Absolutely they should be protected. The more we move over to an economy based on ideas, the more we need to ensure that the people who develop those ideas have a good life.

The earliest use of the term "intellectual property" appears to be an October 1845 Massachusetts Circuit Court ruling in the patent case *Davoll et al. v. Brown* in which Justice Charles L. Woodbury wrote that "only in this way can we protect intellectual property, the labors of the mind, productions and interests as much a man's own...as the wheat he cultivates, or the flocks he rears." (*Woodury & Minot, CCD Mass. 7 F. Cas. 197, 1845*). In Europe, French author A. Nion mentioned "*propriété intellectuelle*" in his *Droits civils des auteurs, artistes et inventeurs*, published in 1846. The term's widespread popularity is a much more modern phenomenon. It was very uncommon until the 1967 establishment of the World Intellectual Property Organization (WIPO), which actively tried to promote the term. Still, it was rarely used without scare quotes until about the time of the passage of the Bayh-Dole Act in 1980.

## TYPES AND CHARACTERISTICS

Intellectual property can be divided into two categories: Industrial property, which includes inventions (patents), trademarks, industrial designs, and geographic indications of source; and artistic and literary property, *i.e.,* copyright and related rights, which includes a broad range of literary and artistic works, written, performed, and recorded. Current technological developments are blurring, to some extent, this distinction, and some hybrid *sue generis* systems are emerging.

Intellectual property is unique, as it is the fruit of personal creation and inventiveness. It might be a poem that a poet writes, the name of a particular person thinks up to sell his or her services, or an inventor's invention for a non-spill cup for babies. It can also be a Picasso painting, a Satayajit Ray's film, a Salman

Rushdie's novel, a new method of irrigation for farmers in arid regions, the invention of the light bulb, a computer chip or a jet turbine engine. The distinctive features, which help us choose the products we buy, like brand names and designs, can fall within the scope of intellectual property. Even the place of origin of a product can have rights attached to it, as is the case with Champagne and Scotch. Much of what we see and use on the Internet, be it a web page or a domain name, also includes or represents some form of intellectual property.

Intellectual property shares many of the characteristics associated with real and personal property. For example, intellectual property is an asset, and as such it can be bought, sold licensed, exchanged, or gratuitously given away like any other form of property. Further, the intellectual property owner has the right to prevent the unauthorized use or sale of the property. The most noticeable difference between intellectual property and other form of property, however, is that intellectual property is intangible, that is, it cannot be defined or identified by its own physical parameters. It must be expressed in some discernible way to be protectable. Because intellectual property is intangible, many people may use it simultaneously without conflict. For example, only one person can drive a car at a time, but if an author publishes a book, many people can read the work at the same time. Intellectual property is also much easier to copy than it is to create. It may take many months of work to write a novel or computer program, but with a photocopy machine or a computer others could copy the work in a matter of seconds.

## IMPORTANCE

Copyright helps bring music to our ears, and art, films and literature before our eyes; industrial design helps shape our world, and trademarks provide reliable signs of quality; patenting helps promote ingenious inventions that make life easier, faster, safer and sometimes completely change our way of living. Works of the mind—intellectual property—such as inventions, designs, trademarks, books, music, and films, are now used and enjoyed on every continent on earth. It is a common observation that intellectual property has applications in all aspects of human existence, across many different human activities: industry, commerce, health, nutrition, communications and culture. This is reflected first in the large number of national, international and regional treaties, conventions and laws, which have an intellectual property application, as well as in the large number of national, international and regional organizations and government departments asserting an intellectual property policy-making role. The protection and enforcement of intellectual property rights should contribute to the promotion of technological innovation and to the transfer and dissemination of technology. The subject of intellectual property rights has also become important for the technological, industrial and economic development of a country. It is being recognized as an important commercial asset and a driving force in technological progress and socio-economic development of the country. The intellectual property system was an important catalyst for the development of indigenous technology by Korean companies, several of which have become global market leaders. Intellectual property is a crucial instrument in the innovation process. It is recognized as an important tool, not only to promote inventiveness but also to ensure adequate returns to the investments made. Intellectual property plays an important role in facilitating the process of taking innovative technology to marketplace. It also plays a major role in enhancing competitiveness of technology-based enterprizes and encouraging the production of a wide range of quality goods and services. The World Economic Forum (WEF) Global Competitiveness Report indicates a correlation between the protection of intellectual property rights and national competitiveness. In 2004, the 20 countries that were perceived as having the most stringent intellectual property protection were classed among the top 27 in the WEF's growth competitiveness index. Conversely, the 20 countries perceived as having the weakest intellectual property regimes were ranked among the bottom 36 for growth and competitiveness. Intellectual property helps in providing access to financial or technical facilities. It provides a negotiating position when it comes to entering into business partnerships. An organization's knowledge and expertise is its intellectual property and it is the lifeblood of every enterprize.

Intellectual property gives the business a competitive edge and also creates multiple revenue streams from licensing those rights to others. It is an important intangible asset for the business firms. Intellectual property is a tradable asset that can be commercially exploited by the owner. Others can also exploit this asset with the permission of the owner. Intellectual properties seek to create a broad-based sustainable improvement in the quality of life and standard of living. Enriching the pool of public knowledge and culture. In the future, intellectual property creators aim to deliver more abundant food resources, clean energy and cures for diseases from cancer to the common cold. Intellectual property stimulates progress, transforming society and adding value to our lives. During the 21st century, intellectual property will play an ever more important role on the international stage. Intellectual property is the currency, the lifeline. The most valuable currency today is not money but intellectual property.

## INTELLECTUAL PROPERTY SYSTEM

The intellectual property system refers to the entire gamut of intellectual property laws, procedures, practices and institutions responsible for protecting, administering, enforcing, and using intellectual assets for social, cultural and economic progress. Every country needs a well-developed and healthy intellectual property system for economic and social well-being.

In law, intellectual property is an umbrella term for various legal entitlements which attach to certain types of information, ideas, or other intangibles in their expressed form. The holder of this legal entitlement is generally entitled to exercise various exclusive rights in relation to the subject matter of the intellectual property. The term intellectual property reflects the idea that this subject matter is the product of the mind or the intellect, and that intellectual property rights may be protected in the same way as any other form of property.

Intellectual property laws vary from jurisdiction to jurisdiction, such that the acquisition, registration or enforcement of intellectual property rights must be pursued or obtained separately in each territory of interest. However, these laws are becoming increasingly harmonized through the effects of international treaties such as the 1994 World Trade Organization's (WTO) agreement on Trade-Related Aspects of Intellectual Property Rights (TRIPS), while other treaties may facilitate registration in more than one jurisdiction at a time. Certain forms of intellectual property rights do not require registration in order to be enforced.

The exclusive right provided by the intellectual property system has, so far, been mainly seen as an opportunity for enterprizes to exclude competitors from the marketplace. Broadly speaking, the right to exclude all others is the essence of a property right, be it over tangibles or intangibles, including patents and all other types of intellectual property. Beyond the right to exclude, there are a number of other possibilities and opportunities that are available to an owner of intellectual property assets, be they owned by enterprizes, large or small. These additional choices enable a multifaceted strategic use of intellectual property assets, beyond the limited possibilities linked to the narrow focus on use of the "concept of exclusivity" or "the right to exclude". Simply put, the key to proper use of intellectual property assets is to treat the tools of the intellectual property system (in the form of trade secrets, patents, trademarks, industrial design, copyright, etc) as instruments for developing business relationships. Intellectual property, if properly managed, can be a powerful tool for growth and progress. To fulfill its potential, intellectual property protection has to be supported by appropriate policies and a deep commitment by governments to establish an effective infrastructure to process and make use of intellectual property rights.

## CONTROVERSIES

The use of the term intellectual property and the concepts it is said to embody are the subject of some controversy. The basic public policy rationale for the protection of intellectual property is that intellectual property laws facilitate and encourage the pursuit and disclosure of innovation into the public domain for the common good, by granting authors and inventor's exclusive rights to exploit their works and invention for a limited period.

However, various schools of thought are critical of the term "intellectual property", the very concept of intellectual property, and some characterize intellectual property as intellectual protectionism. There is ongoing debate as to whether intellectual property laws truly operate to confer the stated public benefits, and whether the protection they are said to provide is appropriate in the context of innovation derived from such things as traditional knowledge and folklore, and patents for software and business methods. Manifestations of this controversy can be seen in the way different jurisdictions decide whether to grant intellectual property protection in relation to subject matter of this kind, and the North-South divide on issues of the role and scope of intellectual property laws. The global harmonization of intellectual property legislation under the WTO has also been criticized, for example by the alter-globalization movement.

## INTELLECTUAL PROPERTY IN DAILY LIFE

Intellectual property surrounds us in nearly everything we do, at home, at school, at work, at rest and at play. Everywhere we look, we see images of intellectual property in action: (1) In the colour and drama of a box office hit movie; (2) In the songs of Lata Mangeshkar; (3) In the intricate weaving of an Iranian carpet; (4) In new medical treatments based on innovative research of one of our national laboratories; or (5) In the best-seller written by Khushwant Singh. What most of us probably do not realize is that intellectual property is everywhere in our world. It is with us everyday of our lives, from dawn to dusk, while we are at work, while we are hanging out with our friends, and even as we sleep. It is found almost everywhere—in creative works like books, films, records, music, art and software, and in everyday objects like cars, computers, drugs and varieties of plants. Almost everyone in society is a user and potential creator of intellectual property. Most people deal with intellectual property everyday of their life. It covers the contents of the morning paper as copyright, the logo of the tea carton as trademark and the safety razor as patent. Similarly, regardless of what product an enterprise makes or what service it provides, it is likely that it is regularly using and creating a great deal of intellectual property. Even in our day-to-day life, knowingly or unknowingly we are concerned and connected either with patents/trademarks/copyright/designs, etc.

*This drawing room is full of intellectual property products such as books (protected by copyright), television (protected by patent), carpet (protected as industrial design), table (protected as industrial design), etc.*

Every product or service that we use in our daily lives is the result of a long chain of big or small innovations, such as changes in designs, or improvements that make a product look or function the way it does today. We may take a simple product, for example, a ballpoint pen. Its inventor has taken a patent on it. But, like him, many others have improved the product and its designs and legally protected their improvements through the acquisition of intellectual property rights. The trademark on our pen is also intellectual property, and it helps the producer to market the product and develop a loyal clientele. This would be the case with almost any product or service in the marketplace. Similarly, in a CD player patent may protect its various technical parts. Industrial design rights may protect its design. A trademark may protect the brand name and the music played in the CD player may be protected by copyright. People are buying and selling words, music, pictures, gadgets, computer software, copyrights, trademarks, patents, reputation, and brands. The goods on sale in this marketplace are the rights to use or, to exploit intellectual property.

## UNDERSTANDING INTELLECTUAL PROPERTY

Although most people have heard of copyright, patents and trademarks, many view them simply as business or legal concerns, with little affect on their own lives. To many, intellectual property is a rather obscure legal concept that can only be properly understood and applied by those, who are specially trained. It used to be an arcane and boring subject. Though intellectual property is a term increasingly in use today, it is still little understood. To many people it has very little relevance to everyday life. There is hardly any understanding of their importance in daily life. This is mainly because of the lack of public understanding of—and respect for—creativity, innovation, and the intellectual property system. These things are often taken for granted; moreover, there is little public awareness of the connection between human creativity and intellectual property in daily life. There is a need for providing an opportunity to reflect on how intellectual property touches all aspects of our lives. How copyright helps bring music to our ears and art, films and literature before our eyes; how industrial design helps shape our world, and how trademarks provide reliable signs of quality; how patenting helps promote ingenious inventions that make life easier, faster, safer and sometimes completely change our way of living. How important are the contributions made by innovators and artists to the development of societies across the globe. In fact, at the heart of understanding intellectual property is recognizing and respecting the creator and appreciating creative potential of future creators, inventors and innovators. To ensure a better and more prosperous future for mankind, it is important to increase awareness of scientific knowledge as well as the creative power of children. Critical to this effort is instilling respect for intellectual property. Respect for intellectual property and its appreciation as a valuable tool for scientific, cultural and social progress should begin at an early age. In today's highly competitive business environment, an understanding of the intellectual property system in general and patents in particular, is central to an effective approach to managing innovation. Everybody in the system needs to know about intellectual property. So everybody who is doing a deal, doing a transaction with someone else has got to know about intellectual property. In the old days, the people in production had to know about raw materials and contract law; now they have to know about intellectual property and contract law. And it all has to do with 'what have I got that I can use as a lever to sell to the other person'. Today, the most valuable currency is not money but ideas and intellectual property, which are intangible and highly mobile. Within the past few years it has become a powerful influence on the way everyone has ideas and owns them, as well as on global economic output. In a knowledge-based economy, there is no doubt that an understanding of intellectual property rights is indispensable to informed policy-making in all areas of human development.

Many countries have recognized the importance of promoting awareness about intellectual property rights. European Commission (EC) established in October 1998, the Intellectual Property Rights (IPR) Helpdesk as the central reference point for intellectual property inquiries and advice throughout the European Union (EU). In order to perform these functions, the IPR-Helpdesk maintains the IPR-Helpdesk Website (www.cordis.lu/ipr-helpdesk). Japan has also recognized the need to stimulate and promote awareness on IPR. There is an emphasis on the study and training on IPR in industry, academia and government. In USA, a special website for independent inventors gives basic information on a number of frequently asked questions about IPR. The Office of the Independent Inventor Programs (OIPP) of the US Patent and Trademark Office, established in March 1999, maintains the site. In China there is an emphasis to enhance the awareness on IPR. The member countries of the ASEAN have also recognized the importance of IPR awareness.

iCopyright has launched a public website for copyright education and compliance—http://poweredby.copyright.com/. iCopyright is the world's first 'intelligent copyright' system for digital content. Internet users can learn about copyright and report copyright piracy. They can also submit a permission request to use any online content. The copyright education website is being promoted in co-operation with hundreds of online publishers.

## PROTECTING INTELLECTUAL CREATIONS

The source of all knowledge and information is creativity and unless it is protected it cannot be further encouraged. However, intellectual property is susceptible for stealing. Without intellectual property laws, it would be easy to duplicate original works and sell them for very low prices, leaving the original creators without any chance to secure economic rewards for their efforts. The legal system avoids this problem by making it against the law to reproduce various forms of intellectual property without the permission of the creator.

In general, intellectual property is protected by giving the creator of a work or an inventor exclusive right to commercially exploit his creation or invention for a limited period of time. The one exception to limited periods of intellectual property rights is in the field of trademark law. Trademark rights never expire, so long as a merchant continues to use the trademark to identify a given product.

These rights can also be sold, licensed or otherwise disposed of by the right holder. Intellectual property rights are granted under the national laws of each country or region. In addition, various international agreements on intellectual property rights harmonize laws and procedures, or allow intellectual property rights to be registered at the same time in several countries. All types of intellectual property are protected on a national basis. Thus, the scope of protection and the requirements of obtaining protection will vary from country-to-country. There are, however, similarities between national legal arrangements. Moreover, the current worldwide trend is toward harmonizing the national laws. In practically all countries the world over, a national legal system of intellectual property rights have evolved; this has been created over varying periods of time during the last 150 years or so. It has enabled the grant of property-like rights over such new knowledge and creative expression of mankind, which has made it possible to harness the commercial value of the outputs of human inventiveness and creativity. Through a system of intellectual property rights, it is possible not only to ensure that an innovation or creation is attributed to its producer or creator, but also to secure "ownership" of it and benefit commercially as a result.

An intellectual property right is a legal right, which comes into existence only when the requirements of the relevant intellectual property law are met and, if required, it is granted or registered after following the prescribed procedure under that law. Intellectual property may only come into existence after an application has been made and/or registration has been obtained. Alternatively, it may come into existence automatically upon creation of an original design or other work or upon the creation of a reputation in the brand name.

Different types of intellectual creations are protected in different ways: (1) Creations in the fields of literature and the arts, such as books, paintings, music, films and records as well as software, are generally protected through copyright or so-called neighbouring rights. (2) Inventions, both technological and scientific, are typically protected by patents. (3) Distinctive features—such as words, symbols, smells, sounds, colours and shapes—that distinguish one product or service from another, can be protected by trademark rights. (4) The specific external appearance given to objects, such as furniture, car body parts, tableware, jewelry, may enjoy design protection; (5) Geographical indications and trade secrets are also considered to be types of intellectual property and most countries provide some form of legal protection for them; (6) Legal protection for safety and efficacy studies data for certain regulated products (*e.g.*, plant science products and pharmaceuticals) is increasingly provided in many parts of the world.

In intellectual property there are also some specialized varieties of intellectual property rights which are known as *sui generis* intellectual property rights such as intellectual property rights in layout designs of integrated circuits, new varieties of plants or databases.

The same product can also be simultaneously protected by more than one type of intellectual property right in different countries. If the innovative ideas, creative designs and powerful brands of any enterprise are not legally protected by intellectual property rights, then these may be freely and legally used by any other enterprise without limitation. However, when intellectual property rights protect them, they acquire concrete value for any enterprise, as they become property rights, which cannot be commercialized or used without owner's authorization.

Generally, pure concepts and notions cannot be protected. Suppose we have an idea to create digital locks. If it is purely an idea and we have not drawn out any plans or attempted to make a prototype, we probably cannot get any protection at that stage.

We may register the following types of intellectual property rights: (1) Patent grants for inventions, (2) Trademarks for business signs, (3) Industrial designs for designs applied to the articles, (4) Grants for protection of plant varieties. However, following forms of intellectual property need not be registered, but may be protected nonetheless: (1) Copyrighted works, (2) Geographical indications, (3) Layout designs of integrated circuits, (4) Confidential information and trade secrets. Each one of the intellectual property rights gives the intellectual property owner the right to prevent others from using, selling, licensing, reproducing, transferring or exploiting his or her intellectual creations without his or her permission for a specific period of time.

If our business has overseas contacts or operations, *e.g.*, if we export our goods, franchise or license our business overseas, we need to protect our intellectual property in foreign markets.

Each intellectual property right has its own requirements. For instance, inventions that are patented must be new or involve an improvement, and have some form of industrial application. Trademarks must be distinctive and distinguish one's goods or services. Intellectual property law limits what can be protected and for how long. Intellectual property rights do not protect ideas. They protect only expressions of ideas, in the case of copyrights, and inventions fulfilling certain strict and well-established criteria in the case of patents. These limitations and conditions are built-in mechanisms to balance the rights of intellectual property owners in the interests of the society.

## LICENSING

Intellectual property rights allow innovators and creators to choose the terms on which they distribute their work. They can choose, for example, to license and sell their works or inventions, to make them available for free, or to allow their use subject to certain conditions. In the patent area, patented technologies are shared on certain terms as common technical standards to improve the interoperability of different systems, thus simplifying the lives of consumers. Licensing is the right granted by an owner of an asset to another to use that asset while still retaining ownership of that asset. To remain competitive in the global arena, companies today need to develop effective mechanisms for intellectual property licensing and technology transfer as these are important factors in strategic alliances, joint ventures and turnkey projects. Licensing offers several advantages both to the licensor and the licensee.

## TOWARDS INTERNATIONAL PROTECTION OF INTELLECTUAL PROPERTY

The World Intellectual Property Organization (WIPO) is an international organization dedicated to helping to ensure that the rights of creators and owners of intellectual property are protected worldwide and that inventors and authors are, thus, recognized and rewarded for their ingenuity. This international protection acts as a spur to human creativity, pushing forward the boundaries of science and technology and enriching the world of literature and the arts. By providing a stable environment for the marketing of intellectual property products, it also oils the wheels of international trade. WIPO carries out many tasks related to the protection of intellectual property rights, such as administering international treaties, assisting governments, organizations and the private sector, monitoring developments in the field and harmonizing and simplifying relevant rules and practices. It strives to contribute to the good of mankind by creating real wealth for nations, and to enhance the quality and enjoyment of life. WIPO works closely with its Member States and other constituents to ensure that the intellectual property system remains a supple and adaptable tool for prosperity and well-being, crafted to help realize the full potential of intellectual property for present and future generations. The main activities of WIPO are to establish international norms and standards in the field of intellectual property, especially through international treaties. The treaties define internationally agreed basic standards of intellectual property protection in each country.

As part of the United Nations, WIPO exists as a forum for its Member States to create and harmonize rules and practices to protect intellectual property rights. Most industrialized nations have protection systems that are centuries old. Many new and developing countries, however, are now building up their patent, trademark, and copyright laws and systems. With the rapid globalization of trade during the last decade, WIPO plays a key role in helping these new systems evolve through treaty negotiation, legal and technical assistance, and training in various forms, including in the area of enforcement of intellectual property rights. WIPO also provides global registration systems—for patents, trademarks, and industrial designs—which are under regular review by Member States and other stakeholders to determine how they can better serve the needs of users and potential users.

In the United States and other countries, intellectual property has gained increased protection with advances in technology and international trade. However, some countries tolerate the widespread sale of counterfeit versions of intellectual property products, such as software, movies on videotape, brand name of athletic goods, and even patented medicines. Violations of intellectual property rights cost the owners of the rights billions of dollars each year. These costs stem from lost royalties and sales in markets dominated by counterfeit products. In an attempt to reverse this situation, most nations of the world signed the Agreement on Trade-Related Aspects of Intellectual Property Rights (TRIPS) in 1994. Administered by the World Trade Organization (WTO), TRIPS strengthened legal protection for intellectual property around the world. TRIPS Agreement requires all WTO Members to provide minimum standards of protection for a wide range of intellectual property rights including copyright, patents, trademarks, industrial designs, geographical indications, semiconductor topographies and undisclosed information. In doing so, TRIPS Agreement incorporates provisions from many existing intellectual property international agreements. It, however, also introduces a number of new obligations, particularly in relation to geographical indications, patents, trade secrets, and measures governing how intellectual property rights should be enforced.

## TRIPS PROVISIONS

Intellectual property was until recently the domain of specialists and producers of intellectual property rights. The Agreement on Trade-Related Aspects of Intellectual Property Rights concluded during the Uruguay Round negotiations has signaled a major shift in this regard. The TRIPS Agreement was the result of concerted efforts on the part of certain governments (in particular, the United States) and private sector organizations to establish adequate and effective levels of protection for intellectual property rights, and to reduce distortions and impediments to international trade arising from differing standards of protection.

TRIPS Agreement addresses a variety of intellectual property rights, including copyright, trademarks, geographical indications, industrial designs, patents, and trade secrets. Protection for plant varieties is also mandated, whether by patents or otherwise (such as by *sui generis* protection, such as plant breeders' rights under the UPOV Convention). In addition to substantive provisions regarding the rights themselves, TRIPS Agreement also specifies enforcement measures, effective dispute settlement mechanisms, and transitional arrangements for World Trade Organization (WTO) member countries lacking a developed intellectual property regime.

The incorporation of intellectual property rights into the multilateral trading system and its relationship with a wide area of key public policy issues has elicited great concern over its pervasive role in people's lives and in society in general. Developing country members of the WTO no longer have the policy options and flexibilities developed countries had in using intellectual property rights to support their national development. Moreover, significant new developments are taking place at the international, regional and bilateral level that build on and strengthen the minimum TRIPS Agreement standards through the progressive harmonization of policies along standards of technologically advanced countries.

TRIPS Agreement requires Member States to provide strong protection for intellectual property rights. For example, under TRIPS Agreement: (1) Copyright terms must extend to 50 years after the death of the author, although films and photographs are only required to have fixed 50 and 25 year terms, respectively. (2) Copyright must be granted automatically, and not based upon any "formality", such as registrations or systems of renewal. (3) Computer programs must be regarded as "literary works" under copyright law and receive the same terms of protection. (4) National exceptions to copyright (such as "fair use" in the United States) must be tightly constrained. (5) Patents must be granted in all "fields of technology", although exceptions for certain public interests are allowed. (6) Exceptions to patent law must be limited almost as strictly as those to copyright law. (7) In each state, intellectual property laws may not offer any benefits to local citizens which are not available to citizens of other TRIPS Agreement signatories by the principles of national treatment (with certain limited exceptions, Articles 3 and 5 [2]). TRIPS Agreement also has a most favoured nation clause.

## RATIONALE FOR PROVIDING PROTECTION

The intellectual property system is designed to benefit society as a whole, striking a delicate balance to ensure that the needs of both the creator and the user are satisfied. This balance is maintained through checks within the intellectual property system itself and in the larger regulatory framework, to ensure that the system is sustainable and beneficial to all stakeholders. Society provides legal rights over intellectual property to encourage the production of inventions and creative works that benefit society and to help innovators and creators make a living from their work. Governments and courts recognize these rights, which can belong to individuals or organizations. Intellectual property rights are governed by the public policy objectives including developmental and technological objectives. By protecting intellectual property, society provides an incentive for people to invest time and resources to foster innovation and expand knowledge. There are two main policy bases that underline intellectual property rights: first is the policy of encouraging new intellectual creations (patents, industrial designs and copyright). The second main policy basis is the orderly functioning of the market through the avoidance of confusion and deception (trademarks, rights in geographical indications and protection against unfair competition).

Most intellectual property rights expire after a specified period. This permits the rest of society to benefit from the work after the creator has had an opportunity to earn a fair reward. For example, after the inventor of a patented telecommunications device has profited from the work for a specified period, anyone may manufacture that same device without paying the inventor royalties, thereby encouraging competition that allows others to benefit from the invention as well. The contributions made by innovators and artists to the development of societies across the globe are enormous. Technologies and creations that have touched and changed millions of lives would probably not exist today without the incentives provided by intellectual property rights. Patent protection has spurred the development of key technologies (*e.g.*, the transistor, telephone communication and electricity), lifesaving drugs, *e.g.*, beta blockers for heart disease, the anti-cancer drug taxol, and other inventions that have helped improve lives in different parts of the world. Copyright has stimulated the development of vibrant local cultures, and encouraged their dissemination worldwide. Copyright system has enhanced the international popularity of different forms of world music, whose growth, distribution and commercial success have been encouraged by it. For example: the multi-billion dollar film, recording, publishing, and software industries, which bring pleasure to millions of people in all parts of the world, would not exist without copyright protection. Consumers would have no means to confidently buy products or services without reliable, international trademark protection and enforcement to discourage counterfeiting and piracy. Without the rewards provided by the patent system, researchers and inventors would have little incentive to continue producing better and more efficient products for consumers worldwide. Intellectual property rights also represent a lasting link between the producer and its product and encourage producers to maintain responsibility for the safety, efficacy and quality of the product even after it has been sold. They add value for consumers and can provide a guarantee of source and quality. Trademarks and geographical indications allow consumers to differentiate between goods and services from different producers and to select products by manufacturers whose reputations they trust. In virtually every instance, intellectual property stimulates progress, transforming society and adding value to our lives.

The dissemination of ideas, knowledge and information necessary to stimulate creation and innovation is encouraged by intellectual property rights, especially patents and copyrights. As patent applicants are obliged to publish the details of their inventions in exchange for patent protection, published patents and patent applications are a rich resource in technical and scientific information accessible to all via patent office databases. This knowledge pool, which would not exist without the patent system, stimulates further research and development, thereby creating a virtuous cycle of innovation. By encouraging the publication of inventions, patents also help avoid duplication of research. Copyright encourages the dissemination of new works and creative expressions, as authors are more likely to make their works public if they know they can retain some control over them.

In fact, there are several compelling reasons for promoting and protecting intellectual property. Protection of intellectual property encourages qualitative competitiveness in international trade; it encourages technology transfer, development of new technology as well as promotion of creative endeavours, and socio-economic progress. Intellectual property protection encourages the use and further development of local inventive and artistic talents and assets; nurtures and safeguards local intellectual property assets such as traditional knowledge and folklore; and attracts investment, providing a stable environment in which investors, both local and foreign, can be confident that their intellectual property rights will be respected. Thus, intellectual property rights reward creativity and human endeavour, which fuel the progress of humankind.

## A TOOL FOR ECONOMIC DEVELOPMENT

Innovation, creativity, cultural diversity and technological development all contribute to economic growth. This is all the more true as knowledge-based industries increase in importance to the economy, particularly as creators of employment. The role that intellectual property protection plays in development is currently at the heart of many debates, including those over technology transfer, intellectual property and public health, access and benefit sharing in relation to genetic resources, and the availability of intellectual property protected information.

The correlation between innovation performance and economic development has strengthened over the past 15 years. Technological progress is now responsible for up to one half of the growth of the US economy and, in 2000, intangible assets represented 70 per cent of corporate assets in the United States. Creative industries, such as publishing, music, film, software and arts, are a powerful generator of economic growth and employment in both the developed and developing world. These industries—heavily reliant on copyright—contributed more than 1.2 trillion euros to the European Union's economy, produced added value of 450 billion euros, equaling 5.3% of the EU's GDP, and employed 5.2 million persons in 2000. India's IT industry continues to chart double-digit growth with expected revenues of US $28 billion in 2004-2005.

Looking forward, as economies develop, the use and value of intellectual capital will gradually replace the value of raw materials as a percentage of capital input toward economic growth. As such, intellectual property is an increasingly important asset that must be continually nurtured, protected and stimulated to grow.

Intellectual property protection is one essential element of the tool-kit necessary for economic growth. To realize its full potential, however, the intellectual property system has to be supported by sound economic management, good infrastructure and the right type of flanking policies. Active national intellectual property policies and efficient institutions, as well as public awareness and support, are key elements of this tool-kit.

Korea's spectacular transformation from a poor farming economy in the 1960s with a per capita income of less than US $100 to a highly industrialized country with a per capita income of US $12,000 today, resulted from a systematic economic and trade development policy that included incentives for technological innovation and the development of domestic intellectual property assets.

In recent decades, the fraction of the total output of the US economy that is essentially conceptual rather than physical has been rising. The trend has, of necessity, shifted the emphasis in asset valuation from physical property to intellectual property and to the legal rights inherent in intellectual property.

Statistics support the positive relationship between economic growth, R&D and intellectual property. The contribution of knowledge-intensive industries to gross national product is increasing (from 21% to 27% in the US from 1982 to 1995) and there is a noticeable upward trend in patent applications and grants worldwide, including in developing countries.

Intellectual property protection contributes to economic growth in both developed and developing countries by stimulating innovation, cultural diversity and technical development as part of a larger policy framework. Properly used, intellectual property rights can also be key tools for the alleviation of poverty through trade.

## INTELLECTUAL PROPERTY AND BUSINESSES

Intellectual property was a fancy and rarely used word few years ago but the same has assumed a great importance in today's competitive business world. The word intellectual property has become a buzzword in the business and industry. Businesses need the intellectual property system to protect manufacturing secrets or other useful information and remain ahead of the competitor. They need to fully exploit their intellectual assets to maintain consistent quality and market products and services to consumers so as to develop long-term customer loyalty. Any industry or business, whether traditional or modern, regardless of what product or service it produces or provides, is likely to regularly use intellectual property to prevent others from encroaching on its due reward or taking advantage of its goodwill in the market place. We can say that none of the businesses of today, either small or large is without a touch of intellectual property rights. Intellectual property has become a factor in the global battle for competitive advantage. The effect is seen in almost every industry; not merely the traditional copyright and patent industries (which are expanding) but in all industries that depend upon trademarks, brands and designs, from food to sport. Companies want to maximize revenue from each creative product, and therefore create as many intellectual properties and as many rights as possible.

Since the early days of trade and economic activity, companies have invested a large portion of their resources in research and development. These investments have allowed them to create new products, to differentiate themselves, and to become leaders in their sectors. The success of such expenditures is due in large part to the protection of each company's intellectual property rights. Over the years, companies have come to expect that spending on research and development will continue to be rewarded with intellectual property protection.

In today's economy, the trend is toward increasing investment in intangible assets. When a company has money to spend, it is more often directed toward research and development than toward new plants and equipment. By its very nature, however, intellectual property is less tangible than physical capital and, therefore, it is more vulnerable to theft.

People and businesses at all levels can use this wide array of intellectual property tools. Almost all businesses in all countries – the vast majority of which are small enterprises—use trademarks for marketing their goods and services. Copyrights are even more easily available. The moment someone writes a text, composes some music or draws an image, he or she will have copyright to the result.

The key to proper use of intellectual property assets is to treat the tools of the intellectual property system (in the form of trade secrets, patents, trademarks, industrial design, copyright, etc.) as instruments for developing business relationships so as to co-operate and partner with other enterprises, rather than merely barring others from entering the market. Other things being equal, such strategic use of intellectual property assets leads to generation of additional revenues/income, access to new technology/markets, access to R&D facilities, and a host of other possibilities that are potentially unlimited. The acquisition of intellectual property rights should be seen more as an investment decision. Businesses should, therefore, consider all possible options, which would result in higher returns on investment.

Businesses have a legitimate interest—for reasons relating to commercial strategy, quality control, brand reputation, safety, etc.—in controlling the distribution of their goods across different markets to ensure that products tailored for one market are not sold in another.

The increasingly international scale on which businesses operate and trade has led to a growing tension with the traditionally territorial nature of most legislation, including that governing intellectual property rights. This tendency is exacerbated by the development of electronic commerce, which allows more companies to operate internationally. Issues concerning the applicable law and jurisdiction with respect to intellectual property transactions and infringements will thus have to be studied in a multi-disciplinary context. The expansion of businesses into a growing number of markets has also made it prohibitively expensive, and often impossible in practice, to obtain and enforce intellectual property rights in all the countries where infringing or counterfeit goods may be manufactured and widely sold. This is equally true for globally active service companies such as insurance, banks and transportation companies.

Businesses reliant on the exploitation of intellectual property assets must, to remain competitive, ensure that the means available to them to protect their intellectual property are still effective in this evolving environment.

## INTELLECTUAL PROPERTY AND PUBLIC HEALTH

Inadequate healthcare systems and epidemics of serious diseases have placed significant pressure on governments and on industry to take immediate and effective action. The WTO is also currently working to resolve the issue of how the TRIPS Agreement can best support public health goals. Article 31(f) of TRIPS Agreement states that production under compulsory licensing must be predominantly for the domestic market. This prevents countries from manufacturing patented pharmaceutical products for export to countries, which do not have the capacity to manufacture these themselves, without the authorization of the patent holder. This is evidenced in the debate on cross border compulsory licensing under Paragraph 6 of the WTO Declaration on TRIPS and Public Health, resulting in the 30 August 2003 decision of the WTO General Council adopting the so-called Motta text in light of the accompanying WTO General Council Chairman's statement. This was by a further decision of the WTO Members on December 6, 2005, made permanent by an amendment to the TRIPS Agreement. Implementation of the December 6, 2005 decision should be done in good faith as to assist developing and least-developed countries in meeting their public health needs, while ensuring commitment to intellectual property protection in general, including the provisions of the TRIPS Agreement.

The role of the patent system in making medicines available to needy consumers, particularly in poor countries, has been the subject of intense debate. In this respect, the linkages between intellectual property rights and public health are being addressed in several fora. The WHO Commission on Intellectual Property Rights, Innovation and Public Health, CIPIH, was set up in early 2004 to study a number of topics, including interfaces and linkages between intellectual property rights, innovation and public health, with emphasis on the importance and effectiveness of intellectual property rights regimes in stimulation of research and creation of new medicines against diseases which particularly affect developing countries. The CIPIH final report was published in April 2006. The issue of public health and access to medicines calls for a variety of policies, including those unrelated to intellectual property. The business community has an important perspective to contribute to the discussion, having participated in a number of public-private partnerships, and as well as in private sector initiatives for supplying needed drugs to developing countries. Business and industry is also providing free or affordable access to biomedical and healthcare information for institutions in low-income countries through public-private initiatives.

## INTELLECTUAL PROPERTY AND DEVELOPING COUNTRIES

The subject of intellectual property rights has been a much-debated issue in the post-GATT Uruguay Round scenario. The value of the TRIPS Agreement for developing and least-developed countries has been questioned. Some point out that, in a modern economy, the minimum standards laid down in TRIPS Agreement will bring benefits to developing countries by creating the incentive structure necessary for knowledge generation and diffusion, technology transfer and private investment flows. It would safeguard results of technology development and at the same time engenders, nourish and sustain creative endeavours of nations. Many countries at all stages of development are increasingly using the protection of intellectual property to grow and expand local innovation-based industries, recognizing that the ability to manage and exploit innovation and resultant intellectual property rights is key to success in today's world. It is believed that the protection of intellectual property assets, supported by other legitimate policies, is a necessary tool for growth and development today. Debates are taking place at the international level on the relationship between intellectual property protection and development, notably regarding proposals for a Development Agenda for WIPO.

The argument that intellectual property rights systems only benefit developed countries and foreign companies and indeed may counteract economic development, for developing and least-developed countries, and prevent access by local populations to technology, continues to resonate in certain countries and among some groups. By placing intellectual property rights under the World Trade Organization, the developed countries would benefit, as they would have controlled on future innovations. The intellectual property, especially some of its elements, such as the patenting regime, will adversely affect the pursuit of sustainable development strategies by raising the prices of essential drugs to levels that are too high for the poor to afford; limiting the availability of educational materials for developing country school and university students; legitimizing the piracy of traditional knowledge; and undermining the self-reliance of resource poor farmers.

National sovereignty over genetic resources, often found in developing countries, is perceived to be undermined by the patenting of inventions based on such resources. Such patenting is also seen as encouraging unsustainable use and "biopiracy". These perceptions, aggravated by profound differences in history and culture, have led to allegations that intellectual property rights are both unjust and incompatible with the protection of the environment, most clearly heard in the context of the Convention on Biological Diversity (CBD). In particular, there is pressure to provide in patent specifications more information about biological materials to which they refer and to make patentability of such inventions dependent on such information: both information about the source of these biological materials, and confirmation that the resources have been obtained legally under the CBD (*i.e.*, with Prior Informed Consent—PIC). Under the CBD, access to biological materials normally entails benefit-sharing of the results from such access.

Developing countries need to know how to protect the knowledge of, and revenues from, indigenous weaves, music and jewelry, as well as traditional medicines. Poor countries and peoples can reap the benefits of turning their own knowledge into commercial success, if they find new ways of protecting and commercializing that information when patent laws and costly compliance with rich countries fail to serve them. There are many tangible and intangible properties such as craft designs, music and other cultural products, as well as medicines and traditional herbal knowledge from which poorer countries can earn income. The United Nations has estimated that developing countries lose at least $5 billion annually in unpaid royalties to multinational corporations that appropriate traditional knowledge. Direct links can be traced between many new medical products on the market and knowledge systems dating back millennia. Of the approximately 120 pharmaceutical products derived from plants in 1985, 75% were discovered through the study of their traditional medical use, yet benefit-sharing agreements between the holders of traditional knowledge and the pharmaceutical corporations are still relatively rare.

It has been observed that: on the cultural front, while some of the impoverished weavers of Andhra Pradesh, India, are committing suicide out of despair over their inability to take care of their families, the size of the markets enjoyed by the copies of their products that are churned out in China and South-east Asia is unknown, but is substantial. African music forms about half of the growing 'world music' scene, but since virtually all African music that enjoys an international market is produced in Paris or London—the agglomeration of jobs that successful African music generates is not in Africa. Similarly, Legal protection for artisans has been in place in the global market for decades, but the issues of protection of ancient designs, symbols and traditional knowledge utilized in artisan crafts have not been well-established.

## MISUSE OF INTELLECTUAL PROPERTY RIGHTS

Traditionally, most enterprises that have used the intellectual property system have done so primarily to create barriers to prevent competitors from entering their market niche. For example, enterprises have viewed their patents essentially as legal walls or barriers to keep out potential competitors. This has been possible as the basic right of the owner of a patent is the right to exclude all others from doing a number of specified acts. The exclusive right has, so far, been mainly seen as an opportunity for enterprises to exclude competitors from the marketplace. The use of intellectual property assets to create market entry barriers has been seen as the primary justification for creation and use of the intellectual property system that seeks to prevent copying, imitation and/or free riding by others. According to the survey undertaken by Nelson and Cohen (2000), one of the prominent motives for patenting has been the prevention of rivals from patenting related inventions (*i.e.,* "patent blocking"). However, such narrow use of the concept of exclusivity results in a lot of missed opportunities. A change of mindset and attitude is required for business to see that the exclusive right provided by intellectual property protection provides an avenue for enterprises to enhance their ability to co-operate with others so as to enhance their competitiveness.

Article 40 of the TRIPS Agreement recognizes that some licensing practices or conditions pertaining to intellectual property rights, which restrain competition, may have adverse effects on trade and may impede the transfer and dissemination of technology. Member countries may adopt, consistently with the other provisions of the Agreement, appropriate measures to prevent or control practices in the licensing of intellectual property rights, which are abusive and anti-competitive. The Agreement provides for a mechanism whereby a country seeking to take action against such practices involving the companies of another Member country can enter into consultations with that other Member and exchange publicly available non-confidential information of relevance to the matter in question and of other information available to that Member, subject to domestic law and to the conclusion of mutually satisfactory agreements concerning the safeguarding of its confidentiality by the requesting Member. Similarly, a country whose companies are subject to such action in another Member can enter into consultations with that Member.

## INTELLECTUAL PROPERTY THEFT

By its very nature, intellectual property is less tangible than physical capital and, therefore, it is more vulnerable to theft. Counterfeiting and piracy are growing exponentially in terms of volume, sophistication, range of goods, and countries affected. This has a significant negative economic and social impact on national economies, governments, consumers and businesses in countries at all stages of development. Theft of intellectual property affects all industry sectors. Piracy and counterfeiting have been shown to decrease employment opportunities, diminish tax revenues for governments, and reduce incentives to invest. Tax and excise losses caused by counterfeiting and piracy are considerable. This deprives governments of revenues needed for the country's infrastructure and other priorities, and translates into higher taxes on taxpayers.

Collectively, the wider economic, social and developmental costs are much more damaging than may be currently understood. A disorder of this magnitude not only discourages innovation and introduces health and safety risks, but also creates a significant drain on the global economy—undermining economic development, a sound market economy system and open international trade and investment. Intellectual property theft stifles innovation and deters honest local entrepreneurs from investing in product and market development. It robs innovators and creators of reward for effort and innovation, undermine local culture by reducing the incentive to invest, and ultimately limit the diversity and availability of high-quality goods and services. As intellectual property theft is a profitable criminal activity, it attracts organized crime and its associated violence. Counterfeiting and piracy therefore become part of a wider criminal network and sometime finances other criminal activity. There is evidence of increasing links between piracy and counterfeiting operations and organized crime.

Local and imported products alike suffer considerably from counterfeiting and piracy. This particularly affects knowledge-based industries, the keystone of the economic strategies of many countries. Countries that aim to increase the value of their exports by using their intellectual capital are also hampered in their efforts by counterfeiting and piracy.

In India, fast-moving consumer goods lose approximately 15% of market share to counterfeits and 38% of auto parts are fake. Approximately 22% of Japanese corporate executives state that counterfeits are their biggest concern in trade negotiations with China. The US and other developed countries are not immune. The California economy loses some US $34.5 billion per year to counterfeiting and piracy, while UK industry reports it lost nearly £10 billion in 2002.

Counterfeiting and piracy are also detrimental to the proper functioning of competition.

Legitimate industries cannot "compete" with pirates and counterfeiters on the price of products, since illegal operators are saved the research, development and marketing costs of the legitimate sector. Pirates and counterfeiters simply take a free ride on all the effort, creative work and investment of others. This illegal activity leads to serious distortions in the marketplace. Businesses are less likely to transfer advanced technology, or invest in production or R&D facilities in countries where they are likely to have their products copied or technology stolen. This is particularly true of industries where intellectual property plays a key role, such as the IT, biotechnology and pharmaceutical sectors, which many countries aspire to develop.

Counterfeiting and piracy likewise have damaging consequences for consumers. Every industry sector is affected, including airplane and car parts, food, beverages, batteries, medicines, film, music, publishing and toys. They generally involve: (1) Potentially serious risks to health and safety when these products are counterfeited without the safety features of the originals; unsafe counterfeit products that can present significant health and safety risks are increasingly harming consumers; (2) Low and inconsistent quality of the counterfeit product. Businesses whose products are pirated and counterfeited suffer from loss of sales.

## ENFORCEMENT

Counterfeiting and piracy require an international multi-sectoral response. The launching of business action to stop counterfeiting and piracy is necessary to increase public and political awareness of the problem and to encourage government action to tackle this. Digital piracy (and other cyber crimes, such as password/ identity theft or "phishing") also continues to be a problem—the application of new technologies allowing perfect copying and immediate mass distribution of digital works poses economic, technological and legal challenges, including that of ensuring the secure distribution of digital works. Despite the efforts of companies and trade associations to stop counterfeiting and piracy, the problem is swelling at a more dangerous rate than ever. The immense adverse economic and social impact of intellectual property theft requires that combating counterfeiting and piracy become a priority for society, and not just right holders. Unless governments, businesses and citizens make a co-ordinated effort to uphold the intellectual property system, society will not reap its benefits.

The ease and speed of reproduction and transmission of digital content on the Internet have made it difficult for right holders to control the distribution of their copyrighted works and to enforce their rights in the digital context. The music sector has been particularly affected, and rights holders have taken a broad range of measures, including the roll out of legitimate services, public awareness campaigns, the use of technological protection measures, and enforcement action against the most detrimental infringements of their rights. Still, infringers are resourceful and try for instance to avoid jurisdiction by using remote servers. The increasing importance of websites as a communication and trading interface with consumers and business partners has also provided new opportunities for abuses of trademark rights (through domain names, metatagging, etc.).

The Internet also exacerbates issues of jurisdiction and enforcement because Internet activity, due to its worldwide reach, may expose parties to litigation in any country of the world where arguably the tort occurs or the injury is suffered. Infringement of intellectual property rights on the Internet raises complex issues of localization of the components of the infringing acts.

In addition to jurisdictional issues, right holders have difficulties in tracing infringers operating on the Internet, because of the lack of reliable information on the identity of persons operating websites or holding domain names. Moreover, the transient nature of the bulk of the content circulating on the Internet renders evidence collection more difficult.

Also, with the growing number of electronic documents that may be needed or discoverable in litigation, questions of admissibility of digital evidence raise complex issues, such as authentication of identity, content and time, confidentiality, and archival policy including deleted files. Therefore, the major focus of attention is the enforcement of intellectual property rights.

## POLICY ISSUES AND NEW DEVELOPMENTS

Several intellectual property policy issues are currently under consideration in the TRIPS Council. These include: (1) The patentability of biotechnological inventions, and the relationship between TRIPS Agreement, the UN Convention on Biological Diversity, and the protection of traditional knowledge, folklore and genetic resources. (2) How TRIPS provisions can best support public health goals; and (3) Geographical indications, which relate to the manner in which places or country names can be used to identify the origin and quality of specific goods.

Intellectual property issues have arisen and are assuming greater importance in respect of traditional knowledge and folklore as well as the conservation, preservation, management, sustainable utilization and benefit sharing of genetic resources.

The commercial application of new technologies—especially digital and communication technologies and biotechnology—has led not only to the development of new types of products and services, but also to new forms of distribution and methods of infringement. New technologies and business players are emerging so fast in these fields that unless traditional business, and governmental and other organizations dealing with intellectual property rights take note and respond quickly and accordingly, they will be overtaken by such developments.

Important economic, social, political and technological developments over the past few years have had a fundamental impact on how intellectual property is created, exploited and used. The main forces changing the intellectual property landscape today and their possible impact on the creation and exploitation of intellectual property are: (1) The globalization of the economy. (2) The development of new technologies. (3) The growth in economic importance of non-technological business innovations and resources not protected by existing intellectual property regimes. (4) The politicization of intellectual property issues. (5) Changes in the ways businesses operate.

4

# PATENTS ENCOURAGE INNOVATION

Patents are a part of intellectual property, which is a legal way to protect all creations of the human mind. It is an exclusive right granted by the State for an invention that is new, involves an inventive step and is capable of industrial application. It gives its owner the exclusive right to prevent or stop others from making, using, selling or importing a product or a process, based on the patented invention, without the owner's prior permission.

A patent is granted by the national patent office of a country or a regional patent office for a group of countries. It is valid for a limited period of time, generally for 20 years from the date of filing of the patent application, provided the required maintenance fees are paid on time. A patent is a territorial right, limited to the geographical boundary of the relevant country or region.

Patents are perceived as a sound intellectual property title, granted after a rigorous examination process. Patented inventions have, in fact, pervaded every aspect of human life, from electric lighting and plastic, to ballpoint pens and microprocessors. A complex product (such as a camera, mobile phone, or a car) may incorporate a number of inventions that are covered by several patents, which may be owned by different patent holders. A patent is a powerful business tool for companies to gain exclusivity over a new product or process, develop a strong market position and earn additional revenues through licensing. They provide competitive advantage to the company in the market. More than assets on company's balance sheet, patents can help companies attract investors. They can be a steady source of income as patents ownership affords a 20-year sanctioned monopoly, granting the right to market a technology or charge a royalty for its use. The proper management of patents is the core of the competitive strategy.

## HISTORICAL BACKGROUND

The term 'patent' originally was used to designate the document (letters patent) by which a sovereign conferred a privilege or right on someone. The term has, however, now come to refer to certain grants in respect of inventions only. Although there is some evidence suggesting that something like patents were used among some ancient Greek cities, the first known 'grant' by a State to an inventor is reported to have taken place in the Republic of Florence in 1421 and an ordinance relating to patents was enacted in Venice in 1474. Such patents for invention gradually came into practice in many other European countries. USA came up with patent statute in 1790 and France in 1791. In Great Britain there was no general statute until 1852. Today there are hardly any countries without a patent regime.

Since its founding in 1790, the United States Patent and Trademark Office (USPTO) has issued over 7 million patents, of that number approximately 70-thousand have become legitimate products. Although most patents are obscure and long forgotten, in the 1% that did become successful are some very significant inventions that have changed the way we live our lives. The first inventor to avail himself of the advantages of the 1790 Patent Act was Samuel Hopkins, born in Vermont and living in Philadelphia, who received a patent on the 31st of July 1790 for an improved method of "Making Pot and Pearl Ashes."

## A TOOL FOR ENCOURAGING CREATIVITY AND INNOVATION

Patents provide rewards and protection for inventors but they also benefit society. In return for patent protection, inventors agree to reveal all the technical information about their invention. This information is available to everyone and has enough details so anyone with basic knowledge of the invention's field can reproduce the invention. The accurate and complete written description of the invention is provided in the patent application.

The purpose is to enrich the total body of technical knowledge in the world. Such an ever-increasing body of public knowledge promotes further creativity and innovation in others, which assures that the quality of human life is continuously enhanced. In this way, patents help to spread new knowledge. This new knowledge can in turn help others to solve different problems, or to make further advances in science and technology. Thus, patents provide not only protection for the owner but valuable information and inspiration for future generations of researchers and inventors. A patent-holder discloses to the world the research and science underlying the invention. The breakthrough of one scientist can become the basis for the breakthrough of others. Patents are crucial because they make it possible for society to realize or secure the benefits of genius creativity and effort. The granted patent and in many countries, the patent application is made public via publication in an official journal or gazette.

## PATENT SYSTEMS

*Telescope (a patented invention)*

The patent system refers to the patent laws, procedures, practices and institutions responsible for protecting, administering, enforcing, and using patents for social, cultural and economic progress. The goal of the patent system is to encourage inventors to advance the state of technology by awarding them special rights to benefit from their inventions. Any country that respects intellectual property has a national policy and provision for patenting an invention. Patent systems have been adopted by many countries over the years because: (1) They encourage the disclosure of information to the public, increasing the public's access to technical and scientific knowledge. Without the assurance of a patent, an individual or corporate inventor may choose to keep the details of an invention secret; (2) They provide an incentive and reward for innovation and investment in R&D and future inventions; (3) The limited duration of a patent encourages rapid commercialization of inventions, so that the public receives a tangible benefit from the invention sooner rather than later; (4) By encouraging the publication of inventions, patents help avoid duplication of research and stimulate further research and competition. (5) The patent system facilitates technology transfer and foreign direct investment, as it provides reassurance to companies considering investing in a country.

*An innovative award-winning drill bit used to make holes on glass and ceramics (Patent No. US2002137433)*

## PATENT PROTECTION

Inventions are the result of hard work. It takes a lot of research and experimentation to turn the idea into a useful and working invention. They deserve a reward for the amount of time they spend developing their ideas. Inventors also need the security of knowing that if they share the invention with the rest of the world, nobody will steal it, use it or copy it without their permission. Such protection is provided by the patents.

Patent protection means that the invention cannot be commercially made, used, distributed or sold without the patent owner's consent. A patent is a monopoly over the potential use and exploitation of an invention for a set period of time. A patent is, therefore, a negative right—it excludes others from exploiting the inventor's achievement. These patent rights are usually enforced in a court, which, in most systems, holds the authority to stop patent infringement. Conversely, a court can also declare a patent invalid upon a successful challenge by a third party. In order to safeguard the right of an inventor, a patent, whether a process or product, may also be filed in other countries. Procedures and steps involved in acquiring this right may vary from country to country but the basic principle followed universally is that the inventor publicly discloses the invention in sufficient details, supplemented by drawings if necessary, so that anyone skilled in the art should be able to reproduce the result(s). In return the inventor is granted for a limited period of time a legally enforceable right to exclude others from exploiting it. Patent protection has great economic importance to a number of industries that rely on technological innovation to remain competitive, such as the chemical, pharmaceutical, and computer industries. Patent law grants patents for machines; compositions of matter, such as new chemical compounds to be used in industry; manufactured items; and industrial processes, provided they meet a number of strict legal tests. Patents are also available for significant improvements on previously invented items.

## INTERNATIONAL PROTECTION

Several international agreements on patent protection exist. For substantive issues, the most important are the Paris Convention for the Protection of Industrial Property (1883) and the WTO Agreement on Trade-Related Aspects of Intellectual Property Rights (TRIPS) (1994), while the main patent treaties for procedural issues are the Patent Co-operation Treaty (1970) and the Patent Law Treaty (2000). TRIPS Agreement has strengthened legal protection for patents worldwide.

## TRIPS PROVISIONS

As per the Agreement, patents shall be available for any inventions, whether products or processes, in all fields of technology, provided that they are new, involve an inventive step and are capable of industrial application. Patents shall be available and patent rights enjoyable without discrimination as to the place of invention, the field of technology and whether products are imported or locally produced. The terms "inventive step" and "capable of industrial application" may be deemed by a member to be synonymous with the terms "non-obvious" and "useful" respectively.

Members may exclude from patentability inventions, the prevention within their territory of the commercial exploitation of which is necessary to protect *ordre public* or morality, including to protect human, animal or plant life or health or to avoid serious prejudice to the environment, provided that such exclusion is not made merely because the exploitation is prohibited by their law.

Members may also exclude from patentability: (*a*) Diagnostic, therapeutic and surgical methods for the treatment of humans or animals. (*b*) Plants and animals other than micro-organisms, and essentially biological processes for the production of plants or animals other than non-biological and microbiological processes. However, members shall provide for the protection of plant varieties either by patents or by an effective *sui generis* system or by any combination thereof.

## CONDITIONS OF PATENTABILITY

Inventions can be as simple as a paperclip or as complicated as a robot but they must meet certain conditions of patentability before they can be patented. An invention must meet several requirements to be eligible for patent protection. These include, in particular, that the claimed invention: (1) Consists of patentable subject matter; (2) Is new (novelty requirement), it could be a new concept or idea or solution to an existing problem or completely a new method/process/device/utility; (3) Involves an inventive step (non-obviousness requirement); (4) Is capable of industrial application (utility requirement); and (5) Is disclosed in a clear and complete manner in the patent application (disclosure requirement).

Patents do not cover every kind of inventive activity in every country. Patents, however, do cover virtually every field of technology although the subject matter excluded from the purview of patents is variable from one country to another. In most national or regional patent laws provide a list of what cannot be patented. While there are considerable differences between countries, following are examples of some of the areas that may be excluded from patentability: Discoveries and scientific theories; Aesthetic creations; Schemes, Rules and Methods for performing mental acts; Mere discoveries of substances as they naturally occur in the world; Inventions that may affect public order, good morals or public health; Diagnostic, therapeutic and surgical methods of treatment for humans or animals; Plants and animals other than micro-organisms, and essentially biological processes for the production of plants or animals other than non-biological and microbiological processes; and Computer programs.

### Novelty Requirement

An invention is new or novel if it does not form part of the 'prior art'. In general, prior art refers to all the relevant technical knowledge available to the public anywhere in the world prior to the first filing date of the relevant patent application. It includes, *inter alia*, patents, patent applications and non-patent literature of all kinds. The definition of prior art differs considerably from country-to-country. In many countries, any information disclosed to the public anywhere in the world in written form, by oral communication, by display or through public use constitutes prior art. Thus, in principle, the publication of the invention in a scientific journal, its presentation in a conference, its use in commerce or its display in a company's catalogue would all constitute acts that could destroy the novelty of the invention and render it unpatentable. It is important to prevent accidental disclosure of inventions prior to filing the patent application. Assistance of a competent patent agent is often crucial for a clear determination of what is included in the prior art. Prior art often includes "secret prior art" such as pending unpublished patent applications, provided they are published at a later stage.

### Non-obviousness Requirement

An invention is considered to involve an inventive step (or to be non-obvious) when, taking into account the prior art, the invention would not have been obvious to a person skilled in the particular field of technology. The non-obviousness requirement is meant to ensure that patents are only granted in respect of truly creative and inventive achievements, and not to developments that a person with ordinary skill in the field could easily deduce from what already exists. The invention must be a significant improvement to existing technology. Simple changes to previously known devices do not comprise a patentable invention.

Some examples of what may not qualify as inventive, as established by past court decisions in some countries, are: mere change of size; making a product portable; the reversal of parts; the change of materials; or the mere substitution by an equivalent part or function.

### Utility Requirement

To be patentable, an invention must be capable of being used for an industrial or business purpose. An invention cannot be a mere theoretical phenomenon; it must be useful and provide some practical benefit. The term "industrial" is meant here in the broadest sense as anything distinct from purely intellectual or aesthetic activity, and includes, for example, agriculture. In some countries, instead of industrial applicability, the criterion is utility.

The utility requirement has become particularly important for patents on genetic sequences for which a utility may not yet be known at the time of filing the application. No patent will be granted for inventions that can only be used for an illegal or immoral purpose.

### Disclosure Requirement

According to the national legislation of most of the countries, a patent application must disclose the invention in a manner sufficiently clear and complete for the invention to be carried out by a person skilled in the specific technical field. In some countries, patent law requires that the inventor disclose the "best mode" for practising the invention.

For patents involving micro-organisms, many countries require the micro-organism to be deposited at a recognized depositary institution.

## OBTAINING A PATENT

When deciding whether or not to patent an invention, the first thing inventors need to do is to find out if their inventions meet the conditions of patentability. Next, inventors should try to find out how interested other people are in their inventions, and if customers would be willing to buy them. The patenting process can be long and expensive so inventors should make sure that once they have the patents they will be able to sell their inventions and recover the patenting and production costs.

It is preferable to apply for patent protection as soon as one has all the information required for drafting the patent application. Generally, the first step is to perform a prior art search. With over 40 million patents granted worldwide, and millions of printed publications, which are potential prior art against ones invention, there is a serious risk that some reference, or combination of references, may render the inventor's invention non-novel or obvious, and, therefore, unpatentable. After a prior art search has been performed and the decision to seek patent protection has been made, a patent application has to be prepared and submitted to the relevant national or regional patent office. The application will include a full description of the invention, the patent claims that determine the scope of the patent applied for, drawings and an abstract.

## Patent Application

A patent application has a range of functions: It determines the legal scope of the patent. It describes the nature of the invention, including instructions on how to carry out the invention; and it gives details of the inventor, the patent owner and other legal information. It is a key document.

Patent applications are similarly structured worldwide and consist of a request, a description, claims, drawings (if necessary) and an abstract. A patent document may be anywhere between a few pages to hundreds of pages long, depending on the nature of the specific invention and the technical field.

### *Request*

It contains information on the title of the invention, the date of filing, the priority date and bibliographic data such as the name and address of the applicant and inventor.

### *Description*

The written description of an invention must describe the invention in sufficient detail so that anyone skilled in the same technical field can reconstruct and practice the invention from the description and the drawings without putting in further inventive effort. If this is not the case, the patent may not be granted or may be revoked after it is challenged in a court action.

### *Claims*

The claims determine the scope of protection of a patent. The claims are absolutely crucial to a patented invention since, if they are badly drafted, even a truly valuable invention could result in a worthless patent that is easy to circumvent or design around. In patent litigation, interpreting the claims is generally the first step in determining whether the patent is valid and in determining whether the patent has been infringed. It is strongly advisable to seek the advice of an expert to draft patent applications, particularly the claims.

### *Drawings*

The drawings show the technical details of the invention in an abstract and visual way. They help to explain some information, tool or result set out in the disclosure. Drawings are not always a necessary part of the application. If the invention is for a process or method of doing something, drawings usually are not required. If drawings are required, formal rules govern their acceptability.

### *Abstract*

The abstract is a brief summary of the invention. When the patent is published by the patent office, the abstract is included on the front page. The abstract is sometimes improved or drafted by the patent examiner in the relevant patent office.

## Processing an Application

A specially trained official, called a patent examiner, reviews the application to determine if it qualifies for a patent. During the patent examination process, the patent examiner may ask the applicant to answer various questions about the invention. The law requires the patent applicant to disclose all information in his or her possession that is relevant to whether the patent should be issued. Because this process often goes back and forth several times between the applicant and the examiner, a patent examination can be very time-consuming and the legal fees can be expensive. The steps taken by a patent office to grant a patent vary but, broadly speaking, follow a similar pattern. It involves following steps:

### *Formal Examination*

The patent office examines the application to ensure that it complies with the administrative requirements or formalities (*e.g.*, that all relevant documentation is included and the application fee has been paid).

### *Search*

The patent office conducts a search to determine the prior art in the specific field to which the invention relates. The search report is used during the substantive examination to compare the claimed invention with the prior art.

### *Substantive Examination*

The aim of the substantive examination is to ensure that the application satisfies the patentability requirements. Not all patent offices check applications against all the patentability requirements, and some only do so upon request within a specified time. The results of the examination are sent in writing to the applicant (or his attorney) so as to provide an opportunity to respond to and/or remove any objections raised during the examination. This process often results in the narrowing of the scope of the claims.

### *Publication*

In most of the countries, the patent application is published 18 months after the first filing date. In general, patent offices also publish the patent once it is granted.

### *Grant*

If the examination process reaches a positive conclusion, the patent office grants the patent and issues a certificate of grant.

### *Opposition*

Many patent offices provide a period during which third parties may oppose the grant of a patent, for example, on the basis that the claimed invention is not new. Opposition proceedings may be pre-grant and/or post-grant, and are possible within the specified time limits.

## Patenting Abroad

Patents are territorial rights, which means that an invention is only protected in the countries or regions where patent protection has been obtained. In other words, if one has not been granted a patent with effect in a given country, his or her invention will not be protected in that country, enabling anybody else to make, use, import or sell his or her invention in that country. It is now faster and easier for people and ideas to travel around the world. Because of this, it is no longer enough for inventors to protect their ideas in only one country.

Patent protection in foreign countries will enable any company to enjoy exclusive rights over the patented invention in those countries. In addition, patenting abroad may enable the company to license the invention to foreign firms, develop outsourcing relationship, and access those markets in partnership with others.

As protecting an invention in many countries is an expensive undertaking, companies should carefully select the countries in which they require protection. It will have to consider where it will benefit from protection and it will also have to take into account the costs of protecting in various countries. Market of the patented product would be the key consideration.

There are three main ways of protecting an invention abroad:

### *The National Route*

One may apply to the national patent office of each country of interest, by filing a patent application in the required language and paying the required fees. This path may be very cumbersome and expensive if the number of countries is large.

### *The Regional Route*

When a number of countries are members of a regional patent system, one may apply for protection, with effect in the territories of all or some of these, by filing an application at the relevant regional office. The regional patent offices are: The African Intellectual Property Organization (OAPI); The African Regional Intellectual Property Organization (ARIPO); The Eurasian Patent Organization (EAPO); The European Patent Office (EPO); and The Patent Office of the Gulf Co-operation Council.

### *The International Route*

The WIPO-administered Patent Co-operation Treaty (PCT) provides for the filing of a single international patent application, which has the same effect as national applications filed in the designated countries. An applicant seeking protection may file one application and request protection in as many signatory states as needed.

If any company wants to have the option of protecting an invention in any number of member countries of the Patent Co-operation Treaty (PCT), then it should consider filing an international PCT application. To be eligible to do so, one must be a national or resident of a PCT Contracting State, or, his or her business must have a real and effective industrial or commercial presence in one of these countries. By filing one international application under the PCT, one may simultaneously seek patent protection for an invention in the more than 125 member countries of the PCT. This application may be filed either at one's national or regional patent office and/or at the PCT receiving office at the World Intellectual Property Office (WIPO) in Geneva, Switzerland. This is an easier and cheaper system to file international patent applications.

The date of inventor's first application for a given invention is called the priority date and any subsequent applications in other countries filed by him within 12 months (*i.e.*, within the priority period) will benefit from the earlier application and will have priority over other applications for the same invention filed by others after the priority date. It is highly advisable to file foreign patent applications within the priority period. After the expiration of the priority period and the PCT provides at least 18 additional months on top of the 12-month priority period, in which applicants can explore the commercial potential of their product in various countries and decide where to seek patent protection. Payment of the fees and translation costs associated with national applications is thus delayed. The PCT is widely used by applicants to keep their options open for as long as possible.

PCT applicants receive valuable information about the potential patentability of their invention in the form of the PCT International Search Report and the Written Opinion of the International Searching Authority. These documents provide PCT applicants with a strong basis on which they can make their decisions about whether and where to pursue patent protection.

A single PCT application, in one language and with one set of fees, has legal effect in all PCT member countries. This effect significantly reduces the initial transaction costs of submitting separate applications to each patent office.

The Patent Co-operation Treaty (PCT) has been a great success since it came into force in 1978, and now has more than 120 member states. It has caused a reduction in both costs and the administrative burden for applicants and has enabled them to delay making heavy payments in the patenting process until such time as the value of the invention is better known. WIPO's attempts to improve the PCT system so that its search and examination procedures better serve applicants and the patent offices of the many member states have been successful. On April 1, 2005, amendments to PCT Regulations, simplifying the procedure before the International Search Authority and the International Preliminary Examining Authority came into force.

## COST OF PATENTING

The costs vary considerably from country to country and within a country depending on factors such as the nature of the invention, its complexity, attorney's fees, the length of the application and objections raised during the examination by the patent office.

There are generally costs associated with performing a prior art search. There are official filing fees that vary widely from country to country. If the services of a patent agent/attorney are taken to assist in the application process (*e.g.*, provide the patentability opinion, draft the patent application, prepare the formal drawings and correspond with the patent office), it will incur additional costs.

Once a patent has been granted by the patent office, one must pay maintenance or renewal fees, generally on an annual basis, to maintain the validity of the patent. In case one decides to patent his invention abroad, he should consider also the relevant official filing fees for the countries in question, the translation costs and the costs of using local patent agents (which is a requirement, in many countries, for foreign applicants). In case of inventions involving micro-organisms, where the deposit of the micro-organism or biological material with a recognized depositary institution is necessary, fees for filing, storage and viability testing of the deposited material will have to be paid.

## HARMONIZATION OF PATENT LAWS

WIPO has launched worldwide discussions for the purpose of preparing a blueprint for the future evolution of the international patent system. Its main purpose is to create mechanizms and programmes whereby inventors and industry have access to national, regional and internationally effective patent protection systems, which enable them to obtain, maintain and enforce their patents globally. Though at present there is no such system, the foundation for it exists in the PCT and Patent Law Treaty (PLT) and TRIPS Agreement. The idea of an international patent system at this point of time is based on mutual recognition of single patent granted from a single application, which should be obtained quickly and inexpensively. Reasons for this thinking are: (*i*) the application and maintenance cost of a patent are burdensome for individual inventors and small businesses, and (*ii*) the duplication of effort involved in granting patents.

A truly worldwide patent system, giving rise to a single patent enforceable within every country within a single legal framework, would however raise major constitutional issues (*e.g.*, concerning a country's right to determine what commercial acts are permissible within its borders and what its citizens are allowed to do in relation to local economic issues and imperatives). This is therefore unlikely but much can be done to harmonize patent grant and enforcement systems by resolving the issues, and by regionalizing patenting and patent enforcement systems. The most likely outcome of a harmonized system will be a network of regional bodies charged with granting patents in a consistent way. Such an outcome will have to be reached by progressive harmonization of laws and practices within existing major national and regional patent offices. While progress has been made, especially in the area of prior art searching, much remains to be done.

## USING PATENTS

Once inventors have patent protection, they can make money by being the only ones allowed to produce, distribute and sell their inventions. Some inventors are too busy working on their next idea to spend time trying to sell their previous inventions. In these cases, inventors may prefer to license their inventions.

When inventors license their patented inventions, they authorize another person or a company (the licensee) to produce, sell or distribute them as long as they pay a licence fee. This licence fee rewards inventors for their creations and allows licensees to "commercialize" inventions so that consumers can benefit from them.

A patent owner has the right to decide who may or may not use the patented invention for the period in which the invention is protected. The patent owner may give permission to, or license, other parties to use the invention on mutually agreed terms. The owner may also sell the right to the invention to someone else, who will then become the new owner of the patent. Once a patent expires, the protection ends, and an invention enters the public domain, that is, the owner no longer holds exclusive rights to the invention, which becomes available to commercial exploitation by others. If people copy, distribute or sell a patented invention without the patentee's permission, they commit a crime called patent infringement. The patentee can sue the patent infringer in a law court.

The exclusive rights granted by a patent give the patent owner the opportunity to prevent or stop competitors from making products and using processes that infringe on its rights and to seek compensation for damages suffered. To prove that infringement has occurred, it must be shown that each and every element of a given claim, or its equivalent, is contained in the infringing product or process. Enforcing ones rights when he or she believes that his or her patented invention is being copied may be crucial to maintain his or her competitive edge, market share and profitability.

## PATENT INFORMATION

"Patent information" is the technical and legal information contained in patent documents that are published periodically by patent offices. It is the sum total of all the information contained in every patent document ever published. A patent document includes the full description of how a patented invention works and the claims, which determine the scope of protection as well as details on who patented the invention, when it was patented, and reference to relevant literature. About two-thirds of the technical information revealed in patents is never published elsewhere. This makes patent information the single most comprehensive collection of classified technological data.

Patent information relates information concerning patented invention disclosed in a patent document. To date this means some 42 million patent documents worldwide in every technical field, with about one million more documents added each year. The patent document and the patent application is worded by the applicant and the document contains three basic parts of information: (*a*) Bibliographic data such as symbols of patent classification, publication number, date of application, name of inventor, etc.; (*b*) A detailed description of the invention, sometimes supported by drawings; (*c*) Claims giving in exact words the essence of the invention and defining the scope of protection. The published patent document includes a condensed version of the content of the patent application known as the abstract. The abstract describes in a few sentences the main features of the invention. It normally appears on the front page of the patent document together with the most relevant drawing. In some countries the abstract is also published separately. Patent document also includes the title of the invention and references to prior art. Thus, the patent document discloses the technology field of the invention, the technical problem solved by it, the prior art, the owner of the patent and its inventor. It also indicates when was the earliest application for a patent filed and where? Whether the technology is in the public domain?

Because of the following reasons patent document is considered a unique source of technological information. A large percentage of technology disclosed in the patents is never published in any other publication. They are effective only in the country of grant and for a limited period. Patents form one of the earliest publications of the patented invention. Patents form a single storehouse of technological information covering the widest range of technologies irrespective of the level of sophistication of the technology. They are written in standard format. Once familiarity is gained, retrieval of relevant is easy. Patent information is easily accessible through the use of classification systems and the use of electronic systems. In recent years, economists, social science researchers, policy-makers, businessmen and professionals have begun to make increasing macro-level and macro-level use of patent information.

Most significant inventions are disclosed to the public for the first time only when the patent or patent application is published. Thus, patents and published patent applications provide means of learning about current research and innovations often long before the relevant innovative product appears on the market. Patent searches should be part of the essential inputs to any company's R&D effort. Patent information may help the researcher/inventor in avoiding duplication of research. Inventors research patent documents to increase their knowledge about the latest technological developments in their field and to find inspiration for their own inventions. They assess the state-of-the-art before initiating research project. They find ready solutions to technical problems in ongoing research and keep up-to-date with developments in the technology fields.

Industry may use patent information to: (1) Improve existing technology to produce newer/better/cheaper products, (2) Find ready solution to technological problem, (3) Increase production and productivity, (4) Locate suppliers of equipment/materials, (5) Assess the state-of-the-art before initiating manufacturing projects, (6) Identify suitable technologies for adaptation/transfer, and (7) Evaluate alternative technologies for transfer.

The technical information contained in patent documents can provide business enterprises with important insights that may be used to: (1) Identify new products for marketing, licence, or distribution, (2) Locate patent owners, (3) Identify competitors, (4) Avoid possible infringement problems, and (5) Locate area of investment. Companies may find patent information, which is a unique source of classified technical information, of great value for their strategic business planning. Investors and companies, who are looking for new products in which to invest also read patent documents.

Consultants and planners use patent information to assess a technology for viability, to undertake technology forecasting by identifying the trend of inventions in a given technology field, and to advise industry/R&D/financial institutions on issues relating to the technology.

Financial institution utilizes patent information to assess a technology/research project for financial support and to monitor the viability and progress of aided projects.

Patent agents/applicants for patents use patent information to ascertain patentability and other aspects in respect of an application for patent, opposition, revocation and other proceedings under the relevant patent law.

### Access to Patent Information

Inventors have to provide detailed information about their inventions in their patent applications. Patent applications are public documents, which means that anyone can read and learn from them. Countries have patent libraries where anyone can go to find information about all the patents that the government of that country has granted.

Patents and patent applications published by many patent offices are accessible on-line, thus making it easier to conduct prior art searches.

While access to patent information is considerably simpler, it is not easy to perform a high-quality patent search. Patent jargon is often complex and obscure and professional searching requires considerable knowledge and expertise. While preliminary searches may be performed through free on-line patent databases, most companies requiring patent information for making key business decisions (*e.g.*, whether to apply for a patent or not) will generally rely on the services of patent professionals and/or use more sophisticated commercial databases.

A prior art search can be done based on keywords, patent classification or other search criteria. The prior art uncovered depends on the search strategy employed, the classification system used, the technical expertise of the person who conducts the search, and the patent database being used. The International Patent Classification (IPC) is a hierarchical classification system used to classify and search patent documents. It also serves as an instrument for orderly arrangement of patent documents, a basis for selective dissemination of information and a basis for investigating the state-of-the-art in given fields of technology. Currently, over 100 countries use the IPC to classify their patents.

### *Patent Databases*

Patent databases provide a deep pool of technical information that countries can use to build up their technological capacity. CD-ROM databases are very convenient for documentary searches, but the information rapidly becomes out-of-date, at least for certain types of analysis. CD-ROM databases are not yet suitable for statistical applications.

The Internet contains many wonderful sites that are patent-oriented and are extremely useful. Internet-based databases are on-line databases. Anyone who has access to the internet may be able to browse the full text of published patent documents via free of charge databases or commercial databases. As access to these kinds of databases is not restricted across national borders, so users worldwide can very easily access patent documents from a computer connected to the internet.

As of now, many national patent offices have launched free-of-charge patent information databases, which are open to the public. For example, the Full-Text and Full-Page Image Database of the United States Patent and Trademark Office (USPTO) is one of the earliest and free online patent information services. Another major on-line free patent database is esp@cenet, which has some 30 million patent documents. WIPO's international Patent Co-operation Treaty (PCT) database is also a free-of-charge database.

The free services work well for simple searches, based on key words, such as a known patent number, name of the inventor(s) or applicant(s), a key word in the title, etc., but are not a suitable tool for executing more complex investigations and legally motivated searches.

There are a number of private companies that have commercial databases. These include Derwent, Dialog, STN, Questel Orbit, Micro-patent, WIPS, etc. These commercial services offer enhanced or value-added patent information, based on the actual requirement of particular end users.

## UTILITY MODELS

Utility models involve some of the inventions in the mechanical field. Therefore, the objects of utility models are sometimes described as devices for useful objects. This type of invention is also referred to as a 'petty invention'. As the name suggests, the degree of the inventive step required in these types of inventions are usually very small as compared to that required for the inventions to be protected by patents. The maximum term of protection under this category of inventions is generally shorter than that available in the case of patents. The examination procedure for securing legal rights under the Utility model law is very simple; the time taken for securing the rights is short and the cost very low. Utility model law is prevalent only in a few countries.

## PATENT PROTECTION FOR SOFTWARE

Computer technology plays an increasingly important role in our society today. It penetrates more and more areas of our life, not only in business environments but also in daily surroundings. A computer cannot operate without instructions. These instructions, so-called computer programs or software, may be incorporated in the computer or apparatus, but are often created, reproduced and distributed. Once created, it is often possible to reproduce software easily at very low cost. Thus, without appropriate protection against unauthorized copying and use, producers of software may not be able to recoup their investments. The unique nature of software is that it performs various functions through expressions written in computer language.

Until a few years ago, most software companies primarily relied on copyright and trade secret protection for software because software was not considered patentable subject matter. Although copyright protects "literal expressions" of software, it does not protect the "concept" behind the software, which often is a core part of its commercial value. Since such concepts behind the software often provide technical functions such as controlling machines or processing data, program developers started seeking protection of software through the patent system. Today software is clearly patentable in the United States. Many other countries grant some patent protection for software related inventions.

In the 1970s and 1980s, there were extensive discussions on whether the patent system, the copyright system, or a *sui generis* system, should provide protection for computer software. These discussions resulted in the generally accepted principle that computer programs should be protected by copyright, whereas apparatus using computer software or software-related inventions should be protected by patent.

One possible definition of a software patent, supported by the Foundation for a Free Information Infrastructure (FFII), is that it is a patent on any performance of a computer realized by means of a computer program.

### Business Method Patents

In recent years, another issue arose, namely the question of the patentability of business methods. Traditionally, business methods have been either in the public domain or protected under trade secret law. Today, however, information technology offers possibilities of applying new business models, using information technology as a tool for processing and transmitting various data and for communication. The internet has provided new prospects of doing business on-line. Due to high economic stakes put on those new business methods and the expansion of e-commerce in our society, the debate on the opportunity of patenting business methods has continued at both the national and international levels. In fact, business method patent for book-keeping was denied in 1908 case of Hotel Security Checking Co. vs. Lorraine Co. From 1908 until now methods of doing business were not considered patentable. But on 23rd July 1998, a three-judge panel of the USA Court of Appeals for the Federal Circuit, definitively ruled that there is no business method exceptions to the patent laws, and that the business methods are subject to the same legal standards as any other process or method. The growth in the use of computer technology in business decided that business methods should enjoy patent protection, even if they do not involve computers. The general idea is that a business patent is one that covers any method of using existing technology, such as the Internet, in some unique manner. There is, however, a sustained debate as to what extent such patents should be granted.

Business method patents are a class of patents and one of many legal aspects of business. They may be constituted as very important assets of some internet-related companies.

## PATENTING IN BIOLOGY

Many years ago when the patent system was evolved, it was the presumption that technology can be developed only using the tools of physics, chemistry and engineering. The possibility of using the tools of biology was not recognized. Further, all matters connected with life were presumed to be the products of nature. Human interventions for the development of inventions employing living matters were not given recognition or importance.

But during the years consequent on the development of technologies based on the tools of biological sciences such as micro-organisms to produce industrial products such as alcohol, enzymes, antibiotics, or ability to select and manipulate genetic materials resulted in the recognition of such tools and steadily patents covered the inventions in the areas of biotechnology also. Accordingly in many countries it is now possible to obtain legal protection for inventions using and/or involving biological materials.

Seven types of patents have emerged in biology with different countries taking different positions. Three of these patents that are universally agreeable are patenting of all micro-organisms and the substances produced by them, methods of agriculture and horticulture, micro-propagation, and genetically modified organisms. However, the other areas where patents have been given in different countries include protection for the plant varieties and in US even methods of treatment to human or animal body such as methods of surgery are also patentable.

**Problems**

For an invention to be patentable, the patent law requires the invention to be new, to have inventive step (non-obvious) and to be industrially applicable (utility). In addition the invention must be repeatable. In other words, the invention disclosed must enable others to repeat the technical solution described. As regards the conditions of novelty, an invention is not new if it has been disclosed to the public either in writing, orally, by use or otherwise, before the filing date or priority date of the patent. A question, therefore, arises as to whether the substances such as micro-organisms or other biological materials, which are present in nature, can be treated as new. As in the other technological fields the requirement of inventive step (non-obvious) also constitutes one of the most complex questions in the field of biotechnology. The consideration of industrial application is yet another obstacle for securing patents for the invention in the field of biotechnology.

Further, it is a mandatory requirement of the patent law to provide detailed information on the invention to be protected. This is commonly referred to as 'sufficiency of disclosure'. In the field of biotechnology, the condition of sufficiency of disclosure poses specific problems due to the fact that the inventions in this field involve living entities (biological materials). Such materials are difficult to describe in words. To satisfy the sufficiency of disclosure requirement condition of patent law in the field of biotechnology a practice has been developed now, *i.e.*, to deposit the sample of the living entity in the invention developed with an authorized depositary authority. Such an authority provides an accession number which when quoted in the patent document (specification) is considered as equivalent description of the invention satisfying the sufficient disclosure of the patent. It is also beneficial to provide in the written form also the information whenever possible in addition to above said deposition. For example, in the case of micro-organisms an international treaty was established in 1977, which is known as the Budapest Treaty on the International Recognition of the Deposit of Micro-organisms. Under the Treaty the deposition of microbial strains with a single internationally recognized depositary is to be internationally recognized.

### Provisions of TRIPS Agreement

The provisions of TRIPS excludes 'plants and animals' from patentability, but makes it obligatory to provide patent protection for micro-organisms and microbiological processes. The term 'micro-organisms' is not defined in the Agreement nor does the Agreement specify any parameters concerning the scope of protection to be provided. TRIPS provision has included a clause binding all members to provide for protection of plant varieties either by patent or by any effective *sui generis* system or any combination thereof.

## CURRENT AND EMERGING ISSUES

As business, trade and the impact of technology have become increasingly global, awareness of the value of intellectual assets has grown and the very high costs of obtaining and enforcing patents have continued to increase, a strong worldwide cost-effective patent system has become a very desirable objective. The cost of patenting is also perceived by business and industry as being too high and the speed of patent office proceedings too slow (*e.g.*, Japan and EU), especially for industries with increasingly short product life cycles.

The US and the rest of the world rely on fundamentally different criteria for deciding to which a patent should be granted. The US awards patents to the first person to invent while other countries work on the basis of who has first filed a patent application. To bring this aspect of the US patent system in conformity with the rest of the world, adoption of the first-to-file system has been proposed in the US in a patent reform bill. There is good support in the US for moving to the first-to-file system but also strong opposition.

Major differences between countries still exist with respect to the patentability of inventions in areas of innovation at the forefront of scientific endeavour (*e.g.*, life sciences) or where the pace of technological change is very fast (*e.g.*, information technologies). An example is the difference between the European and Japanese approaches and the broader US approach to the patentability of computer software. Wide variations occur in the patentability of biological materials: the US allowing organisms of all kinds (humans excepted) to be patented, Europe excluding patents on plant and animal varieties, and some developing countries rejecting all patents on biological materials. Significant differences also remain concerning the precise definition of what constitutes prior art, "technical contribution" and the scope of any grace period.

Andean community countries and some other countries, *e.g.*, Argentina, rely on a fundamentally different criterion for deciding whether patents can be granted with respect to second or further uses of known compounds, even if such use meets the standards of novelty, inventive level and industrial application. In such countries, once a compound is known, and regardless of whether it is patentable or not, only the original use can be protected, as new uses for known compounds are considered to be discoveries and not inventive matter. The Andean Court of Justice has interpreted Article 27 of TRIPS as requiring countries to grant protection for inventions that are related only to products, compounds or processes. It further established that uses are a new category of inventions—different from products, compounds, procedures or processes, and therefore not necessarily patentable under TRIPS. It also held that new uses are lacking in industrial applicability. Second uses of products can involve important and significant new applications of existing inventions. Most developed countries provide for second-use patents and a number of bilateral free trade agreements recently negotiated by the US expressly call for the patentability of all inventions.

The issue of language will have to be addressed in the context of any regional or world patent system. From a strictly economic perspective, the cost benefits of one language for obtaining and enforcing patents are self-evident. However, the choice of language has important implications for national identity, culture and sovereignty. Improvements in machine translation may gradually reduce the significance of this issue in the future.

The statutes of most countries provide for the authorities to work, or authorize third parties to work, a patented invention commercially without the patentee's permission. Such provisions include compulsory licensing and government use (*e.g.*, Crown use in the UK). Generally, the statutes clearly define the relatively limited circumstances under which such working is permitted and require the payment of reasonable compensation to the patentee. Articles 27 and 31 of the TRIPS Agreement lay down minimum standards for allowing such working under compulsory licence. In response to the problem raised in paragraph 6 of the 2001 Doha Declaration on TRIPS and Public Health, the WTO General Council agreed on August 30, 2003 on how countries with insufficient or no manufacturing capacities in the pharmaceutical sector could make use of compulsory licensing under the TRIPS Agreement. This was done through a waiver of the condition in TRIPS Article 31(f) (compulsory licensing only authorized predominantly for supply of the domestic market) thereby allowing compulsory licences to be granted solely for export of the patented product. This waiver was made permanent by a decision on December 6, 2005, by the WTO members to make a corresponding amendment in the TRIPS Agreement.

the recorded music and the artwork on the CD are protected by copyright. The written words inside books are protected by copyright, as is the artwork on the cover of and inside the book. The multi-billion dollar film, recording, publishing, and software industries, which bring pleasure to millions of people in all parts of the world, would not exist without copyright protection.

As consumers, we are exposed to culture in our day-to-day lives—so much so that we hardly think about where it comes from. We read our morning newspaper; we listen to music on the way to work. We learn with the help of books in school, we study scientific research published in journals as university students. We watch television at home, or go to the cinema or a concert in the evening; we may visit an art gallery on the weekend. We may have a pile of books on our bedroom table, or a stack of magazines in the living room. All of these products of creativity that surround us nourish us as human beings. We learn new things. We appreciate art, we learn about different cultures. This is why these works were created in the first place: for our education, our enjoyment, and our enrichment, for improving the quality of our lives.

## RIGHTS PROVIDED

The creators of works protected by copyright, and their heirs and successors (generally referred to as "rights holders"), have certain basic rights under copyright law. They hold the exclusive right to use or authorize others to use the work on agreed terms. The rights holder(s) of a work can prohibit or authorize: its reproduction in all forms, including printing and sound recording; its public performance and communication to the public; its broadcasting; its translation into other languages; and its adaptation, such as a novel into a screenplay for a film. Similar rights of, among others, fixation (recording) and reproduction are granted under related rights.

Many types of works, etc., protected under the laws of copyright and related rights require mass distribution, communication, and financial investment for their successful dissemination (for example, publications, sound recordings, and films); hence, creators often transfer the rights to their works to companies best able to develop and market the works, in return for compensation, in the form of payments and/or royalties (compensation based on a percentage of revenues generated by the work). In some countries, the author does not have the right to prevent certain uses of works but still has a right to be remunerated for its use. In every country, exceptions exist that allow the public to make certain uses of works without either remunerating or obtaining the authorization of the author. An example of this could be the use of limited quotations for illustration or teaching.

Copyright provides economic rights to creators, which allows them—their heirs—to benefit financially from their works. The economic rights of copyright have duration, as provided for in the relevant WIPO treaties, commencing upon the creation and fixation of the work, and lasting for not less than 50 years after the creator's death. National laws may establish longer terms of protection. This term of protection enables both creators and their heirs and successors to benefit financially for a reasonable period of time. Related rights enjoy shorter terms; normally 50 years after the performance, recording or broadcast took place. Once the copyright period ends, the work goes into the public domain and reproduction is free; however, credit for the work, or authorship, will forever belongs to the creator.

Copyright and the protection of performers also include moral rights, which are the right to claim authorship of a work, and the right to oppose changes to the work, which could harm the creator's reputation. Thus, in addition to granting economic rights, copyright also bestows "moral" rights, which allow the creator to claim authorship and prevent mutilation or deformation of his work that might harm his reputation.

Rights provided for under copyright and related rights laws can be enforced by rights holders through a variety of methods and fora, including by instituting civil actions, pursing administrative remedies, and through criminal prosecutions. Injunctions, orders requiring destruction of infringing items, inspection orders, etc., are used to enforce rights.

## RELATED RIGHTS

There exist rights related to, or "neighbouring on", copyright. These rights are generally referred to as "related rights" or "neighbouring rights", in an abbreviated expression. This closely associated field of rights related to copyright provides rights similar or identical to those of copyright, although sometimes more limited and of shorter duration.

It is generally understood that there are three kinds of related rights: the rights of performing artists in their performances, the rights of producers of phonograms in their phonograms, and the rights of broadcasting organizations in their radio and television programmes. Protection of those who assist intellectual creators to communicate their message and to disseminate their works to the public at large is attempted by means of related rights. The beneficiaries of related rights, therefore, are: performers (such as actors and musicians) in their performances; producers of sound recordings (for example, cassette recordings and compact discs) in their recordings; and broadcasting organizations in their radio and television programmes. In some countries performers, producers and broadcasters of copyrighted works are protected by copyright just like authors; in other countries, they are instead protected by neighbouring or related rights based on their role in bringing copyrighted works to the public as consumer products.

## BENEFITS OF COPYRIGHT PROTECTION

Copyright encourages human creativity. It exists to encourage the production of original artistic, literary and musical creations from books and paintings to movies, recordings and software. This provides not only recognition for their work but also incentive to create more. As they create, we all benefit, through a greater access to and wider variety of culture, knowledge and entertainment. In fact, copyright and related rights protection is an essential component in fostering human creativity and innovation. Giving authors, artists and creators incentives in the form of recognition and fair economic rewards increases their activities and output and often enhances the results. The copyright system rewards artistic expression by allowing the creator to benefit commercially from his work. Also, by insuring the existence and enforceability of rights, enterprises and companies can more easily invest in the creation, development, and global dissemination of works; this, in turn, helps increase access to, and enhances the enjoyment of, culture, knowledge, and entertainment all over the world, as well as stimulating economic and social development. Copyright and related rights are legal concepts and instruments, which, while respecting and protecting the rights of creators in their works, also contribute to the cultural and economic development of nations. Copyright law fulfills a decisive role in articulating the contributions and rights of the different stakeholders taking part in the cultural industries and the relation between them and the public.

Copyright is a basic right to receive credit as the author, and to receive remuneration for one's creative work. The protection of this basic right provides the essential basis for pursuing creative activity—recognition and fair reward. Copyright protects not only the fruits of creative work but also the investments made in bringing the resulting products and services to market. Copyright legislation also provides the basic mechanism to prevent unauthorized use of works protected by copyright, such as piracy.

## OWNER OF COPYRIGHT AND ITS ASSIGNMENT

Generally, the author of the work is the first owner of copyright. However, during the course of the author's employment in a newspaper or a magazine, the proprietor of the firm employing him becomes the author of the work in the absence of any agreement to the contrary. Similar is the case with the employment under the government or appointment under contract or apprenticeship. 'Author' means not merely the writer of a book. Author means the author of a literary or dramatic work, the composer of a musical work, the artist, the photographer and the producer of a cinematograph film. The author in relation to any literary, dramatic, musical or artistic work, which is computer-generated, is the person who causes the work to be created.

The author/owner of the work can assign the copyright wholly or partially in favour of any interested party. He/she can assign the work for the whole term of copyright or for a shorter period.

Work can be assigned generally or subject to certain limitations. While entering into an assignment, the assignor and assignee should keep in mind: (1) All the assignment should be in writing, signed by the assignor or his duly authorized agent. (2) The assignment should clearly identify the work. The rights assigned the territorial extent and duration of the assignment. (3) The assignment of copyright should, without fail, indicate the amount of royalty payable, if any, to the author or his legal heirs during the currency of the assignment. He should also provide for revision, extension or termination on terms mutually agreed upon by the parties. (4) If the assignee does not exercise the rights assigned to him within a period of one year from the date of assignment, the assignment shall be deemed to have lapsed after the expiry of one year.

## REGULATION

Copyright and related rights protection is obtained automatically without any need for registration or other formalities. However, many countries provide for a national system of optional registration and deposit of works; these systems facilitate, for example, questions involving disputes over ownership or creation, financing transactions, sales, assignments and transfers of rights. Many authors and performers do not have the ability or the means to pursue the legal and administrative enforcement of copyright and related rights, especially given the increasingly worldwide use of literary, musical and performance rights. In such situations, collective management organizations, or "societies", can provide for their members the benefits of the organization's administrative and legal expertise and efficiency in, for example, collecting, managing, and disbursing royalties gained from the national and international use of a member's work or performance. Certain rights of producers of sound recordings and broadcasting organizations are sometimes managed collectively as well.

### International Regulation

Harmonization of the national laws for protection of the rights of creative mind resulted in formulation of international norms for effective management and protection of copyright and neighbouring rights. Several international agreements on copyright protection and related rights exist. These include the Berne Convention for the Protection of Literary and Artistic Works (1886), the Rome Convention for the Protection of Performers, Producers of Phonograms, and Broadcasting Organizations (1961), the WIPO Copyright Treaty (WCT) (1996), and the WIPO Performances and Phonograms Treaty (WPPT) (1996). The World Trade Organization (WTO) Agreement on Trade-Related Aspects of Intellectual Property Rights (TRIPS) (1994) is the first multilateral trade-related intellectual property agreement. It covers most types of intellectual property and includes copyright and related rights. The Berne and Rome Conventions are milestones in the international efforts to come to terms with the dangers posed to the interest of authors and performers all over the world. The Universal Copyright Convention (UCC)(1952) was developed by UNESCO as an alternative to the Berne Convention for those states which disagreed with aspects of the Berne Convention, but still wished to participate in some form of multilateral copyright protection. These states included developing countries and the Soviet Union. The Berne Convention states also became party to the UCC, so that their copyrights would exist in non-Berne convention states.

WIPO, through its Copyright and Related Rights Sector, is committed to that crucial role. The Sector works currently on the development of international norms and standards in the area of copyright. It works closely with the Standing Committee on Copyright and Related Rights, which is presently discussing the updating of the international protection of broadcasting organizations, as well as the possible introduction of international protection of non-original databases, which presently do not qualify for protection under copyright law.

In addition, the Copyright and Related Rights Sector actively promotes the WCT and the WPPT, known together as the "WIPO Internet Treaties", by arranging meetings and seminars and providing speakers for other meetings arranged by WIPO.

Obtaining and enforcing copyrights in foreign countries requires compliance with the laws and treaties of each individual country.

## MANAGING COPYRIGHT

In principle, copyright owners can decide how and by whom their works are used. It is in their interest that their works are enjoyed by the widest audience, provided that they are rewarded for their work. This requires efficient mechanisms to manage creators' rights so that they can concentrate on their creative activity. There is no way each user could remunerate each individual creator or rights holder every time a work is accessed or enjoyed. Many owners of creative works do not have the means to pursue the legal and administrative enforcement of copyright, especially given the increasingly worldwide use of literary, musical and performance rights. As a result, the establishment of collective management organizations or societies is a growing trend in many countries. These societies can provide members the benefits of the organization's administrative and legal expertise in collecting, managing, and disbursing royalties gained from international use of a member's work.

It is a system that is in place in many countries around the world, and one that is growing in many more countries. It plays an important role in cultural development and dissemination of culture, by making the works of artists, authors, and other creators available to the general public on a large scale. Its role in economic development is also important: the collective management system not only helps individuals make a living from their work, it builds upon and strengthens cultural industries as well. Authors and artists in many fields have established professional organizations—generally called collective management organizations—to manage their copyrights, to facilitate clearance of those rights, and to ensure that they obtain economic reward for their creative output.

In some sectors, copyright can be managed through individual contracts between the authors and users. However, in many cases it is impossible to negotiate individual licences or permissions for dissemination of works. Think of playing songs on a radio station, showing a movie on a cable network, or performing a play in theaters around the world: there is no way each user could remunerate each individual creator or rights holder every time a work is accessed or enjoyed. In many of these cases rights are managed through the system of collective management.

The system of copyright and related rights and collective management of these rights provides a real service to creators and consumers alike. The system not only helps composers, artists, authors and other rights holders make a living from their work, it enables all of us as consumers to gain access to an incredible range of art, knowledge, and culture.

### Collective Management of Musical Works

Taking into account the innumerable places where music can be played, both nationally and internationally, it is in the most cases impossible to license the use of musical works individually. This is why music creators and publishers have established collective management organizations in more than 100 countries, in all regions. These organizations license the public performance and broadcasting of musical compositions, thus they are also called performing rights societies. Music is performed in radio and television studios, concert halls, restaurants, discotheques, cinemas and many other places. Music also plays an important role in the new digital delivery channels such as the Internet. On radio, music accounts for more than 70 per cent of airtime. It would be close to impossible for individual broadcasters to clear the rights with each and every copyright owner. Collective management organizations act as intermediaries between copyright holders and users. They manage the licensing of works to users, collect the payments, and pass them on to the copyright holders. This makes it easy for users to get permission to perform music in many different places. By establishing a network of representation agreements with similar organizations in foreign countries, collective management organizations can offer an international music repertory for licensing in their country, representing more than 1.4 million composers, song writers, music arrangers and publishers worldwide.

### Collective Management of Performances and Phonograms

When recorded music is played publicly on radio and television, performers and producers of sound recordings are entitled to receive remuneration. In many countries, the same rights apply to the playing of phonograms in discotheques and other public places. Often, performers and phonogram producers establish joint management organizations to manage these rights; sometimes they are handled by separate organizations. These organizations work closely together to make it easy for users to pay the necessary fees.

Because of the large number of participants in these productions, as well as the heavy investments involved in film-making and distribution, legislation in many countries contains specific rules concerning the ownership of copyright in audio-visual works. Audio-visual authors have also established their own collective management organizations in many countries to manage their interests in areas such as the rental of videotapes and DVDs, the private copying of audio-visual works, and the distribution of television channels over cable.

Collective management organizations facilitate the clearing of multiple copyright licences of thousands of individual programmes transmitted via satellite and cable. The rights cover those of original creators, performers, film producers and broadcasters—all of whom benefit from cable revenues.

## TECHNOLOGICAL ADVANCES AND COPYRIGHT

The field of copyright and related rights has expanded enormously during the last several decades with the spectacular progress of technological developments, which have in turn brought new ways of disseminating creations by such forms of worldwide communication as satellite broadcasting, compact discs and DVDs. Copyright has become increasingly important with the development of digital technology and the Internet, where it is a major form of intellectual property protection for content distributed online—and where it faces difficult enforcement issues. Dissemination of works via the Internet is but the latest development, which raises new questions concerning copyright and related rights in this global medium. WIPO is deeply involved in the on-going international debate to shape new standards for copyright protection in cyberspace. In this regard, the Organization administers the WIPO Copyright Treaty (entry into force on March 6, 2002) and the WIPO Performance and Phonogram Treaty (entry into force on May 20, 2002). These Internet Treaties have clarified international norms aimed at preventing unauthorized access to and use of creative works on the Internet.

## SOFTWARE PATENTS *VS* COPYRIGHT

In the 1970s and 1980s, there were extensive discussions on whether the patent system, the copyright system, or a *sui generis* system, should provide protection for computer software. These discussions resulted in the generally accepted principle that computer programs should be protected by copyright, whereas apparatus using computer software or software-related inventions should be protected by patent.

Copyright law and patent law provide different types of protection. Copyright protection extends only to expressions, and not to ideas, procedures, methods of operation or mathematical concepts as such, whereas a patent is an exclusive right granted for an invention, which is a product or a process that provides a new way of doing something, or offers a new technical solution to a problem. Copyright protection is formality-free in countries party to the Berne Convention for the Protection of Literary and Artistic Works (the Berne Convention), which means that protection does not depend on compliance with any formalities such as registration or deposit of copies. A patent is generally granted after completing an examination procedure by a government agency. Copyright protection of computer software is established in most countries and harmonized by international treaties to that effect. The law relating to the patentability of software is still not harmonized internationally, but some countries have embraced the patentability of computer software and others have adopted approaches that recognize inventions assisted by computer software. In view of the complexity of these matters, it is recommended to contact a practising lawyer, who is

industries expanded in the 1970s, so did the interest in determining how copyright's contribution to development could be described in economic terms.

The contribution of the copyright-based industries was shown to be considerable, and indeed higher than suggested by previous research in those countries. This reflects the development of the copyright industries, but also the more detailed scope of the surveys. (1) These industries showed a higher overall growth rate than the rest of the economy. By the same token, compared to traditional sectors of the economy, they both contract and expand more rapidly in response to fluctuations in the economy. (2) Unsurprisingly, those copyright industries linked to the digital revolution grew faster than in previous periods.

Overall, the economic contribution of cultural industries to a nation's economic wealth is considerable. Surveys conducted in numerous countries indicate that the value added by cultural industries ranges between three and six per cent of gross domestic product (GDP). These industries often grow at a faster rate than the economy in general, and employ an increasing number of people. In fact, the economic value of copyright protection is quite considerable in an economic age as it covers mass media communication including virtually all forms and methods of public communication, not only printed publications but also sound and television broadcasting, films and, in a number of countries, extends to the protection of computer programs and to computer systems for storage of information. Copyright industries can be divided into the following three categories:

### Core Copyright Industries

Core copyright industries, defined as wholly engaged in the creation, production, performance, exhibition, communication or distribution and sales of copyright protected subject matter. These include literature, music, theatre, film, the media, photography, software, visual arts, advertising services and collective management societies. These are industries that create copyright materials as their main product. They include book publishers and related industries, the music publishing industry, theater, film and television production companies, the visual arts industry, and computer software, etc.

## Print and Publishing

Prior to the invention of the printing press in the 15th century, there was no mass market for publications, as books were copied by hand. The introduction of this new technology led to the rise of mass publishing, which brought about the introduction of the first copyright law, the Statute of Anne in 1710 in England. Today, print and publishing is the biggest single cultural industry in many countries, covering books, newspapers, magazines, periodicals and scientific journals. Consider just a few statistics: Some one million book titles are published yearly. Some 6,600 newspapers are circulated everyday. More than 1,10,000 magazine titles are on offer to both the consumer and business markets. Thousands of scientific articles are published monthly in journals, in books, and on-line. The content of these publications is created by writers of fiction and non-fiction, translators, journalists, scientists and other professional writers. Their works are brought to the market by publishers: book, newspaper, magazine, periodical and journal publishers in many different formats, including on-line. Generally, a writer enters into a publishing contract with a publisher and gives the company a right to bring the work to the market. In return, the writer gets a share of the sales price as a royalty and thus benefits from the economic success of the work. Journalists are often employed by newspaper companies and their copyrights are dealt with in an employment contract. A scientist may entrust a scientific journal to publish his work and profits.

## Music and Sound Recordings

Rhythm comes naturally to man. Music is his oldest impulse. From time immemorial, music has served as an outlet for his every emotion and has been part of every occasion. To appease the God he feared, to invoke the blessings of natural elements, to sooth, calm or excite his senses, music provided the completeness to the life he led. Music is perhaps the most universal, accessible and widespread of all copyright-based creative expressions. It is used in many different media, such as films, videos, and theaters, and is performed on radio and television. Digital recordings are delivered via the Internet. Music is played everywhere—in restaurants, nightclubs, and shopping malls. Every country has some form of local music. The music itself is created by composers and the words of a song are created by lyricists. Music publishers bring their compositions to the market, as sheet music for example. They are all owners of copyright in musical works. Singers and musicians, as performers, have rights based on copyright and related rights legislation as well. Phonogram producers invest in making music available through recordings and online delivery.

### Film and Television

The industry today—known variously as the film, movie or audio-visual industry—has changed dramatically. Creators and performers are drawn from a large number of professions, including script writers, directors, and directors of photography, narrators and actors. Their work is enjoyed in cinemas and on television, via satellite and cable, as home video or DVD rentals, and now even through delivery of files over the Internet. Because of the large number of participants in these productions, as well as the heavy investments involved in film-making and distribution, legislation in many countries contains specific rules concerning the ownership of copyright in audio-visual works. Television plays a major role in disseminating audio-visual works to a large audience. Broadcasters produce a great number of television programmes themselves; they also acquire rights for showing films and other independent productions on their channels. This involves an enormous amount of individual rights. A single television channel may broadcast more than 10,000 programmes a year, including films, documentaries and animated cartoons produced both in-house and independently.

### Visual Art and Photography

A wide variety of creators work in the field of visual arts including painters, sculptors, graphic artists, illustrators, and photographers. They all have copyrights in their works. Artists and photographers usually sell their works through individual contracts. A painter, for example, sells his painting to an art collector, and a photographer gives a right to publish its photograph in a book through a licensing contract.

### Dramatic Works and Theatre

In the field of dramatic works—such as plays, musicals, ballets and operas—a large number of artists usually collaborate: dramatists and script writers, directors and choreographers, scene designers, actors and singers. All of them are entitled to some form of remuneration based on copyright.

### Partially Copyright-based Industries

These are industries in which part of their product is directly related to the creation or exploitation of copyrighted works. Such industries include advertising agencies, computer consultants, architectural services, stationary manufacturing, commercial or job printing services, web page design services, etc. In this only part of the production is linked to copyright protected material, such as design, architecture, jewelry, furniture and other crafts.

### Copyright-based Distribution Industries

This category includes businesses involved in paper product wholesaling, computer and software retailing, film and video distribution, and motion picture projection as well as libraries, museums, performing arts' venues, video hire outlets, photographic film processing, etc.

Besides, there are inter-dependent copyright industries, which deal with products jointly consumed with the core industries, or with facilitation equipment. They include the manufacture and sale of equipment such as television sets, CD recorders and computers; of musical and photographic instruments; of photocopying and recording material, etc. They provide the means for the production, dissemination and consumption of copyright goods and services.

## COPYRIGHT AND BUSINESSES

All businesses own or use copyrighted material. Protecting such materials from abuse, misuse and/or piracy may be critical to prevent erosion of a competitive advantage. Yet many companies do not focus on management of copyright assets while planning their competitive strategies. Active management of copyright, along with other intellectual property rights, is essential for all businesses, big or small, as it impacts directly or indirectly on their performance, profitability and competitiveness. In order to sustain their competitiveness and success in business, copyright industries need to safeguard the fruits of their creativity and innovations from free-riders, imitators, and copiers. In fact, the viability of these industries rests on the existence and proper functioning of the copyright system in domestic and international markets. Most businesses, although not directly involved in the copyright area, print brochures or publish advertisements that create and/or use copyright-protected materials. Even shopping malls, bars, nightclubs, hotels, airlines, restaurants and other retail outlets play music—protected by copyright—to attract customers and influence their behaviour, entertain employees, and increase turnover and profits. Thus, proprietors of these businesses must understand the basics of copyright law as safeguarding copyright and securing the permission of others before using copyrighted material is not only a legal necessity but also good business sense. Many businesses, especially small ones, do not have a sufficient understanding of the importance and relevance of copyright to their business success or bottom-line.

## COPYRIGHT INFRINGEMENT AND PIRACY

One of the greatest fears among copyright holders is infringement of their rights in the form of piracy and plagiarism. The recent controversy over peer-to-peer networks and file sharing, for example, deals with issues of copyright infringement and piracy, since in many cases copyright owners are not being compensated for the reproduction of their works. Copyright infringement is the unauthorized use of copyrighted material in a manner that violates one of the copyright owner's exclusive rights, such as the right to reproduce or perform the copyrighted work, or to make derivative works that build upon it. In many jurisdictions copyright infringement is a strict liability tort or crime. This means that the plaintiff or prosecutor must only prove that the act of copying was committed by the defendant, and need not prove *mens rea*. Good faith, standing alone, is no defense. For electronic and audio-visual media, unauthorized reproduction and distribution is often referred to as piracy or theft.

Infringement of copyright can happen when works—such as paintings, books, computer software, films and music—are reproduced or communicated (including communication over the Internet) without permission from the copyright owners. Infringement can also occur when works such as plays and films are performed or screened without permission from the copyright owner. A person, who sells infringing versions of a work, even if somebody else made them, is also in breach of copyright, as is a person who authorizes someone else to make an infringement. If a work is very distinctive and original, reproducing part of it may be a breach of copyright.

Some examples of activities that involve copyright infringement (where the material is in copyright term) are where: (1) A company buys 100 licences from a computer software developer and then issues 200 copies of the software to its employees without permission from the developer; (2) Photographs or computer images of an artwork are reproduced and distributed, in hard copy or over the Internet, without permission from the copyright owner; (3) Music or computer software CDs are 'burnt' without permission and then given away or sold; or (4) A script for a play is interpreted and performed without permission from the copyright owner.

There are many different ways copyright owners may find their copyright has been infringed. For example, in the music industry, infringing activities include: (1) Bootlegging—where recordings are made of live performances without the performers' consent; (2) Piracy—the illegal copying of music products that have been released without permission from the copyright owner. Common ways this is done are by copying music onto or from a cassette, CD, a hard drive or the Internet. Pirate products are not necessarily packaged in the same way as the original, as opposed to counterfeit products. (3) Counterfeiting—involves duplication of both the music product and of its packaging. For this reason unwitting buyers are less able to recognize counterfeit copies than is the case with some pirate copies.

Rights provided for under copyright and rights holders through a variety of methods and fora, including by instituting civil actions, pursing administrative remedies, and through criminal prosecutions, can enforce related rights laws. Injunctions, orders requiring destruction of infringing items, inspection orders, etc., are used to enforce rights.

## COPYRIGHT NOTICES

In some jurisdictions, in order to obtain a copyright when a work such as a book or movie is created the work generally should contain a copyright notice. This notice is comprized by a letter C inside a circle (*i.e.*, ©), or the word "copyright", followed by the year(s) of the copyright and the name of the copyright holder. (*e.g.*, © 2005 Knobbe Martens Olson & Bear LLP). If a sound recording is copyrighted, use P with the first publication date and owner. If the copyrighted material is revised, add the year of the revision to the copyright notice. It is also advisable to add "All Rights Reserved."

If the work has been modified (*i.e.*, a new edition) and recopy righted, there will be more than one year listed. A copyright notice serves to inform any potential users that the work is copyrighted. With the exception of a small number of countries which still require notices to be on works, this requirement is generally optional except for works which were originally created before the particular country became a member of the Berne Convention. A copyright notice is no longer required for a work to be covered by copyright in jurisdictions which have acceded to the Berne Convention. In most jurisdictions a work may be copyrighted from the moment of its creation regardless of whether or not it bears a copyright notice. However, the existence of a copyright notice may make it easier to claim certain damages for infringement in legal proceedings, as a defendant may be presumed to have ignored the notice and intentionally infringed copyright.

The phrase, 'all rights reserved', was a formal notice that all rights granted under existing copyright law are retained by the copyright holder and that legal action may be taken against copyright infringement. It was provided as a result of the Buenos Aires Convention of 1910, which required some statement of reservation of rights to grant international coverage in all the countries that were signatory to that convention. While it is commonplace to see it, this notice is now superfluous, as every country that is a member of the Buenos Aires Convention is also a member of the Berne Convention, which requires copyright to be valid without any formality of notice. This phrase is sometimes still used even on some documents to which the original author does not retain all rights granted by copyright law. This is a habitual formality and is unlikely to have legal consequences.

## CURRENT AND EMERGING ISSUES

The protection of copyright and related rights, within the ever-changing digital infrastructure and applications, is taking place within a framework of complex legal, economic and social issues. New ways of perfecting inexpensive and virtually instantaneous reproduction, distribution and display of works and other subject matter have created great opportunities and challenges for right holders. At the same time, the new technology is seen as providing opportunities for an increasing number of new players, ranging from new commercial content providers/publishers of copyrighted material and the IT, telecom and consumer electronic industries, to private persons making copyrighted material they created themselves available on the Internet.

Important contributions to the new framework are the 1996 WIPO Treaties on Copyright (WCT) and on Performances and Phonograms (WPPT) (collectively the "WIPO Internet Treaties"), which both entered into force in 2002. In addition to the WIPO Internet Treaties, discussions on the protection of broadcasters and audio-visual performers are in progress within WIPO.

The contribution of copyright-based activities to the national economies is growing. Yet, the copyright-dependent nature of different commercial activities is often not generally acknowledged as such, nor is the contribution of copyright-dependent industries to the national economy understood or fully credited. Consequently, there may be a lack of awareness among national decision-makers and opinion leaders about the economic importance of copyright. Consequently, WIPO is working with a group of national governments from each region of the world to analyse the impact of copyright-dependent industry on the respective national economies.

New media and technology create new ways for right holders to distribute and exploit their works, including on-line, thus potentially creating additional opportunities for direct licensing. Digital rights management systems are being designed to better distribute and protect the right holder's investment while allowing an increased variety of terms and conditions for use of those works. It is expected that increased market implementation of such systems will increase consumer choice and availability of copyright works such as software and entertainment products in digital format and permit price points that reflect the consumer's actual use rather than an assumption that the consumer will use the product in a variety of formats.

The WIPO Internet Treaties require signatories to provide adequate legal protection for technological measures and effective legal remedies when they are circumvented which rights holders may employ in connection with the exercise of their rights.

There is a need for multi-faceted means to commercialize and distribute copyrighted works. Existing systems should not be allowed to be taken over by illegal activities. Effective and balanced actions are necessary to stop international illegal exploitation of copyrighted works.

Creators and performing artists are seeking reassurances that their moral rights are respected, especially by third parties, and that their works and performances are not unduly manipulated in the digital-networked environment.

Audio-visual performers have been seeking an update of their rights at international level since negotiations began for the WIPO Internet Treaties. Broadcasters have been seeking an update of their rights in response to market changes and technological developments, currently embodied at an international level in the Rome Convention.

6

# TRADEMARKS: NAMING THE INVENTIONS

A trademark is a sign capable of distinguishing the goods or services produced or provided by one enterprise from those of other enterprises. In other words, trademarks allow consumers to differentiate between goods and services from different producers, and to select products by manufacturers whose reputation they trust. A trademark serves a guarantee of quality for consumers. The enhanced circulation of goods and services has made it necessary to use a distinctive mark or name to identify a product, service or enterprise. Any distinctive words, letters, numerals, drawings, pictures, shapes, colours, logotypes, labels or combinations used to distinguish goods or services may be considered a trademark. That is, any sign which is capable of performing the essential trademark function may qualify as a trademark. Throughout history, makers of goods have put their names or other marks on things they produce.

Trademark is an important tool in commerce. It is a central element in the marketing and branding strategy of any company. The exclusive right to the use of the mark, which may be of indefinite duration, enables the owner to build goodwill and reputation in its enterprise and to prevent others from misleading consumers by false association with an enterprise with which they are not connected. Almost all businesses, large and small, rely on trademarks. Most of the countries of the world legally protect trademarks. Trademark law is one branch of the larger legal field known as intellectual property. Because consumers often continue to buy products they trust, well-known trademarks can be extremely valuable.

The trademark concept extends to include a range of non-conventional signs such as shapes (*i.e.*, three-dimensional registration is not available globally, international branding for companies such as Deutsch Telekom, Nokia, Yahoo and Intel include registration of sound marks in multiple jurisdictions. Perhaps the expanded use of unconventional sound marks in wireless technology and the Internet will increase the demand for global registration of sound marks as intellectual property. Several jurisdictions have recognized the registrability of sound marks. Despite the recognition which must be accorded to sound trademarks in most countries, the graphical representation of such marks sometimes constitutes a problem for trademark owners seeking to protect their marks, and different countries have different methods for dealing with this issue.

## Scent Marks

A scent mark (also known as smell trademark) was first recognized in 1990 in the United States, where a scent, described as a high impact, fresh, floral fragrance reminiscent of plumeria blossoms, applied to sewing thread, was deemed a registrable trademark. There are a few registrations of scents as trademarks currently in force, including "a scent mark is having the scent of bubble gum" for use with oil-based metal cutting fluid and oil-based metal removing fluid for industrial metal working. In 2001, a "cherry scent" was registered for synthetic lubricants for vehicles. However, scent marks are still not common. Although scent trademarks are sometimes specifically mentioned in legislative definitions of "trademark", it is often difficult to register such marks if consistent, non-arbitrary and meaningful graphic representations of the marks cannot be produced.

## Shape Marks

The possibility of registering product shapes as trademarks became a reality in the UK with the implementation of the Trade Marks Act 1994 ("TMA") when such shapes were specifically included within the definition of trademarks. Since the definition of trademarks was broadened in this way, there has been much debate over the issue of what exactly may be registered. However, in the past few years both the Office for the Harmonization of the Internal Market (OHIM) and the European Court of Justice

(ECJ) have offered valuable guidance on how to assess inherent distinctiveness of three-dimensional trademarks including shapes of products. As a result, it is clear that inherent distinctiveness of product shapes will be difficult to prove. It is noteworthy that most of the decisions in respect of product shape trademark applications have involved rejections of shapes where the owners have not filed evidence of use to support a claim to distinctiveness. Solid evidence of distinctiveness can make all the difference. Shape trademarks are also known as three dimensional trademarks or 3D trademarks.

### Slogans

Advertisers have recognized the power of advertising slogans for decades. Modern advertising campaigns are often defined by a catchy slogan. If a company can successfully implant a slogan in the public's mind, it can trade on that goodwill for years to come. In the United Kingdom, many purchasers of Audi-branded cars may not even know what the advertising slogan "Vorspung durch Technik" means in English, but the slogan has become iconic and recognized throughout the country. Although the laws of copyright can often protect slogans, the registration of a slogan as a trademark affords them a broader scope of protection. Nevertheless, the path to the registration of a slogan is far from straightforward.

### Trade Dress

Trade dress refers to characteristics of the visual appearance of a product or its packaging (or even the facade of a building such as a restaurant) that may be registered and protected from being used by competitors in the manner of a trademark. These characteristics can include the three-dimensional shape, graphic design of the product and its packaging. It is one type of trademark. Under trademark law, the total commercial image of a product is known by the term trade dress. It refers to the manner in which a product—or place of business—is "dressed up" to go to market. Trade dress is a form of commercial shorthand that provides a "source-associating cue" for the unthinking purchaser. Trade dress law may protect the total packaging and design of a product. There are two basic requirements that must be met for trade dress protection. The first is that those features must be capable of functioning as a source indicator—identifying a particular product and its maker to consumers. While trade dress originally referred exclusively to a products packaging, the concept has grown to include product designs for everything from bedroom furniture to sweaters.

A use of a few new types of marks is growing commercial adoption in the marketplace. Such marks are motion trademarks (also known as animated marks, moving marks, moving image marks or movement marks) and a hologram trademark, where a picture sequence is used to perform the trademark function of uniquely identifying the commercial origin of products or services.

## BRAND

Although the term "brand" is sometimes used as a synonym for a "trademark", in commercial circles the term "brand" is frequently used in a much wider sense to refer to a combination of tangible and intangible elements, such as a trademark, design, logo and trade dress, and the concept, image and reputation which those elements transmit with respect to specified products and/or services. Some experts consider the goods or services themselves as a component of the brand. Although, strictly speaking, a brand is composed of the sum of its individual parts, the brand ultimately exists independently of and its value is greater than the mere sum of those parts. In fact, the value-added of a brand is precisely the concrete and direct result of the synergy that is created among its component parts. The brand thus takes up a life of its own and leads us beyond the limited functions of such objects of intellectual property protection as a trademark or a design and the generic product or service differentiated and rendered more appealing by those objects of protection. The concept of a brand reminds us that creating and protecting a trademark or design is not an end in itself. These are only tools (albeit important ones) in the process of developing an effective brand image for one's goods or services. It is the brand image as a whole, and not merely a trademark or design as a stand-alone element, that differentiates one's goods and/or services from those of competitors, denotes a certain quality, and over the long-term attracts and nourishes consumer loyalty.

A brand is a collection of images and ideas representing an economic producer; more specifically, it refers to the concrete symbols such as a name, logo, slogan, and design scheme. Brand recognition and other reactions are created by the accumulation of experiences with the specific product or service, both directly relating to its use, and through the influence of advertising, design, and media commentary. A brand is a symbolic embodiment of all the information connected to a company, product or service. A brand serves to create associations and expectations among products made by a producer. A brand often includes an explicit logo, fonts, colour schemes, symbols, which may be developed to represent implicit values, ideas, and even personality.

The brand can be in one of the following forms: (*i*) Brands, which are associated with the product and have no association with the manufacturers' name; (*ii*) Brands where the manufacturers' name is attributed to a product; (*iii*) Brands where the company and product name is blended; and (*iv*) Brands that are personalized.

The brand, and branding and brand equity have become increasingly important components of culture and the economy, now being described as cultural accessories and personal philosophies.

Brand, in the literary sense, is small word but the meaning and the power that it conveys is significant. A brand sells itself. The American Marketing Association defines a brand as a name, term, sign, symbol or design, or a combination of these intended to identify the goods and services of one seller or group of sellers and to differentiate them from those of the competitors. Therefore, brands are denoted not only by things, but also by replicas of people or even actual people. For instance, some of the popular brands today are: Coke, Pepsi, McDonalds, Cadburys, Microsoft, Dell, etc.

Consumers perceive branded products as higher quality and reliability, and better value than non-branded products. Generally speaking, the number one brand in a category can features embodied in the products bearing such trademarks. Therefore, the very ownership of a trademark with a good image and reputation provides a company with a competitive edge. The development of international trade has led to greater use of trademarks in all countries and in different fields of activity. Trademarks have an increasingly important role in a country's commerce and trade. Once a trademark has acquired a reputation, it makes it easier to get into new markets, which could stimulate exports. Industrial and business enterprises use trademarks for diversifying their market strategies in their own as well as in other countries. Trademark protection also hinders the efforts of unfair competitors, such as counterfeiters, to use similar distinctive signs to market inferior or different products or services. This ensures fair competition between competitors in the marketplace and encourages producers to invest in the quality and reputation of their products or services. A trademark is a useful tool in launching new product segments or entirely new products through brand extension. In addition, trademarks can be very effective in penetrating new markets. Use of trademarks for ensuring efficient marketing of products, however, requires indepth knowledge of trademark law and practice at the national and international levels.

## TRADEMARK PROTECTION

Trademark protection can be obtained through registration or, in some countries, also through use. Even where trademarks can be protected through use, one is well-advised to register the trademark by filing the appropriate application form at the national trademark office. While it is not compulsory, it is highly advisable to register a trademark, as registration provides exclusive rights to prevent unauthorized use of the trademark. Some trademark offices have facilities for applying for registration on-line. Registering a trademark will provide stronger protection, particularly in case of conflict with an identical or confusingly similar trademark. For the registration of a trademark, the services of a trademark agent in some countries are compulsory. In general, any person who intends to use a trademark or to have it used by third parties can apply for registration. It can be either an individual or a legal entity. For registration of trademark, first, an application for its registration must be filed with the appropriate national or regional trademark office. The application must contain a clear reproduction of the sign filed for registration, including any colours, forms, or three-dimensional features. The application must also contain a list of goods or services to which the sign would apply.

## Regulation

Almost all countries in the world register and protect trademarks. Each national or regional office maintains a Register of Trademarks, which contains full application information on all registrations and renewals, facilitating examination, search, and potential opposition by third parties. The effects of such a registration are, however, limited to the country (or, in the case of a regional registration, countries) concerned.

While the term of protection may vary, in a large number of countries, registered trademarks are protected for 10 years. Registration may be renewed indefinitely (usually, for consecutive periods of 10 years) provided renewal fees are paid in time. The legal rights arising out of a trademark registration are normally limited to the territory to which they pertain; so, ordinarily, valid registration of a trademark in one's home country gives him rights only in his own country unless his mark is considered to be a well-known mark.

All the main reasons for registering one's trademark in his home country also apply to the commercialization of his products in foreign markets. It is, therefore, highly advisable to register trademark abroad if one is currently engaged in export operations or intend to do so in the near future. Exporting goods bearing a distinctive trademark will enable export products to be recognized in foreign markets, allowing the concerned company to build a reputation and image among foreign consumers that may result in higher profits for the company. If one has registered the trademark of his company in the country where it is located (home country) but now wishes to export or grant a licence to use the trademark in other countries, then it is advisable to register the trademark abroad.

In order to avoid the need to register separately with each national or regional office, WIPO administers a system of international registration of marks. Two treaties, the Madrid Agreement Concerning the International Registration of Marks and the Madrid Protocol, govern this system. A person who has a link (through nationality, domicile or establishment) with a country party to one or both of these treaties may, on the basis of a registration or application with the trademark office of that country, obtain an international registration having effect in some or all of the other countries of the Madrid Union. At present, more than 60 countries are party to one or both of the agreements.

The first international agreement dealing with trademark law was a treaty known as the Paris Convention. Adopted in 1883, it required members to recognize the trademark rights of foreign producers. Most of the nations of the world are members of the Paris Convention. In 1994 most countries signed another significant treaty dealing with international trademark law. This agreement, called the Agreement on Trade-related Aspects of Intellectual Property Rights (TRIPS), strengthened legal protections for trademarks around the world.

## Importance of Protecting Trademarks

Without trademark registration, one's investments in marketing a product may become wasteful as rival companies may use the same or a confusingly similar trademark for identical or similar products. If a competitor adopts a similar or identical trademark, customers could be misled into buying the competitor's product thinking it is particular company's product. This could not only decrease the company's profits and confuse its customers, but may also damage the reputation and image of the company, particularly if the rival product is of inferior quality. Given the value of trademarks and the importance that a trademark may have in determining the success of a product in the marketplace, it is critical to make sure that it is registered in the relevant market(s). In addition, a registered trademark may be licensed to other companies, thus providing an additional source of revenue for the company, or may be the basis for a franchising agreement. On occasion, a registered trademark with a good reputation among consumers may also be used to obtain funding from financing institutions that are increasingly aware of the importance of brands for business success.

## SELECTING OR CREATING A TRADEMARK

A carefully selected and nurtured trademark is a valuable business asset for most companies. Selecting or creating an appropriate trademark is a critical step, as it is an important element of the marketing strategy of a business. However, there are no hard and fast rules for selecting an appropriate trademark for any product(s). But the following five-point checklist may be useful. The trademark of choice should meet all the legal requirements for registration.

A trademark search is advised to make sure that it is not identical or confusingly similar to existing trademarks. The trademark should be easy to read, write, spell and remember and is suitable to all types of advertising media. One should be sure the mark does not have any undesired connotations in his own language or in any of the languages of potential export markets.

While selecting one or more words as trademark one should also take into consideration the implications of selecting certain types of words: (1) Coined or "fanciful" words. These are invented words without any intrinsic or real meaning. Coined words have the advantage of being easy to protect, as they are more likely to be considered inherently distinctive. On the negative side, however, they may be more difficult to remember or consumers requiring greater effort to advertise the products. (2) Suggestive marks. These are marks that hint at one or some of the attributes of the product. The appeal of suggestive marks is that they act as a form of advertising. A slight risk, however, is that some countries may consider a suggestive mark to be too descriptive of the product. (3) Arbitrary marks. These are words that have a meaning that has no relation to the product they advertise. While these types of marks will also be easy to protect, they may also require heavy advertising to create the association between the mark and the product in the minds of consumers.

## USING TRADEMARKS

One may apply for registration before he has used the trademark but some countries will not officially register it until the party has shown proof of use. Also, in most of the cases, a trademark that has not been used for a given period of time following registration may be taken off the trademark register.

If a mark is registered with a specific design or font, care should be taken that the trademark is used exactly as it is registered. Its use should be monitored closely as it is crucial for the image of the company's products. It is also important to avoid using the trademark as a verb or noun so that it does not come to be perceived by consumers as a generic term.

Different trademarks may be used for the different products lines of a company. Depending on its branding strategy, each company will decide whether to use the same trademark for its products, extending the brand every time a new product is released, or to use a different mark for each product line. Extending an existing brand to new products enables the new product to benefit from the image and reputation of the mark. However, the use of a new mark, more specific and relevant to the new product, may also prove advantageous and enable the company to target the new product to a specific customer group or to create a specific image for the new product line. Many companies also choose to use a new brand in conjunction with an existing brand. Different companies adopt different strategies. Whatever be the choice, it should be made sure that the trademark is registered for all categories of goods and/or services for which it is, or will be, used. The conflict between trademarks and domain names sometime takes place while using the trademark on the Internet.

## LICENSING

Trademarks can be licensed to other companies. In such cases, the trademark owner retains ownership and merely agrees to the use of the trademark by one or more other companies. This is usually done on payment of royalties and involves the consent of the trademark owner, which is usually specified in a formal licensing agreement. Depending on the nature of the agreement, the licensor often retains some degree of control over the licensee to guarantee that a certain quality is maintained. In practice, trademark licences are frequently granted within broader licensing agreements, for example, franchising agreements or agreements including the licensing of other intellectual property rights such as patents, know-how and some degree of technical assistance for the production of a given product.

The licensing of a trademark is central to a franchising agreement. In franchising agreements the degree of control of the trademark owner over the franchisee is generally greater than is the case for standard trademark licensing agreements. In the case of franchising, the franchiser allows another person (the franchisee) to use his way of doing business (including trademarks, know-how, customer service, software, shop decoration, etc.) in accordance with a set of prescriptions and in exchange for compensation or royalty. It is increasingly possible to sell or assign a trademark independently from the business that currently owns it. In the case of sale or assignment of a trademark, it may be required to deposit a copy of the agreement, or parts of it, at the trademark office.

## ENFORCING

The burden of enforcing a trademark is mainly on the trademark owner. It is up to the company, as a trademark owner to identify any infringement and to decide what measures should be taken to enforce trademark rights.

It is always useful to seek expert advice if one believes that someone is infringing his trademark. As an effective deterrent to infringement, the judicial authorities may order, upon request of the owner of the trademark, that infringing goods and materials be destroyed or disposed of outside the channels of commerce without compensation of any sort.

In order to prevent the importation of counterfeit trademark goods, measures at the international border are available to trademark owners in many countries through the national customs authorities. As a trademark owner, the company may seek the assistance of the customs authorities at the border, that is, before the counterfeit goods have been distributed in the country concerned. The assistance of customs would generally require payment of prescribed fees.

In some instances, an effective way of dealing with infringement is through arbitration or mediation. Arbitration generally has the advantage of being a less formal, shorter and cheaper procedure than court proceedings, and an arbitral award is more easily enforceable internationally. An advantage of mediation is that the parties retain control of the dispute resolution process. As such, it can help to preserve good business relations with another enterprise with which the company may like to collaborate in the future.

## USE OF TRADEMARK SYMBOL

The TM symbol may be used when trademark rights are claimed in relation to a mark, but the mark has not been registered with the government trademarks office of a particular country or jurisdiction, while the ® is used to indicate that the mark has been so registered. The use of ®, TM, SM or equivalent symbols next to a trademark, however, is not a requirement and generally provides no further legal protection. It is not mandatory to use either symbol, although the force of convention is such that the symbols are widely used around the world. It may be a convenient way of informing others that a given sign is a trademark, thus warning possible infringers and counterfeiters. The ® symbol is used once the trademark has been registered, whereas TM denotes that a given sign is a trademark; SM is sometimes used for service marks. However, it is generally unlawful to use the ® symbol with a mark when that mark is not registered.

## TRADEMARKS ON INTERNET

Trademarks carry as much significance on the Internet as in the off-line world. They are of essential importance in electronic commerce. Online enterprises are focussing on building recognition and goodwill so as to inspire confidence in them and in their brands and to remain competitive. Since in e-commerce face-to-face interaction does not exist and there is no opportunity to inspect goods or services before purchase, in such circumstances consumers prefer to reward trusted sources offering competitive products. Trademark owners, however, face challenges with respect to use of their marks in the digital environment. Therefore, Internet environment requires trademarks owners to defend their rights against all forms of trademark abusive practices. There is a general international consensus that trademark protection under law should extend to the Internet, and that its scope should be neither less nor more extensive than the protection granted in the physical world.

## TRADEMARKS AND DOMAIN NAMES

One of the important issues of Internet world is the interface between domain names and trademarks. A domain name is what we type in our web browser to get to a particular site. Domain names are the human-friendly forms of Internet addresses, and are commonly used to find websites. They were originally intended to facilitate connectivity between computers through the Internet. The domain name system is essentially a global addressing system.

As they are easy to use and remember, domain names have come to constitute a form of business identifiers. While designed to serve the function of enabling users to locate computers (and people) in an easy manner, domain names have acquired a further significance as business identifiers and, as such, have come into conflict with the system of business identifiers that existed before the arrival of the Internet and that are protected by intellectual property rights. By using trademarks as their domain names, businesses hope to attract potential customers to their websites and increase their market visibility. Anyone can get their own domain name, and it can be used for personal or business purposes. A few people pick up domain names identical to existing trademarks or products that they do not have ownership of. These persons are called cyber squatters and their act is called cyber squatting. Squatters may purchase domain names to misrepresent or malign the trademark holder of such a name. Others buy domain names simply to make some cash. Domain name disputes arise largely from the practice of cyber squatting, which involves the pre-emptive registration of trademarks by third parties as domain names. Cyber squatters exploit the first-come, first-serve nature of the domain name registration system to register names of trademarks, famous people or businesses with which they have no connection. Since registration of domain names is relatively simple, cyber squatters can register numerous examples of such names as domain names. As the holders of these registrations, cyber squatters often then put the domain names up for auction, or offer them for sale directly to the company or person involved, at prices far beyond the cost of registration. Alternatively, they can keep the registration and use the name of the person or business associated with that domain name to attract business for their own sites. Thus, with the growth of the Internet, domain names have come into conflict with trademarks which presents unusual features.

The possibility of such conflict arises from the lack of connection between the system for registering trademarks, on the one hand, and the system for registering domain names, on the other hand. The former system (trademarks) is administered by a public (governmental) authority on a territorial (either national or international) basis which gives rise to rights on the part of the trademark holder that may be exercised within the pertinent territory. The latter system (domain names) is usually administered by a non-governmental organization without any functional limitation. The potential for conflicts inherent in the two different systems of registration has been exploited by persons, who have made it a practice to register, as domain names for themselves, the trademarks of other persons or enterprises.

There is no agreement within the Internet community that would allow organizations that register domain names to pre-screen the filing of potentially problematic names. Furthermore, the increasing business value of domain names on the Internet has led to more cyber squatting, which results in more disputes and litigation between the cyber squatters and the businesses or individuals whose names have been registered in bad faith. The Internet grew rapidly over the last decade as a place to do business, although no international legal standards existed to resolve domain name disputes. The Internet Corporation for Assigned Names and Numbers (ICANN), the organization responsible for management of domains, was in urgent need of a solution to the dispute resolution problem. With the support of its member States, WIPO—which is mandated to promote the protection of intellectual property worldwide—conducted extensive consultations with members of the Internet community around the world, after which it prepared and published a report containing recommendations dealing with domain name issues. Based on the report's recommendations, ICANN adopted the Uniform Domain Name Dispute Resolution Policy (UDRP). The UDRP went into effect on December 1, 1999, for all ICANN-accredited registrars of Internet domain names. Under the UDRP, WIPO is the leading ICANN-accredited domain name dispute resolution service provider. Based in Geneva, Switzerland, the WIPO Arbitration and Mediation Center was established in 1994 to offer Alternative Dispute Resolution (ADR) options, in particular arbitration and mediation, for the resolution of international commercial disputes between private parties. Developed by leading experts in cross-border dispute settlement, the procedures offered by the Center are widely recognized as particularly appropriate for technology, entertainment and other disputes involving intellectual property.

The publication on WIPO's website of the decisions of the UDRP panels for generic as well as many country-code domain names provides useful guidance for trademark owners. A body of case law is being built up, both under the WIPO dispute resolution procedure and elsewhere, treating each case on its particular circumstances but following the general principle that domain name registrants need to show that there is no intention to detract from, or make use of, the goodwill associated with a trademark.

## TRIPS PROVISIONS

TRIPS Agreement specifies that procedures for registering trademarks should be both transparent and independent of the characteristics of the goods and services for which protection is sought. An important requirement is that countries must extend protection to internationally well-known trademarks in order to head off speculative registration and fraudulent use of those marks. Equally significant is that countries may no longer put use requirements onto trademark registrations. A typical example is the practice of requiring that a product be present on the market in order to maintain registered rights but preventing importation, as a means of accomplishing this presence, via a trade restriction, thereby invalidating the trademark. Such practices are no longer permissible for WTO members. While TRIPS article 21 permits authorities to regulate the licensing and sale of trademarks, it prohibits their compulsory licensing.

## CURRENT AND EMERGING ISSUES

In an increasingly global economy, especially in e-commerce, national regimes for protection of trademarks are becoming an anachronism. Global protection should be available at a reasonable cost and effort, and enforcement of such rights should be effective.

The scope of protection afforded to trademarks needs to be clarified and harmonized, for instance: (1) The flexibility of registration requirements for less than conventional signs, such as colours, smells, shapes, packaging, retail sale services, etc.; (2) How to assess likelihood of confusion in the context of infringement, versus a mere risk of association; (3) What is "genuine" trademark use for purposes of maintaining in force trademark rights; (4) What should be the scope of protection against use of a well-known trademark for dissimilar products; etc. (5) The legal and taxation implications of choosing not to record a trademark licence on the register.

The use of trademarks on the Internet raises many issues, which are being resolved as the law develops. One well-known category of issues relates to conflicts arising from contested registrations of domain names identical or similar to trademarks. A second category of issues relates to new uses of trademarks on the Internet, in many forms that are not all clearly perceptible. The incorporation into websites of trademarks owned by others, either overtly or covertly (as metatags) in order to attract "hits" by "search engines" is generally considered an actionable unfair business practice.

Debates also arise from: (1) The use of trademarks for advertising purposes, for instance as keywords for the purpose of search engine ranking; or for pop up displays on computer screens; (2) The scope of permitted trademark parody, as exercise of freedom of speech, on non-commercial websites including blogs; and (3) The linking and framing of web pages which can also be used for phishing (*i.e.*, basically setting up bogus pages to steal users' information).

These uses of trademarks on the Internet raise many issues of how an act of trademark infringement should be characterized, which law(s) should be applicable to trademark-related transactions and such infringements, and in which jurisdictions actions can be brought. Judgments in national courts are setting precedents to the effect that courts have jurisdiction in the country in which an infringement of rights occurs.

The domain name system, unlike the territorial trademark system, is global in scope and does not differentiate between different categories of goods and services. The problem now is to reduce to a minimum the conflicts between the system of domain names and the territorial trademark system, and to simplify the resolution of disputes when such conflicts arise.

Since well-known marks are especially vulnerable to abuse, it has long been recognized in the Paris Convention, and reaffirmed in TRIPS, that special protection is needed for such marks. However, enhanced protection through concepts broader than mere trademark infringement may be needed, *e.g.*, through rules of unfair competition, dilution, or "indication of connection".

The lack of full, world-wide, national search possibilities using the Internet for all forms of trademarks creates uncertainty for companies wishing to register such marks as they are unable to verify if such marks are already registered.

# 7

# INDUSTRIAL DESIGNS FOR VISUAL APPEAL TO INVENTIONS

Industrial design refers to the creative activity of achieving a formal or ornamental appearance for mass produced items. These designs make an article attractive and visually appealing, thus adding to its commercial value. Additionally, it helps to promote more innovative and aesthetically attractive products, thus providing consumers with a wider choice. Consumers attach particular importance to the visual appeal of shoes and clothes they buy, or the look and style of gadgets or cars. The appearance of an article certainly counts in marking a first impression on a customer, and often plays a decisive role in the final decision to buy or not.

In legal sense, industrial design is a branch of intellectual property right, which was established to give the proprietor of innovative designs asset of competitive advantages in manufacture and trade. As a category of intellectual property rights, it refers only to the aesthetic nature of a finished product, and is distinct from any technical or functional aspects. Definitions of what constitutes an industrial design vary from country to country. Common elements include aesthetic appearance and multi-dimensional nature embodied in an article with utility, and the exclusion of shape dictated by function.

The design may consist of three-dimensional features, such as the shape or surface of an article, or of two-dimensional features, such as patterns, lines or colour, as they can be expressed in two-dimensional (drawing) or three-dimensional (model) formats. Example of two dimensional designs are textile, wallpaper and carpet designs, and of three-dimensional ones are the shape of a toy, package, car, electrical appliance, mobile phone, piece of furniture or the shape and ornamentation of kitchenware. In certain circumstances, the features constituting a design may be the colour, texture or material of an article. In some countries, computer icons have recently been protected as industrial design.

The principle or the mode of construction of the article, mere mechanical contrivances, the building and structure, the part of an article not sold separately, variations commonly used in the trade, mere workshop alterations of components of an assembly, stamps, labels, token, cartoons and mere change in size will not be the subject matter of registration of design.

## HISTORICAL BACKGROUND

The concept of industrial design existed since the production of useful articles. From the days of ancient civilization, efforts have been given to the outline and the ornamentation of the articles produced by the craftsman himself.

The first Act dealing with copyright in industrial designs was the Designing and Printing of Linens Act 1787, came into force on 1st June 1787 in United Kingdom. It was concerned with design for certain specified textile materials namely: linens, cottons, calicos and muslins. By virtue of this Act, the sole right and liberty of printing and reprinting them was for two months from the date of first publication, that too with condition that the name of the proprietor was marked on each piece. Thereafter many Acts came into force, namely, 1794 Act, 1839 Act, 1942 Act, 1850 Act, 1858 Act, 1861 Act, etc. etc. The 1839 Act provided for appointment of a register of designs by the Board of Trade and this responsibility was transferred from the Board of Trade to Patent Office in 1875. Thus in 1911, the Patents and Designs Act, 1907 came into force in England. It did away with substantially all the existing copyright legislations which had been accumulating over a period of two centuries, repealing no less than 18 Acts most of them substantially in toto. Every branch of subject was brought within the statutes. As per the Design Act 1911, the 'design' means only the features of shape, configuration, pattern or ornament applied to any article by any industrial process or means, whether manual, mechanical or chemical, separate or combined, which in finished article appeal to and are judged solely by the eye. The word article as stated in the definition of design has been defined as any article of manufacture and any substance, artificial or natural, or partly artificial and partly natural.

## IMPORTANCE OF INDUSTRIAL DESIGN

An industrial design can serve a function similar to that of a trademark in that a product with a certain shape or look can just as easily be identified as a trademark. Designs contribute significantly to the marketability of goods and are crucial assets in several industries, for instance textiles, fashion, automobiles and furnishing and decoration. Quality is no longer enough to make ones company distinguishable from others. Every class of consumer wants nicely designed things now. Even in the poorest nations, movies, TV, and other media make consumers aware of design too. Turning out a safe, decent product would not make our money automatically, so we have an emphasis on innovation, *i.e.*, on design of the innovation. In today's highly competitive global economy, a visually attractive design alone may enable one to captivate a demanding and extremely diversified clientele. Through creative designs, enterprises could reach out to and appeal to customers from different age groups, regions, cultures, etc. In a highly competitive marketplace, design plays a critical role in adding to the commercial value and marketability of a product by making it more attractive and appealing. Market success, as also the market retention, is often determined by the visual appearance of an article. Companies, therefore, invest large sums of money and expertise in developing winning designs that appeal to changing consumer tastes. Smart businesses take note of changing consumer tastes and choices in order to develop and deliver better products, both in functional and aesthetic terms. Design, therefore, makes a critical contribution to overall corporate business strategy and success. Many companies have successfully redefined their brand image through strong focus on product design. They have started recognizing that design excellence brings stronger brand recognition and better profitability. Businesses have also started devoting attention to the creation and management of distinctive designs as part of their corporate strategy for identity and brand management.

Industrial designs are applied to a wide variety of products of industry and handicraft: from technical and medical instruments to watches, jewelry and other luxury items; from house wares and electrical appliances to vehicles and architectural structures; from textile designs to leisure goods. Over the years improved designs have helped make items like television and telephones more efficient more attractive and more in tune with our needs. Enterprises often devote a significant amount of time and resources to enhancing the design appeal of their products. Effective use of design adds value to a product by creating variety in a world of commodities. Attractive designs help in differentiating between competing products and also in customizing and segmenting the market for a particular product, ranging from ordinary items such as locks, cups and saucers to potentially expensive items such as watches, jewelry and cars. Creating higher perceived value through aesthetically pleasing industrial designs help build trust and lasting customer relationship, which translate into higher market share, better prices and bigger profit. Nevertheless, articles like steel almirahs, water tanks, voltage stabilizers, and geysers are just some of the products that play an integral role in our homes, they are so strongly intertwined with the fabric of our lives that we have learnt to ignore their sheer ugliness and have learned to live with them relatively uncomplainingly. Perhaps design element in their production has not been taken into consideration.

## PROTECTING INDUSTRIAL DESIGNS

*Furniture*
*(A three-dimensional design)*

Industrial designs help companies to differentiate their products from those of competitors and enhance the brand image of their products. This is why ensuring the proper protection of industrial designs is so important. Industrial designs can be relatively simple and inexpensive to develop and protect. To be protected under most national laws, an industrial design must appeal to the eye. This means that an industrial design is primarily of an aesthetic nature, and does not protect any technical features of the article to which it is applied.

While patents protect the technical solution or innovative technical improvement in a process or product, the new or original shape and external appearance of a useful object is protected by an industrial design right. Industrial design rights are intellectual property rights that protect the visual design of objects that are not purely utilitarian. The terms 'design' 'industrial designs', or 'design patent', when used in intellectual property law and practice, have a specific connotation. In most cases they refer to the visual appeal—that is, the features of shape, configuration, pattern or ornament, or any combination of these features—of a finished article made by hand, tool or machine, as opposed to functional features which may be protected by other types of intellectual property rights, such as patents, utility models or trade secrets. In many countries, the requirement of visual appeal of an article of manufacture or handicraft has been modified to that of perceptible features of appearance, and the rule of novelty has been replaced or supplemented by the individuality requirement. If a design combines functional improvements with aesthetic features then it might also be protected under patent or utility model protection.

*Textile Design*

When an industrial design is protected, the owner—the person or entity that has registered the design—

*Car Design*

is assured an exclusive right against unauthorized copying or imitation of the design by third parties. Having design rights on an attractive shape or style of a product may give the much-needed edge over the competitor. An effective system of protection also benefits competitor and the public at large by promoting fair competition and honest trade practices, encouraging creativity, and promoting more aesthetically attractive products.

Depending on the particular national law and the kind of design, an industrial design may also be protected as a work of art under copyright law. In some countries, industrial design and copyright protection can exist concurrently. In other countries, they are mutually exclusive: once the owner chooses one kind of protection, he can no longer invoke the other. Under certain circumstances an industrial design may also be protectable under unfair competition law, although the conditions of protection and the rights and remedies ensured can be significantly different. Thus, legal options may include one or more of protection under industrial design law, copyright law, trademark law—as two or three-dimensional mark—and under unfair competition law. The owner of a protected design may prohibit the making, selling, importing or exporting of products incorporating or applying the design. Depending on the countries, the owner may concurrently avail himself of the protection of copyright, trademark, and patent law (as design patent). In some countries, the protection of these different laws may be mutually exclusive; in others it is cumulative to varying degree. Good design strategy must compare these different legal ways for protecting industrial designs to prevent unscrupulous competitors from unauthorized copying.

The formulation of a legal system for the protection of industrial designs, like the provision of legal protection for all forms of intellectual property, requires the establishment of a balance of interests. On the one hand, there is the need to provide efficient and effective protection, in order that the law may fulfill its function of promoting the design element in production. On the other hand, there is the need to ensure that the law does not unnecessarily extend protection beyond what is necessary to create the required incentive for design activity, so that the least number of impediments are introduced to the free use of available designs.

The subject matter of the legal protection of industrial designs is not articles or products, but rather the design, which is applied to or embodied in such articles or products. While the subject matter of design protection is an essentially abstract conception, one of the basic purposes of industrial design protection is the stimulation of the design element of production.

## REGISTRATION

The diligent design management requires cost-effective protection of valuable designs to prevent the look of the product from becoming a commodity and freely imitated in less expensive look-alike products. This entails timely registration of new, novel or original designs at the national or regional design office. Industrial design registration involves a number of techno-legal issues that need to be appreciated. The regime for design protection differs from one country to another, although harmonization has been achieved within the European Union (EU), leading to the introduction of Community design rights effective in all 25 EU Member States. In most of the countries, design protection is subject to registration, although there is a trend to extend protection for a short-term to unregistered designs, *e.g.*, for 3 years in the EU. In some countries, mainly in Europe, there is an unregistered design right associated with any aspect of the shape or configuration of an article. The unregistered design right comes into existence automatically whenever an original design is created, but is generally a weaker form of right. Registered designs can generally benefit from protection for 25 years. Industrial design protection is usually granted pursuant to a procedure for the registration of such designs. By registering designs and obtaining intellectual property rights over them, companies are better placed to defend themselves against unlawful imitation. A registered design right makes it easier for the owner to bring an action for infringement. But registration may be expensive, as it requires professional advice, drawing up of detailed specifications, and payment of registration and renewal fees.

Most of the countries require registration of an industrial design as a condition for protection. Registration gives an absolute right that excludes all others, from using the design for making, importing for trade or business or selling any article in respect of which the design is registered, and to which the design or a design not differing substantially from it has been applied. This right is for a limited period of time and subject to renewal. The maximum term of protection is 10 to 25 years, depending on the national legislation. Once a design is registered, a registration certificate is issued. In many countries, an industrial design cannot be registered as such if it has been used or published before applying for design registration. Only the owner of a design, namely the creator/author, or depending on the legislation and the context, his employer or his successor in title, may apply for and obtain registration for an industrial design. If a number of persons have worked together to create a design, then they must file for registration as joint owners—unless all of them are working under contract or on commission. Industrial design protection is territorial. While the application must be filed with the office competent for the country or region for which protection is sought, the Hague Agreement concerning the international deposit offers the possibility of obtaining protection for industrial design in a number of countries through a single deposit made with WIPO.

Where regional protection is sought through a single application, this could be filed at the concerned regional intellectual property office related to a group of countries that are bound through regional agreements for providing registration of industrial designs. These are, for example, (*a*) The Office for Harmonization in the Internal Market (OHIM) for community designs in the countries of the European Community; (*b*) The African Regional Industrial Property Office (ARIPO) for industrial design protection in English-speaking African countries; (*c*) *The Organization Africaine de la properiete Intellectuelle* (OAPI) for protection in French-speaking African countries; (*d*) The Benelux Design Office (BDO) for protection in Belgium, the Netherlands and Luxemburg.

By introducing a community system of designs registration and a community-based unregistered design right, and harmonizing the European designs law, efforts are being made by the European Commission to simplify the protection of aesthetic designs, the Commission's work has resulted in the enactment of a Directive harmonizing the law of registered designs in the member states and a Council Regulation that introduces both community-wide registered design rights and community-wide unregistered design rights. The advent of the community unregistered designs right gives automatic protection to designs, which are published within the European Union. Designers should be able to enforce this community unregistered designers right in any European country in which a copy of a protected design is discovered. Besides, a new European-wide registered design system is also taking place, which allows a single design application to be filed in order to gain protection for a design in every member state.

Basic information for filing an industrial design application and the possibility, where available on request, of the deferred publication of a design, which may be critically important for marketing fashion articles such as textiles, clothing or jewelry, can be obtained from the respective national or regional office. The procedure for filing an application varies from country to country. Any person claiming to be the proprietor of a design is required to apply for the registration of his design in prescribed forms, in a prescribed manner and accompanied by the prescribed fee. As a general rule, to be registrable, the design must be "new" or "original". However, different countries have varying definitions of such terms, as well as variations in the registration process itself. Generally, "new" means that no identical or very similar design is known to have existed before.

The most commonly adopted examination system provides for a formal examination only of an application for a registered design. According to this system, an application is examined to ensure that it meets with each of the formal requirements for an application which are imposed by the relevant law (for example, whether the requisite number of representations or specimens of the design are filed with the application), but no search is made of the prior art to determine whether the substantive criterion of novelty or originality is satisfied by the design for which registration is sought.

A system requiring only formal examination has the effect of shifting the burden of assessing novelty to those interested persons in the market who may wish to use, or who may have used the design or a substantially similar design. Any person interested in using such a design will have the opportunity either to oppose the registration of the design for which application has been made, if the relevant law provides for an opposition procedure, or of bringing proceedings for the cancellation of a registration which it is alleged is invalid. The system thus offers a means of reducing the administrative burden of the maintenance of a system of registration of industrial design.

## Essential Requirement

Design rights protect new and original visual aspects of a product or its packaging. Requirements for protection typically borrow concepts from both patent law (novelty) and copyright law (originality). The design eligible for protection must display aesthetic features and must not be predated by a known overall identical or similar design. The design should be new or original, not previously published, at the date of application for registration. Clear statements on the novelty of the designs in terms of its shape and or configuration, ornamental surface pattern must be indicated. The novelty must also be clearly marked in the design submitted. The novelty or the originality of a design is judged by the eye with reference to the external appearance of the finished article to which the design is applied is compared to the published design. It may be noted that the novelty or the originality of a design is destroyed by the publication of design.

## Novelty or Originality

It is a requirement of all industrial design laws that protection through registration shall be granted only to designs which are novel or, as it is sometimes expressed, original. The novelty of the design constitutes the fundamental reason for the grant of a reward to the originator through protection by registration of the industrial design.

While the requirement of novelty is to be found in all laws, the nature of the novelty that is required as a condition of protection differs amongst the laws of various countries. The novelty required is sometimes absolute or universal, meaning that the design for which registration is sought must be new as against all other designs produced in all other parts of the world at any previous time and disclosed by any tangible or oral means. On the other hand, a qualified standard of novelty is sometimes required. In this latter situation, the qualification may relate to time, meaning that novelty is judged by reference to designs published within a limited preceding period of time; or may relate to territory, meaning that novelty is judged by reference to all designs published within the relevant jurisdiction, as opposed to anywhere in the world; or may relate to means of expression, meaning that novelty is assessed by reference to written or tangible disclosures anywhere in the world and to oral disclosures only within the relevant jurisdiction.

The broad policy argument in favour of a standard of unqualified universal novelty is that exclusive rights by registration should be granted only where the originator of the design has produced something which is truly novel, and which therefore justifies the reward of exclusive rights. The broad policy argument in favour of a qualified standard of novelty is that one purpose of design registration is to encourage new design within the relevant jurisdiction, so that a novel design registered within that jurisdiction should not be deprived of protection by the publication elsewhere of a design which its originator did not introduce into the jurisdiction to add to the designs available to industry. It should be noted, however, that it would not necessarily follow from a qualified standard of novelty that a person could obtain valid rights within the jurisdiction simply by registering a design which he had seen overseas and copied, since it is often also a requirement of design law that the applicant be the author of the design.

## RIGHTS

When an industrial design is protected by registration, the owner is granted the right to prevent unauthorized copying or imitation by third parties. This includes the right to exclude all others from making, offering, importing, exporting or selling any product in which the design is incorporated or to which it is applied. The law and practice of a relevant country or region determine the actual scope of protection of the registered design.

The right to prevent others from exploiting an industrial design usually encompasses the exclusive right to do any of the following things for industrial or commercial purposes:

(1) Make articles to which the design is applied or in which the design is embodied; (2) Import articles to which the design is applied or in which it is embodied; and (3) Sell, hire or offer for sale any such articles.

The term for an industrial design right varies from country to country. The usual maximum term goes from 10 to 25 years, often divided into terms requiring the proprietor to renew the registration in order to obtain an extension of the term. The relatively short period of protection may be related to the association of designs with more general styles of fashions, which tend to enjoy somewhat transient acceptance or success, particularly in highly fashion-conscious areas, such as clothing or footwear.

The right to legal protection in respect of an industrial design belongs to the creator (or author or originator) of the industrial design. The law usually provides that the entitlement to legal protection of the design shall belong the employer, or to the person, who has commissioned the design. The basis for this rule is that the creation of the design falls within the duties, which the employee is paid to perform, so that the employee should seek the reward for his creative activity in an appropriate level of remuneration, responsibility and other conditions of employment. Likewise, in the case of the contractor, the thing for which the contractor is being paid is the production of the design for the use of the person commissioning the design. In the case of a computer-generated design the person by whom the arrangements necessary for the creation of the design are undertaken shall be taken to be the designer.

## REGISTER OF DESIGN

On receipt of an application for registration of design, the same is numbered, dated and examined, and defects (objections) if any are communicated to the applicant(s) or his agent. When an application for registration of a design is in order, it is registered and notified and a certification of registration is issued to the applicant, and registration is recorded in the 'register of design'. The register of design is maintained by the patent office as statutory requirement. This document contains number of design, class number, date of filing, name and address of the proprietor(s) of design and notifications of assignments and of transmissions if any and other matters. WIPO is working to develop an electronic design register.

Register of design is open to public inspection on payment of prescribed fee. When a person is in possession of the registration number of a design, on the request of any person on a prescribed form with requisite fee, the patent office shall inform in writing whether the registration still exist in respect of the said design, and if so in respect of what classes of goods, date of registration and name and address of the registered proprietor.

When a person is not in possession of registration number and submits a representation or specimen of design, on the request of on a prescribed form with requisite fee and annexed with representation or specimen of the design in duplicate, the patent office shall inform in writing whether registration of such design exists, if so its registration number, date of application, name and address of the registered proprietor and the status of it.

If a person become entitled by assignment, transmissions or other operations of law to a design right in a registered design, or to any interest therein as mortgagee or licensee, he shall make a request on prescribed form with requisite fee and necessary documents for the entry in the register of his name as proprietor of the design or notice of such interest.

For exploiting an enterprise's exclusivity over its registered designs and also for creating an additional source of revenue, industrial designs are licensed. The designer grants permission to another person to use the design for some mutually agreed purposes.

## INTERNATIONAL PROTECTION

Generally, industrial design protection is limited to the country in which protection is granted. For companies seeking to protect their designs in many countries, WIPO offers a service, known as the "Hague System" which provides an easy and cost-effective way to obtain such protection. Under The Hague Agreement Concerning the International Deposit of Industrial Designs, a WIPO-administered treaty, a procedure for an international registration is offered. An applicant can file a single international deposit either with WIPO or the national office of a country, which is party to the treaty. The design will then be protected in as many member countries of the treaty as the applicant wishes. The application filed is in one language, with one set of fees in one currency (Swiss Francs). An international registration produces the same effects in each of the designated countries as if the design had been registered there directly unless the competent office of that country refuses protection. The 'Hague System' simplifies greatly also the subsequent management of the industrial design, since it is possible to record subsequent changes or to renew the registration through a simple single procedural step with the International Bureau of WIPO. Design protection is an area, which has benefited lately from significant and promising harmonization.

## INTERNATIONAL CLASSIFICATION

The Locarno Agreement, concluded in 1968, establishes an international classification for industrial designs, referred to as the Locarno Classification. The Agreement requires the industrial property office of each contracting country to include in the official documents for the deposit or registration of industrial designs, and, if they are officially published, in the publications in question, the numbers of the classes and sub-classes of the Locarno

Classification into which the goods incorporating the industrial designs belong. Recommendations of the Committee of Experts deal with the manner in which the classes and sub-classes should be indicated in the said documents and publications.

The International Bureau of the World Intellectual Property Organization (Geneva) and the Benelux Designs Office (The Hague) also use the Locarno Classification in their registers and in the publications they issue under the Hague Agreement Concerning the International Deposit of Industrial Designs and the Benelux Designs Convention, respectively.

List of classes based on International Classification for Industrial Designs of the Locarno Agreement:

1. Foodstuffs,
2. Articles of clothing and haberdashery,
3. Travel goods, cases, parasols and personal belongings, not elsewhere specified,
4. Brush ware,
5. Textile piece goods, artificial and natural sheet material,
6. Furnishing,
7. Household goods, not elsewhere specified,
8. Tools and Hardware,
9. Packages and containers for the transport or handling of goods,
10. Clocks and watches and other measuring instruments, checking and signaling instruments,
11. Articles of adornment,
12. Means of transport or hoisting,
13. Equipment for production, distribution or transformation of electricity,
14. Recording, communication or information retrieval equipment,
15. Machines, not elsewhere specified,
16. Photographic, cinematographic and optical apparatus,
17. Musical instruments,
18. Printing and office machinery,

19. Stationery and office equipment, artists' and teaching materials,
20. Sales and advertising equipment, signs,
21. Games, toys, tents and sports goods,
22. Arms, pyrotechnic articles, articles for hunting, fishing and pest-killing,
23. Fluid distribution equipment, sanitary, heating, ventilation and air-conditioning equipment, solid fuel,
24. Medical and laboratory equipment,
25. Building units and construction elements,
26. Lighting apparatus,
27. Tobacco and smokers' supplies,
28. Pharmaceutical and cosmetic products, toilet articles and apparatus,
29. Devices and equipment against fire hazards, for accident prevention and for rescue,
30. Articles for the care and handling of animals,
31. Machines and appliances for preparing food or drink not elsewhere specified,
32. Miscellaneous.

## TRIPS PROVISIONS

TRIPS introduced few concrete international rules (apart from the minimum protection period). As is the case with regard to patents, members of the TRIPS Agreement must comply with the substantive provisions of the Paris Convention (1967), whether or not they are also members of the Paris Union. Thus, most of the relevant substantive provisions set out for patents would also apply to industrial designs.

Requirements for protection of industrial designs in TRIPS Agreement are: (1) Members shall provide for the protection of independently created industrial designs that are new or original. Designs will not be considered new or original if they do not significantly differ from known designs or combinations of known design features. However, such protection shall not extend to designs dictated essentially by technical or functional considerations. (2) Each member shall ensure that requirements for securing protection for textile designs, in particular in regard to any cost, examination or publication, do not unreasonably impair the opportunity to seek and obtain such protection. Members shall be free to meet this obligation through industrial design law or through copyright law.

The owner of protected industrial design shall have the right to prevent third parties not having the owner's consent from making, selling or importing articles bearing or embodying a design which is a copy or substantially a copy, of the protected design, when such acts are undertaken for commercial purposes.

Members may provide limited exceptions to the protection of industrial designs, provided that such exceptions do not unreasonably conflict with the normal exploitation of protected industrial designs and do not unreasonably prejudice the legitimate interests of the owner of the protected design, taking account of the legitimate interests of third parties. The duration of protection available shall amount to at least 10 years.

## MARKING OF ARTICLE

Before delivery or sale of any article to which a registered design has been applied, the proprietor of the design is required to mark the articles with the word 'REGISTERED' or with abbreviation REGD or RD as he may choose and also with the number of registration of the design. If the proprietor fails to do so he shall not be entitled to recover penalty or damage in respect of any infringement of design right in the design.

## PIRACY OF REGISTERED DESIGN

Piracy of a design means application of design or its imitation to any article belonging to the particular class of goods in which the design has been registered for the purpose of sale or importation of such articles without the consent of the registered proprietor. In this case the registered proprietor may bring a suit for the recovery of the damages for any such contravention and for injunction against repetition of the same.

## CURRENT AND EMERGING ISSUES

National differences in substantive rules, *e.g.*, the criteria of protectability, the procedure for granting protection, scope of protection, remedies against infringement, etc., make it difficult for design owners to obtain international protection. The situation should improve with the possibility of applying for registration in several countries through the 'Hague System' that was eased by the Geneva Act. Also, since April 2003, business enterprises can apply for a single community registration covering all 25 EU member States. In the near future, a link should be established between the community design system and the international registration system under the Geneva Act.

One complex substantive issue is ensuring availability of design protection with respect to alternative or cumulative protection by trademark, copyright and, as the case may be, patent law.

Business and industry needs easy user-friendly access to central international registration of designs. The lack of full search possibilities for designs creates uncertainty for companies wishing to register designs, as they are unable to verify if the designs have already been registered. While some countries provide easy access to protection, many others still do not do so.

8

# GEOGRAPHICAL INDICATIONS: SOURCE IDENTIFIERS

Geographical indications (GIs) are a kind of intellectual property, defined as indications, which identify a good as originating in the territory of a country, or a region or locality in that territory, where a given quality, reputation or other characteristic of the good is essentially attributable to its geographic origin. They are a special kind of distinctive sign used in commerce. The use of a GI may act as a certification that the product possesses certain qualities, or enjoys a certain reputation, due to its geographical origin. GI creates 'good will' among consumers, which will assist product's distribution and sale. Most commonly, a geographical indication consists of the name of the place of origin of the goods.

Swiss chocolates are a good example of a geographical indication of source. The taste and quality of chocolates manufactured in Switzerland are expected to meet a certain standard due to characteristics specific to Switzerland. Names such as Champagne, Roquefort, Darjeeling, Chianati and Havana are not only the names of places. They are also geographical indications of source applied to a particular product—in these cases sparkling wine, cheese, tea, red wine and cigar—that have particular characteristics closely identified with their geographical place of origin. Because these names—and the products associated with them—often acquire a valuable reputation for a particular quality or characteristic, they are protected by various laws and international agreements. For this reason, for example, the sparkling wine from Champagne region of France is called champagne, and other similar products are simply identified as sparkling wine.

Agricultural products typically have qualities that derive from their place of production and are influenced by specific local factors, such as climate and soil. Geographical indications may be used for a wide variety of agricultural products, for example, "Tuscany" for olive oil produced in a specific area of Italy or "Roquefort" for cheese produced in France. However, the use of geographical indications is not limited to agricultural products. They may also highlight specific qualities of a product, which are due to human factors that can be found in the place of origin of the products, such as specific manufacturing skills and traditions. That place of origin may be a village or town, a region or a country. An example for the latter is "Switzerland" or "Swiss," which is perceived as a geographical indication in many countries for products that are made in Switzerland and, in particular, for watches.

Geographical indications are of considerable importance for developing countries. For example, India is richly endowed with natural and agricultural products, products of handicraft and industry. Darjeeling tea, *basmati* rice, *Alphonso* mangoes, *Malabar* pepper, etc. are a few examples of products which enjoy reputation for higher intrinsic quality and are known in the world market by reference to the geographical indications traditionally applied to them.

Indications of geographical origins are amongst the oldest category of distinctive signs. They are a type of collective monopoly rights. The concern shown by the World Intellectual Property Organization (WIPO) and World Trade Organization (WTO) gave new impetus to protection of geographical indications. Their importance has emerged with the Trade-related Aspects of Intellectual Property Right (TRIPS) Agreement, which came into force with effect from 1st January 1995. Certain European Union Member States and Switzerland were eager to establish an agreement protecting geographical indications. What emerged, in Article 23 of the Agreement, was additional protection for the place names used in identifying wines and spirits, even if products made outside the legitimate region are modified by words such as 'type' or 'imitation.' However, Article 24 set significant limitations and an agreement was reached whereby members would work toward a new solution. Those negotiations have not begun, though many countries have lists of geographical names they wish to see protected and have submitted proposals on how to go about such negotiations.

In recent years, geographical indications has emerged as one of the most important instrument of protecting the quality, reputation or other character of goods essentially attributable to their geographical origin. Like trademark geographical indication is valuable to providence. It is a source identifier and indicator of quality. It helps to promote goods of particular region or country and eligible for relief from acts of infringement and/or unfair competition. Geographical indications have much wider application and for some countries constitute one of the most important categories of intellectual property. This is reflected in TRIPS Agreement.

## CONCEPT OF GEOGRAPHICAL INDICATIONS

The 'geographical indications' owes its origin from the Paris Convention, 1883. Even though the Convention did not use the said expression, Article 1(2) of the Convention used the expressions 'appellation of origin' and 'indications of source'. The scope of the aforesaid expression has been delineated in Lisbon and Madrid Agreements. The former delineates the appellation of origin to mean:

"Geographical name of a country, region, or locality, which serves to designate a product originating therein, the quality and characteristics of which are due exclusively or essentially to the geographic environment, including natural and human factors."

The country of origin is the "country whose name, or the country in which is situated the region or locality whose name constitutes the appellation of origin which has given the product its reputation."

An appellation of origin is a special kind of geographical indication, used on products that have a specific quality that is exclusively or essentially due to the geographical environment in which the products are produced. The concept of geographical indication encompasses appellations of origin. Examples of appellations of origin, which are protected in states that are party to the Lisbon Agreement for the Protection of Appellations of Origin and their International Registration are "Bordeaux" for wine produced in the Bordeaux region of France, "Havana" for tobacco grown in the Havana region of Cuba or "Tequila" for spirits produced in particular areas of Mexico.

The latter defines the expression 'indications of source' to mean:

"Goods bearing a false or deceptive indications by which one of the countries to which this agreement applies, or a place situated therein, directly or indirectly indicated as being the country or place of origin."

However, the expression 'geographical indications' under the TRIPS Agreement has been defined as "indications which identify a good as originating in the territory of a member, or a region or locality in that territory, where a given quality, reputation or other characteristic of the good is essentially attributable to its geographical origin."

### "Generic" Geographical Indication

If the name of a place is used as the designation of a particular style of product, rather than an indication of the place of origin of that product, the term no longer functions as a geographical indication. For example, "Dijon Mustard", is a style of mustard that originated many years ago in the French town of Dijon; however, over time it has come to denote a certain style of mustard that is made in many places. Hence, "Dijon mustard" is now a generic indication and refers to a type of product, rather than a place.

## GEOGRAPHICAL INDICATIONS *VS* TRADEMARKS

When considering geographical indications as a special kind of distinctive sign used in commerce and thus as a particular category of intellectual property, it is important to distinguish them from trademarks. Whereas a trademark identifies the enterprise (*e.g.*, Toyota or Coca-Cola), which offers certain products or services in the market, a geographical indication identifies a geographical area in which one or several enterprises are located which produce the kind of product for which the geographical indication is used (*e.g.*, champagne or Darjeeling tea, both refer to places of origin of a product). Thus, there is no "owner" of a geographical indication in the sense that one person or enterprise can exclude other persons or enterprises from the use of a geographical indication, but each and every enterprise which is located in the area to which the geographical indication refers has the right to use the said indication for the products originating in the said area, but possibly subject to compliance with certain quality requirements such as prescribed, for example, in administrative decrees governing the use of appellations of origin.

However, geographical indications are valuable to producers for the same reason that trademarks are valuable. Geographical indications serve the same functions as trademarks, because like trademarks they are: (1) Source-identifiers, (2) Guarantees of quality, and (3) Valuable business interests.

As for the linkage between trademarks and geographical indications, Article 22.3 of the TRIPS Agreement provides that a Member State shall "refuse or invalidate the registration of a trademark which contains or consists of a geographical indication with respect to goods not originating in the territory indicated, if use of the indication in the trademark for such goods in that Member State is of such a nature as to mislead the public as to the true place of origin." Both geographical indications and trademarks can be used to promote the competitiveness of businesses and growth of national economies.

## PROTECTION OF GEOGRAPHICAL INDICATIONS

Geographical indications are protected in accordance with national laws and under a wide range of concepts, such as laws against unfair competition, consumer protection laws, laws for the protection of certification marks or special laws for the protection of geographical indications or appellations of origin. In essence, unauthorized parties may not use geographical indications if such use is likely to mislead the public as to the true origin of the product. Applicable sanctions range from court injunctions preventing the unauthorized use to the payment of damages and fines or, in serious cases, imprisonment.

Protection of geographical indications means the right to prevent unauthorized persons from using geographical indications, either for products, which do not originate from the geographical place indicated, or not complying with the prescribed quality standards. The second aspect related to the issue of protection is the question of protecting geographical indications against becoming generic expressions: in that case they have lost all their distinctiveness and, consequently, will lose their protection. The question whether a geographical indication is a generic term and void of any protection is, in the absence of an international agreement, to be determined by national law. It might well be that a geographical name is regarded in one country as a geographical indication and is protected accordingly, whereas it is considered to be a generic or semi-generic term in another country. Examples for such diverging treatment of geographical names are the French names "Champagne" and "Chablis" which, in France, are only allowed to be used for products originating from a certain geographical area and produced according to certain quality standards, whereas, in the United States of America for example, they are regarded as being semi-generic names, and therefore may also be used for wines not originating from the French area of production.

### Protection on the National Level

Geographical indications are protected in accordance with national laws. A significant number of developing countries have also in recent years, provided for their protection.

As regards the various forms of protection of geographical indications on the national level, three main categories can be distinguished. The first category comprises all possibilities of protection which are not based on a decision taken by the competent authority establishing protection with respect to a particular geographical indication, but which results from the direct application of legislative provisions or principles established by jurisprudence. The second category covers the protections of geographical indications through registration of collective marks (including agricultural labels) or certifications marks (or guarantee marks). The third category includes all special titles of protection of geographical indications, which result from a decision made by the competent government authority establishing the protection. This category, in particular, comprises the protection of appellations of origin—whether they result from a registration with the industrial property office or from the adoption of decrees.

*Darjeeling Tea*

### Protection on the International Level

Protection of geographical indications has also been on the international agenda for quite some time. It is addressed to some extent in the Paris Convention (Article 10), and is dealt with more specifically by the Lisbon Agreement for the Protection of Appellations of Origin and their International Registration (1958, revised at Stockholm 1967, and amended in 1979; the latest regulations as in force on April 1, 2002). A broader and more concrete effort in this context was the inclusion in the TRIPS Agreement (Articles 22 and 23) of international minimum standards for protection of geographical indications.

*Swiss Watch*

### Through Multilateral Treaties

Three multilateral treaties administered by WIPO contain provisions for the protection of geographical indications: the Paris Convention for the Protection of Industrial Property, the Madrid Agreement for the Repression of False or Deceptive Indications of Source on Goods (hereinafter referred to as the Madrid Agreement), and the Lisbon Agreement for the Protection

International Registration
ı Agreement). Furthermore,
ner interested parties explore
enhancing the international
ions.

### rotection of Industrial Property

is Convention deal specifically
ppellations of origin: Article 1(2)
tions of source" and "appellations
ects of industrial property; Article
n of indications of source; Article 9
ns which are applicable, *inter alia*, in
use of false indications of source; and
ie provisions of Articles 9 and 10.

that the protection of industrial property
ng others, "indications of source" or
ı." The obligation to protect indications
y provided for in Article 10, but there are
in the Paris Convention for the protection
rigin. Nevertheless, Articles 9, 10 and 10*ter*
pellations of origin since each appellation of
ı constitutes an indication of source.

s the basic provision of the Paris Convention on
urce. It provides that the sanctions prescribed by
pect of goods unlawfully bearing a trademark or
pply to any use of a "false indication of the source"
t. This means that no indications of source may be
refer to a geographical area from which the products
ion do not originate. For the provision to be applicable
s no need for the false indication to appear on the product,
any direct or indirect use, for example in advertising, is
ctionable. However, Article 10(1) does not apply to indications
which, without being false, may mislead the public, or at least the public of a certain country: for example, where certain geographical areas in different countries have the same name but only one of those areas is internationally known for particular products, the use of that name in connection with products

originating from another area may be mislead
sanctionable.

As regards the sanctions in the case of the u
indication of source, Article 9 establishes the principl
upon importation must be provided for, or at least pr
importation or seizure inside the country but, if thos
do not exist in a particular country, the actions an
available in such cases are to be applied.

Article 9(3) and Article 10(2) determine who m
seizure on importation or the imposition of other s
the public prosecutor, any other competent autho
any interested party. Article 10(2) defines what i
by "interested party", stipulating that "any pr
manufacturer, or merchant, whether a natural person o
entity, engaged in the production or manufacture of or
such goods and established either in the locality falsely in
as the source, or in the region where such locality is si
or in the country falsely indicated, or in the country wh
false indication of source is used, shall in any case be d
an interested party."

Article 10*bis* concerns the protection against u
competition and as such provides a basis for protection ag
the use of confusing, false or misleading geographical indicati

Article 10*bis* obliges countries of the Paris Union to as
effective protection against unfair competition, sets a gen
definition of what constitutes an act of unfair competition a
contains a non-exhaustive list of three types of acts which,
particular, must be prohibited.

Article 10*ter* is also relevant inasmuch as it obliges countri
of the Union to provide, on the one hand, appropriate leg
remedies and to permit, on the other, federations and association
representing interested industrialists, producers or traders to take
action, under certain conditions, with a view to the repression of
false indications of source.

The main advantage of the protection afforded by the Paris Convention to indications of source lies in the extent of the territorial area covered by the member countries of the Paris

Union. On the other hand, the question of indications which, in countries other than the country of origin, are generic names of a product in other countries is not dealt with in the Paris Convention, so that member States of the Paris Union can be entirely free in that respect. Finally, sanctions, although specifically mentioned in the Paris Convention, are not in all cases mandatory and apply only to false but not to misleading indications of source.

### *The Madrid Agreement for the Repression of False or Deceptive Indications of Source on Goods*

All goods bearing a false or deceptive indication by which one of the countries to which this Agreement applies, or a place situated therein, is directly or indirectly indicated as being the country or place of origin shall be seized on importation into any of the said countries.

### *The Lisbon Agreement for the Protection of Appellations of Origin and their International Registration*

The countries to which this Agreement applies constitute a Special Union within the framework of the Union for the Protection of Industrial Property. They undertake to protect on their territories, in accordance with the terms of this Agreement, the appellations of origin of products of the other countries of the Special Union, recognized and protected as such in the country of origin and registered at the International Bureau of Intellectual Property.

## Through the Provisions of Bilateral Agreements

A further possibility of international protection of geographical indications is the conclusion of bilateral agreements between two states. A number of countries have entered into such agreements. In general, such bilateral agreements consist of lists of geographical indications, which were drawn up by the contracting parties and an undertaking to protect the geographical indications of the respective contracting parties. The agreement usually also specifies the kind of protection that is to be granted. Although in general useful, bilateral agreements cannot constitute an entirely adequate solution to the problem of the lack of international protection because of the multiplicity of negotiations required and, resulting there from, an inevitable diversity of standards.

## GI-PROVISIONS OF THE TRIPS AGREEMENT

The TRIPS Agreement prescribes minimum standard of protection for geographical indications and additional protection for wines and spirits. It requires World Trade Organization (WTO) members to provide legal means to prevent the use of a geographical indication that misleads the public as to the geographical origin of the goods or constitutes an act of unfair competition. It defines and specifies the minimum standards of protection that WTO members must provide for geographical indications. Protection required under this agreement is defined in two articles.

All products are covered by Article 22, which defines a standard level of protection. This says geographical indications have to be protected in order to avoid misleading the public and to prevent unfair competition. According to Article 22.2(*a*) in respect of geographical indications, the TRIPS Agreement requires Member States to "provide the legal means for interested parties to prevent the use of any means in the designation or presentation of a good that indicates or suggests that the good in question originates in a geographical area other than the true place of origin in a manner which misleads the public as to the geographical origin of the good." It is also incumbent on WTO Member States to prevent, according to Article 22.2(*b*) of the TRIPS Agreement, any use which constitutes an act of unfair competition within the meaning of Article 10*bis* of Paris Convention. It should be noted that an obligation to protect geographical indications exists only with regard to such indications that are protected in their country of origin.

Article 23 provides a higher or enhanced level of protection for geographical indications for wines and spirits: subject to a number of exceptions, they have to be protected even if misuse would not cause the public to be misled.

The TRIPS Agreement also provides for certain exceptions where Members are not required to provide this protection. These include where the product term is considered generic in the market of a particular Member (Article 24.6) (for example, "cheddar" now refers to a particular type of cheese not necessarily made in Cheddar, in the UK), or where prior trademark rights exist in the same or a similar term (Article 24.5).

### The Debate

In the Doha round of negotiations in the WTO, a group of countries, led by the EC, was looking to strengthen exclusive rights over terms with geographical reference as a form of protecting their trade interests in some valuable products. The EC had three interrelated demands: (*i*) to extend the enhanced level of protection afforded to wines and spirits in Article 23 of the TRIPS Agreement to all products; (*ii*) to create a legally binding multilateral register for GIs; and (*iii*) to 'claw-back' the use of 41 product terms for exclusive use by EC producers.

A number of WTO Members from around the world, opposed these proposals for a range of reasons, including the costs to producers and consumers associated with having to re-name, re-label and re-brand products. The TRIPS Agreement already obliges WTO Members to provide the legal means to protect genuine GIs additional protection is not warranted, particularly if it creates new barriers to trade without any gain to global consumers. This has been an issue in global trade negotiations for some time.

### Multilateral Register

Besides providing increased protection for geographical indications on wines and spirits, TRIPS also requires negotiations to be undertaken in the TRIP Council concerning the establishment of a multilateral register of geographical indications for wines. The Doha Ministerial Conference extended this mandate to negotiate the establishment of a system that includes spirits. However, the purpose of the register has not been clearly defined. Groups of countries differ in their views; some wish to use it as a full international register that would oblige all member countries to provide protection to geographical indications meeting the requirements for registration. Others want it as a voluntary system of registration and source of information.

Different models for a multilateral register have been presented. The EU envisages a register that has an effect on all WTO members irrespective of whether or not they have any geographical indications included on the register. Any WTO member wishing to challenge the inclusion of a geographical indication in the register is required to notify the country concerned and enter into negotiations with a view to resolving the disagreement. The Hungarian proposal provides that where one WTO member has successfully challenged the inclusion of a geographical indication on certain specified grounds, then that geographical indication will not need to be protected by other WTO members. In both these proposals, inclusion of a geographical indication in the register would constitute a presumption of eligibility for protection under any legal means provided for protecting geographical indications in any WTO members.

By contrast, the joint proposal from the US, Canada, Chile and Japan provide a system of registration that is binding only on those seeking to participate in the system. Participating members would make use of the register when, for example, examining trademark applications containing or consisting of a geographical indication. Non-participating WTO members would be encouraged to make similar use of the register.

## PROTECTING INDIGENOUS KNOWLEDGE

The rationale for protecting GIs also extends to public policy areas concerning rural development and indigenous knowledge. There is a symbiotic relationship between protecting provenance and promoting rural development. Due to the increasing interest of consumers in qualitative aspects of foodstuffs, it is felt that protection of provenance, *i.e.*, indications of geographical origins, will have substantially wider benefits because concerned goods tend to be land-based and/or exhibit a strong historical and cultural link between place and people. Protection, it is hoped, will provide producer groups with the means to differentiate their product from others in the same category whilst simultaneously using the indication as a barrier to entry into this niche market segment. Due to consumers' growing interest in qualitative aspects of foodstuffs, labels denominating geographical origin on them will provide information concerning product characteristics (*i.e.*, origin, quality, etc.) and promote goodwill between consumers and producers.

GIs have potentially positive implications towards the protection of indigenous knowledge and as a means for generating livelihood and income. They are being increasingly considered as part of a wider policy measure aimed at protecting and rewarding indigenous peoples' knowledge. The use of GIs to protect indigenous knowledge has been discussed in a range of multilateral forums. Notable in this respect are observations of WIPO's Inter governmental Committee on Intellectual Property and Genetic Resources, Traditional Knowledge and Folklore that some forms of IPRs cover the content of knowledge, others a specific expression and others a distinctive sign or symbol. Thus, the very real possibility of a product being protected by these complementary, though overlapping, instruments of intellectual property. For example, consider handicrafts: the technical content may be protected as a technical idea, while the cultural value as form of expression and its distinctive characteristics through marks or indications. One important finding of the Committee's review of existing intellectual property protection of traditional knowledge was that while many countries considered few intellectual property instruments as suitable for protecting traditional knowledge some looked favourably at GIs.

GIs as an instrument of intellectual property protection have specific features, which in contrast to other IPRs, are considered relatively more amenable to the customary practices of indigenous communities. As no institution (firm or individual) exercises exclusive monopoly control over the knowledge/information embedded in the protected indication (or the good), it remains in the public domain. As such, fears of the commodification of traditional knowledge on account of GIs are not entirely valid. Protection involves the codification of well-established practices into rules that become part of public knowledge. However, as the knowledge embedded in the good is not protected, apprehensions concerning the misappropriation (biopiracy) of traditional knowledge remain.

Yet, it is also the case that the codified rules do not disclose the entirety of local (indigenous) knowledge associated with the product and its production process.

The particular indication is protected as long as the good-place-quality link is maintained and the indication not rendered generic. Many indigenous communities consider their knowledge as a heritage to be protected for the lifetime of their culture. In recognizing this element of compatibility, it is also useful to be aware that the codes of practices associated with a GI can evolve and change with time.

To begin with, GIs are a collective rights owned by all producers across the supply chain that observe the specified codes and produce in the demarcated geographical region. The holders of a GI do not have the right to assign the indication, which is provided to holders of trademarks and patents.

Closely following this, the product-quality-place link underlying GI-protection automatically prohibits the transfer of the indication to producers outside the demarcated region. Nor can the indication be used on similar goods that either originate from outside the designated geographical area or, if from within the region, are produced differently.

In effect, the result of protection is to limit the class and/or location of people who may use the protected indication.

In addition to the above, GIs are considered to be free of the many adverse socio-economic results of corporate control and accumulation of IP rights that occur with patents and copyrights. The rights available under GIs are not in any way comparable to the unconditional right of a patent holder. While it is true that any one community or association cannot acquire control over a number of indications in a style akin to the strategic use of patents, evidence of country-level concentration in the distribution of indications by product category exists.

Moreover, viewed from an economist's perspective, indications are a form of collective monopoly right that erects entry barriers for producers wishing to enter a market.

Finally, it is important to recognize that GIs do not protect the knowledge embodied within the good and/or the associated production process. Consequently, as noted earlier, GI protection is no guarantee against the misappropriation of traditional knowledge and other strategies to protect traditional knowledge must be adopted. Yet, GIs remain meaningful in enabling people to translate their long-standing, collective, and patrimonial knowledge into livelihood and income.

## EMERGING ISSUES

Improved protection of goods (and eventual services) other than wines and spirits is not only attractive for some developing countries, but also of interest for many agricultural and industrial sectors of developed countries wishing to protect local products, techniques and know-how. Some producers of products other than wines and spirits (*e.g.*, agricultural and consumer goods) in both developed and developing countries have expressed an interest in using a system for the protection of geographical indications for their products. Business enterprises urge governments to carefully study the implications of such an extension, notably for the interests of trademark holders. These discussions are taking place in the TRIPS Council in order to take account of any bearing on other intellectual property rights, notably trademarks. Integration into negotiations on agricultural issues would lead to an isolated view and a risk of undue interference with established rights.

Pursuant to the Doha Declaration, the WTO is discussing both the establishment of a multilateral system of notification and registration of geographical indications for wines and spirits, and the extension of the stronger protection accorded to wines and spirits to other products. Governments should keep discussions of the extension of the protection for geographical indications separate from the negotiations of the Special Negotiating Session on the notification and registration system for wines and spirits. The negotiations on the latter shall be completed within the overall time-frame foreseen in the Doha Declaration.

## ECONOMIC IMPACT

The main economic benefit of geographical indications would be to act as a quality mark, which will play a part in enhancing export markets and revenues. But increased protection, particularly applied internationally, may adversely affect local enterprises, which currently exploit geographical indications that may become protected by another party. Thus, there will be losses to countries producing substitutes for goods that become protected by geographical indications. A proliferation of geographical indications would tend to reduce their individual value. Geographical indications may be of particular interest to a number of developing countries that might have, or might be able to achieve, a comparative advantage in agricultural products and processed foods and beverages. For these countries, seeking and enforcing protection for geographical indications abroad may have economic gains. However, the costs involved in such actions, especially enforcement, might be prohibitively high. In addition, prior to seeking protection abroad, it is necessary both to develop and protect the geographical indication in the country of origin. Resources may need to be deployed to ensure that the required quality, reputation or other characteristics of the product covered by the geographical indication are developed and maintained. Effort will also be needed to ensure that the geographical indication does not become an accepted generic term, freely useable by all.

9

# TRADE SECRETS PROTECT UNDISCLOSED INFORMATION

A trade secret is information of any type that is actually or potentially valuable to its owner and not generally known or readily ascertainable by the public, and which the owner has made a reasonable effort to keep secret. It generally has some cost associated with its development. Broadly speaking, any confidential business information, which provides an enterprise a competitive edge, may be considered a trade secret. It encompasses manufacturing or industrial secrets and commercial secrets.

The following are a few sample categories of subject matter of trade secret: (1) Data compilations, for example lists of customers, lists of suppliers and clients (the more information a list contains, the more likely it is to qualify for trade secret protection), including certain databases; (2) Designs, drawings, architectural plans, blueprints and maps; (3) Algorithms and processes that are implemented in computer programs, and the programs themselves; (4) Instructional methods; (5) Manufacturing or repair processes, techniques and know-how; (6) Document tracking processes; (7) Formulas for producing products; (8) Consumer profiles, advertising strategies; (9) Business strategies, business plans, methods of doing business, marketing plans and sales methods, distribution methods; (10) Financial information; (11) Personnel records; (12) Schedules; (13) Manuals; (14) Ingredients; (15) Information about research and development activities. An extremely diverse range of business information may qualify to be trade secrets, provided the employer has made reasonable efforts to keep such information confidential, and has also made it known to all employees concerned that it is so.

Trade secrets exhibit the following characteristics: (1) They are in some basic way unique, original or novel; (2) They are generally unknown to others (*i.e.*, relate to something that the competitor does not know or have access to); (3) They provide a competitive advantage for an unlimited duration as long as they remain secret; and (4) They could cause harm if a competitor had access to them.

## KNOW-HOW

Know-how is practical information that may give a person or company a competitive advantage. In all countries the applicable law governing the grant of patents for inventions requires only that the patent specification disclose all necessary information regarding the invention, so as to enable a person reasonably skilled in the field to carry out the invention in the laboratory without the help of the inventor/applicant. It need not contain the optimum conditions. 'Know-how' on the other hand, covers each bit of information that is necessary to set up a production plant or to commercialize the invention. Such information includes, for example, minute details (such as optimum conditions) of the production methods applicable to the invention or, in the case of mechanical inventions, the details of the engineering designs, drawings, etc. It is this know-how, which is traded while transferring technology from a laboratory to an enterprise or from an enterprise to another. Know-how is usually kept commercially confidential and separately disclosed only under the terms of licensing agreement executed between the seller and the buyer of the technology. It is this know-how, which imparts commercial value to an invention disclosed in a patent.

Procedural knowledge or know-how is the knowledge of how to perform some task. Know-how is different from other kinds of knowledge such as propositional knowledge in that it can be directly applied to a task. Procedural knowledge about solving problems differs from propositional knowledge about problem-solving. For example, in some legal systems, this knowledge or know-how has been considered the intellectual property of a company, and can be transferred when that company is purchased.

One limitation of procedural knowledge is its job-dependence; thus it tends to be less general than propositional knowledge. One advantage of procedural knowledge is that it can involve more senses, such as hands-on experience, practice at solving problems, understanding of the limitations of a specific solution, etc. In intellectual property law, the know-how is a parcel of closely-held information relating to industrial technology, sometimes also referred to as a trade secret which enables its user to derive commercial benefit from it. It is a component of the intellectual property rights on its own merits in most legislations but most often accompanies the licence to the right-of-use of patents or trademarks owned by the party releasing it for circumscribed use. Know-how does not, however, solely comprise of secret information that is not in the public domain; it is a combination of secret and related non-secret information which would be novel to an expert in the field of its usage.

As long as only a few people know it, such information can be legally recognized and protected as a trade secret even though it fails to fulfill the criteria of patentability. A claim for protection of know-how as a trade secret requires that efforts be made to prevent disclosure. Law makes the taking without permission of a trade secret an illegal act, but not the discovery by proper means, *i.e.*, by independent discovery, accidental or actual disclosure, or by reverse engineering.

Discovery of trade secrets by fair means, that is, by legitimate reverse engineering, means that the originator has no rights to exclude its use by those, who discover it in a fair manner. Unfair competition includes such activities as industrial espionage, inducing employees to reveal trade secrets, and encouraging defection of technical employees to produce their own versions of a product based on proprietary information.

## PROTECTION OF TRADE SECRETS

Most businesses want to know their competitors' secret of success, including any proprietary information of commercial value. Generally, the value of trade secrets is lost if they are disclosed either willfully or inadvertently. An enterprise-wise information security and protection is imperative for protection of trade secrets. Companies and enterprises safeguard confidential information of commercial value against accidental or willful misappropriation, misuse or loss. Secret information and data need proper protection and management for ensuring competitive advantage.

Unlike other forms of intellectual property, trade secrets are essentially internal instruments, the responsibly for protection remaining with owner of the secrets. They are not disclosed to anyone including the government and are kept confidential. The most quoted trade secret and the one which has established the credibility that trade secrecy can be ensured in the case of the Coca-Cola formula, which is kept locked in a bank volt in Atlanta, can be opened only by a resolution of the Company's board and is known to only two employees at the same time. The public has no access to the names of those employees and they are not allowed to fly on the same airplane. It is obvious that such extreme systems and standards for protection of trade secrets are neither necessary nor practised by many other corporations.

*A Formula Protected by Trade Secret*

Traditionally, confidential business information of commercial value was not considered to be intellectual property. In fact, even today most countries do not have a specific law for protection of such information, which is often also simply called 'trade secret'. But given the growing importance and enormous potential of such information in providing a competitive edge in the market place, as also protecting the business against future competitors, it is now generally agreed that trade secrets are not just a starting point but also an integral part of the intellectual property system and often one of its most valuable parts. Many enterprises and industries are not aware that secret information is considered intellectual property, and is often also protected by legislation. With technology changing rapidly, trade secret protection is, in some cases, being considered the most attractive, effective and rapidly available intellectual property right.

The unauthorized use of secret information by persons other than the holder is regarded as an unfair practice and a violation of the trade secret. Today's business environment has increased the importance of trade secret protection for business by developing and implementing information protection practices that address the risks associated with a global marketplace. A common way of protecting trade secrets is through confidentiality or non-disclosure and non-compete clauses in an employment contract. As trade secrets have to be used in business and industry, those who need to know such trade secrets are generally bound by contractual clauses in employment agreements, which prohibit disclosure of such secrets during or after leaving the employment. In addition, an ex-employee cannot use trade secrets of the former employer to set up competing business, or use such secrets while working for a competitor of the former employer. In addition, a company should have similar rules and requirements for the protection of confidential information from contractors, consultants, vendors, customers, prospective or temporary staff, interns, visitors, non-employees working on site, etc.

Contrary to patents, trade secrets are protected without registration, that is, trade secrets are protected without any procedural formalities. Consequently, a trade secret can be protected for an unlimited period of time. There are, however, some conditions for the information to be considered a trade secret. Compliance with such conditions may turn out to be more difficult and costly than it would appear at first glance. While these conditions vary from country to country, some general standards exist which are referred to in Article 39 of the Agreement on Trade-related Aspects of Intellectual Property Rights (TRIPS Agreement): (1) The information must be secret (*i.e.*, it is not generally known among, or readily accessible to, circles that normally deal with the kind of information in question). (2) It must have commercial value because it is a secret. (3) It must have been subject to reasonable steps by the rightful holder of the information to keep it secret (*e.g.*, through confidentiality agreements). In general, information is eligible for trade secret protection if it is identified, substantial and secret.

Worldwide, the law protecting confidential business information (or trade secrets) is very varied. It is important to bear in mind, however, that trade secret protection is generally weak in most countries, that the conditions for, and scope of, its protection may vary significantly from country-to-country depending on the existing statutory mechanisms and case law, and that the courts may require very significant and possibly costly efforts to preserve secrecy. Patent or utility model protection, wherever possible, will provide much stronger protection. Depending on the legal system, the protection of trade secrets forms part of the general concept of protection against unfair competition or is based on specific provisions or case law on the protection of confidential information.

In USA, unlike patents, trademarks and copyrights, which are regulated by federal law, trade secrets are regulated by state laws. Each individual state has its own unique trade secret law. The United State is the one of the few countries where civil protection against trade secret misappropriation is provided expressly by the Uniform Trade Secrets Act (UTSA), enacted by 43 states. In addition, a federal law, the Economic Espionage Act 1996 (EEA) gives the Attorney General sweeping powers to criminally prosecute a person for appropriating trade secrets. The EEA has provision to punish both the provider as well as the receiver of unauthorized trade secrets.

Similarly, Brazil which in the 1996 revision of its intellectual property law, has provided criminal sanctions against a person releasing or using, without authorization, a trade secret to which such an individual has had access through employment contract with the concerned company or institution. Canada in its trade secret law has provided, among others, for breach of confidence, etc., as a cause for action; France in its criminal code has provisions relating to theft of trade secrets, know-how, and confidential business information; Germany and Italy, in their law, provide strong protection for trade secrets, the latter treating trade secrets theft as a crime; Japan, effective from June 1991, has enacted a national trade secret law. The United Kingdom also provides for effective protection of trade secrets, including search and seizure orders, which could be issued to protect trade secrets and to preserve evidence. In countries, which follow the common law tradition, trade secrets are protected even without legislation. The law relating to trade secrets/confidential information/ commercial secrecy is not well-developed in India. There is no legislation regulating this area of law. India follows common law approach of protection based on the case laws. However, there is Contract Act, 1872.

Thus, the existing laws vary widely. In countries, which apply a civil law procedure, there is probably a specific written law that applies. The title may include the words "unfair competition" or "unfair business practice" or be about "marketing practices". In countries, which operate in this area on common law principles, there is no written law. Over the years the courts have decided what is equitable, what is fair and reasonable, in the circumstances of disputes brought before them, and these principles apply to similar cases in future.

One weakness of legal protection for secrets is that once they have been published in some way they cannot be "made secret" again. Even if the owner of the secret goes to court and wins a payment for the damage suffered, this will not be as good as having the information kept confidential. Competitors will be free to use the owner's hard-won secrets. So the best practice is to make sure that the secrecy is kept in the first place.

## PROVISIONS OF TRIPS AGREEMENT

The TRIPS Agreement requires undisclosed information—trade secrets or know-how to benefit from protection. According to Article 39.2, the protection must apply to information that is secret that has commercial value because it is secret and that has been subject to reasonable steps to keep it secret. The Agreement does not require undisclosed information to be treated as a form of property, but it does require that a person lawfully in control of such information must have the possibility of preventing it from being disclosed to, acquired by, or used by others without his or her consent in a manner contrary to honest commercial practices. "Manner contrary to honest commercial practices" includes breach of contract, breach of confidence and inducement to breach, as well as the acquisition of undisclosed information by third parties who knew, or were grossly negligent in failing to know, that such practices were involved in the acquisition.

The expression 'undisclosed information' is defined in Article 39(2)(*a*) as "secret in the sense that it is not, as a body or in the precise configuration and assembly of its components, generally known among or readily accessible to persons within the circles that normally deal with the kind of information in question."

The Agreement also contains provisions on undisclosed test data and other data whose submission is required by governments as a condition of approving the marketing of pharmaceutical or agricultural chemical products, which use new chemical entities. In such a situation the Member government concerned must protect the data against unfair commercial use. In addition, Members must protect such data against disclosure, except where necessary to protect the public or unless steps are taken to ensure that the data are protected against unfair commercial use.

The TRIPS Agreement enjoins on Member States to ensure effective remedies for trade secret misappropriation, injunctive relief and damages. With the spread of trade secrets legislation, strong remedies are being prescribed against trade secret misappropriation.

### Methods of Protecting Trade Secrets

While TRIPS includes provisions for the protection of trade secrets, under the general terms 'undisclosed information,' it is silent on the modalities of achieving this and has left it to the individual members as to how to provide such protection. Many countries have legal instruments to protect trade secrets. The nature and methodology used differ, in some cases, it falls under privacy laws, in others under unfair competition and in yet others under breach of contracts, trust or confidence. It has to be appreciated that trade secrets *per see* cannot be legally protected, since they are secrets; what is enforceable with the consequential effects of breach of trust or legal contracts. There have been several litigations in recent times on this issue. For example, the source code of Windows, kept as a trade secret by Microsoft, against which Bristol Technology filed a suit terming it as an anti-competitive practice by denial of free access, was decided in favour of Microsoft. Similarly, a company in Singapore, got a court injunction against three of its former employees from starting a business for 18 months, in any area where trade secret acquired during their employment will be used. The court ruled that the non-disclosure agreements signed by them were valid, binding and enforceable. However, if a competitor, who had no access to the secret, but decoded by reverse engineering the secret from a product obtained lawfully, there is no violation of trade secrets, since he has discovered the secret independently.

Since the maximum number of trade secrets appropriation takes place through current or past employees, corporates, as a rule, enforce a non-disclosure agreement on every employee at the time of joining, so that, breach of contract can be used as the legal instrument for prosecution in case of violation. Some MNCs prevent through a contract, former employees from working for a competitor for a limited period of time.

The various ways to ensure that trade secrets are kept as secrets include marking all documents "confidential", limiting access to trade secrets and critical materials to only identified employees, maintaining computer security and insisting that all persons to whom the secrets are to be divulged sign non-disclosure agreements. Without these precautions, no information can be deemed to be secret and as such will not enjoy any legal protection, even when appropriate legislations exist for such protection.

It is necessary for business enterprises in respect of their trade secrets, to identify them, to develop an effective protection policy through employee education, through monitoring compliance, restricting access to trade secrets to the minimal of employees concerned, maintaining and ensuring secrecy about them, including computer secrecy, restricting public access to the enterprise's facilities, etc.

## DATA EXCLUSIVITY

Many countries recognize marketing approval data as 'trade secret' of the drug developer. Therefore, the obligation on the authorities would be to keep the test data secret and to prohibit others from accessing this test data for unfair commercial use, such as sale to rival firms and this substantive obligation would exclude use by the authorities without disclosure of the data.

TRIPS Agreement specifically recognizes the 'protection of undisclosed information' as being a category of intellectual property subject to protection. The structure of Article 39 of the Agreement suggests that the regime for test data has been conceived by the negotiating parties as a particular case in the framework of the protection of "undisclosed" information. Governments are encouraged to protect the confidentiality of these data against its unauthorized use or disclosure, to protect the proprietary interest of scientists and others, and to maintain the economic incentives for further pharmaceutical research and development.

Article 39.1 of TRIPS Agreement says: "In the course of ensuring effective protection against unfair competition as provided in Article 10*bis* of the Paris Convention (1967), Members shall protect undisclosed information in accordance with paragraph 2 and data submitted to governments or governmental agencies in accordance with paragraph 3."

Article 39.3 states: "Members, when requiring, as a condition of approving the marketing of pharmaceutical or of agricultural chemical products which utilize new chemical entities, the submission of undisclosed test or other data, the origination of which involves a considerable effort, shall protect such data against unfair commercial use. In addition, members shall protect such data against disclosure, except where necessary to protect the public or unless steps are taken to ensure that the data are protected against unfair commercial use." Thus, if in respect of pharmaceutical or agricultural chemical products which utilize a 'new chemical entity', the regulatory authority of a Member Country requires submission of 'undisclosed clinical and test data' for granting marketing approval it is under obligation to:

(1) Protect the data against 'unfair commercial use', and (2) Protect the data against 'disclosure' except where it is necessary to protect the public or unless steps are taken to ensure that the data are protected against 'unfair commercial use'.

All WTO members, with the exception of its least developed country members, have been obligated since 1st January 2000 to implement these provisions and many WTO members, including some developing countries, have already done so. Other WTO members, however, including some newly industrializing countries (NICs), have failed to do so and are challenging the accepted interpretation of the obligations contained in TRIPS Article 39.3 through various interpretations.

It has been argued that the Article 39.3 of TRIPS Agreement does not grant data exclusivity rights but requires the protection of undisclosed information against unfair commercial use. Inclination of Article 39.3 is to prevent clinical data from being accessible to third parties, not to create market exclusivity right. This is because Article 39.3 allows considerable discretion as to what Member States must do. As it is evident from the language of the Article, latitude is given to the individual members to take such steps as they deem fit for protecting data against 'unfair commercial use'. The purpose of Article 39.3 can be inferred from paragraph 1 of the same article that is to 'ensure effective protection against unfair competition'. Unfortunately, TRIPS Agreement refrains from defining the practices that would constitute 'unfair commercial use', thus allowing the several interpretations to creep in. It does not specify a minimum term of protection. More importantly, it is not clear whether the phrase "unfair commercial use" includes use of the originator's data by the regulatory agency to assess applications by generic competitors. This has been argued not to amount to "unfair commercial use" so long as the regulatory agency does not disclose the data to the generic competitor. Under this interpretation, Article 39.3 does not require data exclusivity. On the other hand, the research-based pharmaceutical industry, the United States Trade Representative and others have argued strenuously that Article 39.3 does require data exclusivity. Both the Office of the United States Trade Representative and the EU has urged that Article 39.3 of the TRIPS Agreement established an exclusivity obligation. According to the EU, all that is left to Member Countries is the determination of the duration thereof. The US and the EU currently do not allow reliance either on information that is supplied to regulatory authorities for new chemical entities, or on evidence of prior approval of the product in another country requiring such information, for a period between 5-10 years, according to the industry segment.

Article 39.3 does not require protection be given to already public data. Protection is required only for new chemical entities. Members have considerable discretion in defining "new," and may exclude applications for second indications, formulations and dosage forms. And, prior to granting protection, national regulatory authorities may request the applicant to prove that the information for which protection is sought is the result of significant investment.

In fact, there are certain controversial and unsettled provisions in TRIPS Agreement, which have triggered considerable deliberations and debate in the international fora. The scope, meaning and the manner of their implementation remain nebulous. Article 39.3 dealing with data protection is one such provision. The actual impact of Article 39 on competition and access to drugs is quite unclear, because the language in the Article is not precise regarding country's obligations.

## SHARING A SECRET

In a normal business it is sometimes necessary to share a secret with another company. A manufacturer may need to have specialized tests carried out on a prototype, and does not want competitors to know details of the new product. An assembly company may wish to know if a supplier can meet a new, tough specification, which will give a quick market advantage, but does not want anyone else to use the same specification. In both of these examples the prototype and the new specification must pass out of the owner's hands, but the owner will of course wish to retain control. The solution is to get the company to which the confidential information is to be disclosed to sign a confidentiality agreement, sometimes called a non-disclosure agreement (NDA).

### Non-disclosure Agreement

In the NDA, the Agreement names the owner of the information (owner), the company receiving it (recipient), and the reason for handing over the information—the permitted purpose. It briefly defines what the information is, and records of the information (which may be documents or drawings or software) are marked "confidential" or "proprietary".

The NDA sets out how the recipient must look after the information, what the recipient is allowed to do with the information (use it only for the permitted purpose), and what the recipient is not allowed to do (tell anyone who does not need access to the information). The Agreement states how long the information must be kept secret—this can be set as the length of time the secret will give the owner a market advantage, plus a little bit of leeway. Two or five years are common periods. Once the recipient has signed the NDA, the owner can pass over the confidential information. As always, local checks of the applicable law must be made for applying the law.

In a cross-border disclosure, often the owner of the secret will provide the text of the NDA and will suggest use of the law applying in the owner's home country. This is not essential; if the parties can agree, the law of any country could apply.

Companies should not use a NDA if a secret really must be shared, tell as little as necessary to achieve the commercial objective; sometimes a general outline is all that is needed, although for a technical appraisal the full detail of the know-how will need to be passed over for review. Sometimes an NDA sets out a period of time so that information disclosed, say within a defined year, falls within the agreement. This is useful for complex technical deals, such as joint ventures (JV), although a separate JV agreement will eventually be needed. Also, choose the recipient very carefully and be sure that a promise of secrecy will really be kept.

Sometimes the flow of information is two-way, with both parties disclosing confidential information to the other, such as when a joint venture is being set up between them. A few changes to the one-way NDA can cover such an arrangement.

### What an Employee Needs to Know about Trade Secrets

Whatever country one lives in and work in as an employee, there is almost certainly a law that relates to the way he should deal with confidential information that he has access to by reason of his employment. In the broadest terms it can be almost any sort of information that is not freely or easily available. Whatever its nature, it is something of value to his employer, and something that his employer's competitors would like to know. Whether one has been given this information because he needs it for his work, or he has come across it by chance, or even if he generated it himself, it does not matter. He is not allowed to disclose it to anyone outside the company, and sometimes he should not even tell others within the company.

In fact, whatever the system, the principles are the same. Employees must protect secrets belonging to their employer. They must not disclose them outside the company in any way. They must respect any marking on documents such as "restricted access". They must take notice of warnings that the information is confidential. Even further, employees should be aware that they may well have what is known as a "duty of care" or a "fiduciary duty" to their employer. Even if there is nothing written into their employment contract, or if there is no such contract, this applies. Even if they have not been explicitly warned that this information is confidential, but it is clear that it is a trade secret, then employees must not disclose it. The obligation applies, to some degree, even after the employee changes job. After all, one may go and work for a competitor but the new employer still has no right to the secret information. Certainly one should never take documents with him. On the other hand, the courts will protect his/her right to earn him living by using his general skill and knowledge.

If one ignores this advice, many countries clearly state that an unfair disclosure of information by an employee is a criminal act. A maximum jail term may be specified, such as three years. Best practice is to be aware of what is fair to one's employer. In return for his salary, it is only reasonable to keep his employer's confidential information a secret.

## PATENTS OR TRADE SECRETS

Trade secrets are essentially of two kinds. On the one hand, trade secrets may concern inventions or manufacturing processes that do not meet the patentability criteria and therefore can only be protected as trade secrets. This would be the case of customers' lists or manufacturing processes that are not sufficiently inventive to be granted a patent (though they may qualify for protection as a utility model). On the other hand, trade secrets may concern inventions that would fulfill the patentability criteria and could therefore be protected by patents. In the latter case, the inventor will face a choice: to patent the invention or to keep it as a trade secret. So, business enterprises may, as a matter of corporate strategy, sometimes choose whether to apply for a patent for a formula or manufacturing process or hold the information secret.

Some advantages of trade secrets include: (1) Trade secret protection has the advantage of not being limited in time (patents last in general for up to 20 years). It may therefore continue indefinitely as long as the secret is not revealed to the public. (2) Trade secrets involve no registration costs (though there may be high costs related to keeping the information confidential). (3) Trade secrets have immediate effect. (4) Trade secret protection does not require compliance with formalities such as disclosure of the information to a government authority.

There are, however, some concrete disadvantages of protecting confidential business information as a trade secret, especially when the information meets the criteria for patentability: (1) If the secret is embodied in an innovative product, others may be able to inspect it, dissect it and analyze it (*i.e.*, "reverse engineer") and discover the secret and be thereafter entitled to use it. Trade secret protection of an invention in fact does not provide the exclusive right to exclude third parties from making commercial use of it. Only patents and utility models can provide this type of protection. (2) Once the secret is made public, anyone may have access to it and use it at will. (3) A trade secret is more difficult to enforce than a patent. The level of protection granted to trade secrets varies significantly from country to country, but is generally considered weak, particularly when compared with the protection granted by a patent. A trade secret may be patented in someone else, who developed the relevant information by legitimate way.

While a decision will have to be taken on a case-by-case basis, in the following circumstances it would be advisable to make use of trade secret protection: (1) When the secret is not patentable. (2) When the likelihood is high that the information can be kept secret for a considerable period of time. If the secret information consists of a patentable invention, trade secret protection would only be convenient if the secret can be kept confidential for over 20 years (period of protection of a patent), and if others are not likely to come up with the same invention in a legitimate way. (3) When the trade secret is not considered to be of such great value to be deemed worth a patent (though a utility model may be a good alternative in countries where utility model protection exists). (4) When the secret relates to a manufacturing process rather than to a product, as products would be more likely to be reverse engineered. (5) When one has applied for a patent and is waiting for the patent to be granted.

## CURRENT ISSUES

The Article 39.3 of TRIPS Agreement obligates WTO members to provide a period of data exclusivity for safety and efficacy studies submitted by the research-based pharmaceutical and plant science industries to obtain regulatory clearance. During such period, all proprietary information submitted to the regulatory body shall be protected from unfair commercial use. Once this period has expired, the competent national authority may grant registration through summary approval procedures but shall always protect the studies against disclosure. All WTO members, with the exception of its least developed country members, have been obligated since 1st January 2000 to implement these provisions and many WTO members, including some developing countries, have already done so. Other WTO members, however, including some newly industrializing countries (NICs), have failed to do so.

Business enterprises, however, are still waiting for all developing country members of the WTO to implement their obligations pursuant to TRIPS Article 39.3. They urge governments to require original safety and efficacy data from all applicants for marketing approvals of regulated products, or authorization for reliance from the title-holder during the period of non-reliance. Business enterprise also urges governments to provide for specific minimum terms of protection.

The US and the EU currently do not allow reliance either on information that is supplied to regulatory authorities for new chemical entities, or on evidence of prior approval of the product in another country requiring such information, for a period between 5-10 years, according to the industry segment. This may serve as the model for the implementation by all WTO members of the TRIPS Article 39.3 obligation, as it is currently being done through FTA Agreements with several countries and regions.

10

# SPECIALIZED INTELLECTUAL PROPERTY RIGHTS

In intellectual property there are also some specialized varieties of intellectual property rights which are known as *sui generis* intellectual property rights such as intellectual property rights in layout designs of integrated circuits, new varieties of plants or databases. In Latin, literally meaning of *sui generis* is 'of its own kind/genus' or unique in its characteristics.

## CIRCUIT DESIGN RIGHTS

Circuit design rights are called mask work rights in USA law, protected under the Integrated Circuit Topography Act in Canadian law, and in European Community Law by Directive 87/54/EEC of 16th December 1986 on the legal protection of topographies of semiconductor products. It refers to the intellectual property right conferring time-limited exclusivity to reproduction of a particular layout-design of integrated circuits. The layout is called a mask work because, in photolithographic processes, the multiple etched layers within actual

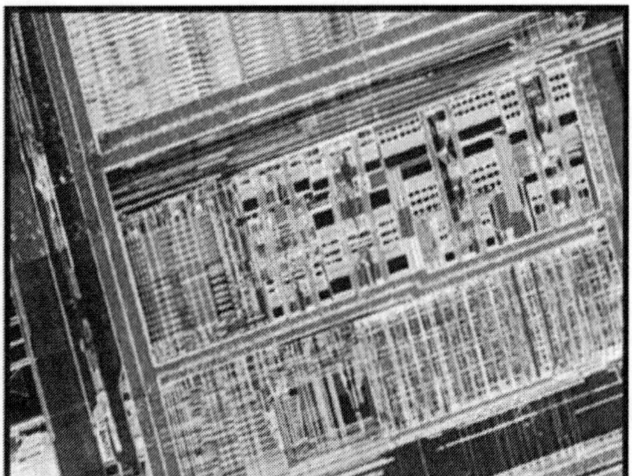

Pentium Microprocessor (an example of layout design of integrated circuit)

integrated circuits are each created using a mask, called the photo mask, to permit or block the light at specific locations, sometimes for hundreds of chips on a wafer simultaneously. A mask work is a two or three-dimensional layout of an integrated circuit (IC or "chip"), *i.e.*, the arrangement on a chip of semi-conductor devices such as transistors and passive electronic components such as resistors and interconnections.

Because of the functional nature of the mask geometry, the designs cannot be effectively protected under copyright law (except perhaps as decorative art). Similarly, because individual lithographic mask works are not clearly protectable subject matter, they also cannot be effectively protected under patent law, although their combined functions and structure certainly may.

Mask work exclusive rights were first granted in the US by the Semi-conductor Chip Protection Act of 1984. In Canada these rights are protected under the Integrated Circuit Topography Act (1990, c. 37). Equivalent legislation exists in Australia and Hong Kong.

### TRIPS Provisions for Layout-designs (Topographies) of Integrated Circuits

Members of WTO agree to provide protection to the layout-designs (topographies) of integrated circuits (referred to in this Agreement as "layout-designs") in accordance with the Treaty on Intellectual Property in Respect of Integrated Circuits. Members shall consider unlawful the following acts if performed without the authorization of the right holder: importing, selling, or otherwise distributing for commercial purposes a protected layout-design, an integrated circuit in which a protected layout-design is incorporated, or an article incorporating such an integrated circuit only in so far as it continues to contain an unlawfully reproduced layout-design.

According to the Agreement, no Member shall consider unlawful the performance of any of the acts referred to in that Article in respect of an integrated circuit incorporating an unlawfully reproduced layout-design or any article incorporating such an integrated circuit where the person performing or ordering such acts did not know and had no reasonable ground to know, when acquiring the integrated circuit or article incorporating such an integrated circuit, that it incorporated an unlawfully reproduced layout-design. Members shall provide that, after the time that such person has received sufficient notice that the layout-design was unlawfully reproduced, that person may perform any of the acts with respect to the stock on hand or ordered before such time, but shall be liable to pay to the right holder a sum equivalent to a reasonable royalty such as would be payable under a freely negotiated licence in respect of such a layout-design.

In the case of Members requiring registration as a condition of protection, the term of protection of layout-designs shall not end before the expiration of a period of 10 years counted from the date of filing an application for registration or from the first commercial exploitation wherever in the world it occurs. In the case of Members not requiring registration as a condition for protection, layout-designs shall be protected for a term of no less than 10 years from the date of the first commercial exploitation wherever in the world it occurs.

## PLANT VARIETY RIGHTS

Plant variety protection, also called a "plant breeder's right" (PBR) or "plant variety rights" (PVR), is a form of intellectual property right granted to the breeder of a new plant variety. According to this right, certain facts concerning the exploitation of the protected variety require the prior authorization of the breeder. Plant variety protection is an independent *sui generis* form of protection, tailored to protect new plant varieties and has certain features in common with other intellectual property rights. PVR protects newly bred varieties of plants. They enable the breeders of successful varieties to control their reproduction, and by licensing to obtain a return on the substantial investments of time and resources needed to produce them. The rights are specifically adapted to the needs of breeders and farmers, but coexist easily with patent rights on genetic inventions.

*PVR protects farmers' right*

These laws typically grant the plant breeder control of the seed of a new variety and the right to collect royalties for a number of years. This guarantees income for the breeder to cover the costs of research and development. The purchase of protected varieties gives farmers the benefits of superior varieties. In return, farmers are expected to pay a small royalty, included in the purchase price, and not sell the seed that they produce. Farmers may store the production in their own bins for their own use as seed, but further sales for propagation purposes are not allowed without the written approval of the breeder. Violations of plant breeders' rights (PBR) can result in litigation and court-ordered restitution to the breeder.

Plant breeders' rights contain a wider array of exceptions than the general regime of patent law. Commonly, there is a defence for farm-saved seed. However, this does not necessarily extend to brown-bag sales of seed. There is also a breeders' exemption—in respect of research and experimentation on new varieties of plants. There is also scope for compulsory licensing to allow public access to new varieties.

Any person who creates, or discovers and develops, a plant variety may apply for PBR. Once the PBR has been granted to the breeder, it means in practice that the title holder is the owner of the variety and anyone else, who wants to commercialize that protected variety requires the authorization of the holder of the PBR (*i.e.*, the breeder of the variety). This authorization is normally in the form of a licence agreement between the titleholder and those who sell the variety.

## Need for Protection

New varieties of plants with improved yields, higher quality or better resistance to pests and diseases increase quality and productivity in agriculture, horticulture and forestry, while minimizing the pressure on the environment. The tremendous progress in agricultural productivity in various parts of the world is largely based on improved plant varieties. More so, plant breeding has benefits that extend beyond increasing food production.

*New plant variety (Protected by PVR)*

The development of new, improved varieties with, for example, higher quality, increases the value and marketability of crops. In addition, breeding programmes for ornamental plants can be of substantial economic importance for an exporting country. The breeding and exploitation of new varieties is a decisive factor in improving rural income and overall economic development. Furthermore, the development of breeding programmes for certain endangered species can remove the threat to their survival out in nature, as in the case of medicinal plants.

While the process of plant breeding requires substantial investments in terms of money and time, once released, a new plant variety can be easily reproduced in a way that would deprive its breeder of the opportunity to be rewarded for his investment. Clearly, few breeders are willing to spend years making substantial economic investment in developing a new variety of plants if there were no means of protecting and rewarding their commitment. Therefore, an effective system for the protection of plant variety is essential to encourage breeders to invest in plant breeding and contribute to the development of agriculture, horticulture and forestry and for the benefit of the society as a whole.

## Requirements for the Grant of the Plant Breeder's Right

To be granted a PBR under the UPOV system of plant variety protection, it is necessary to file an application for examination by the designated authority. A variety is granted protection if it is: new, distinct, uniform and stable. The grant of protection is not subject to any further conditions, provided the variety is designated by a suitable denomination and the applicant complies with all the formalities and pays the required fees.

### *Novelty*

To be eligible for protection, a variety must not have been sold, or otherwise disposed of, in the territory of the member of the Union concerned for more than one year prior to the application for a breeder's right, or more than four years (six years for trees or vines) in a territory other than that of this member of the Union. In the case of new members of the Union, or members extending the plant genera or species for which protection is offered, these novelty periods may be extended for varieties which have been created only recently before the time that protection becomes available.

### *Distinctness*

A variety is deemed to be distinct if it is clearly distinguishable from any other variety whose existence is a matter of common knowledge at the time of filing of the application. A variety whose existence is a matter of common knowledge (a "variety of common knowledge") must fall within the definition of a variety set out in Article 1 (vi) of the 1991 Act of the UPOV Convention, but this does not necessarily require fulfillment of the Distinctness, Uniformity and Stability (DUS) criteria required for grant of a breeder's right under the UPOV Convention. Thus, a variety of common knowledge does not have to be a protected variety and includes ecotypes or landraces, which fall within the definition of variety. Furthermore, if protection was wrongly granted to a variety that was not distinct, the breeder's right shall be declared null and void, *i.e.*, considered that the right was never granted.

### *Uniformity*

A variety is deemed to be uniform if, subject to the variation that may be expected from the particular features of its propagation, it is sufficiently uniform in its relevant characteristics. The uniformity requirement within the Convention has been established to ensure that the variety can be defined as far as is necessary for the purpose of protection. Thus, the criterion for uniformity does not seek absolute uniformity and takes into account the nature of the variety itself. Furthermore, it relates only to the characteristics relevant for the protection of the variety.

### *Stability*

A variety is deemed to be stable if its relevant characteristics remain unchanged after repeated propagation or, in the case of a particular cycle of propagation, at the end of each such cycle. As with the uniformity requirement, the criterion for stability has been established to ensure that the identity of the variety, as the subject matter of protection, is kept throughout the period of protection. Thus, the criterion for stability relates only to the relevant characteristics of a variety.

The distinctness, uniformity and stability criteria are often grouped together and referred to as the "technical criteria." They are most easily understood by considering the criteria together with the way in which they are examined. Guidance on this is provided by document TG/1/3, "General Introduction to the Examination of Distinctness, Uniformity and Stability and the Development of Harmonized Descriptions of New Varieties of Plants".

*Denomination:* Each member of the Union must register the denomination of a new plant variety at the same time as it issues the title of protection for the new variety. Anyone who, within the territory of one of the members of the Union, offers material of the protected variety for sale or markets propagating material of the variety is obliged to use the denomination, even after the expiration of the breeder's right of that variety. The denomination is chosen by the breeder of the new variety but it must conform to all the criteria set out in Article 20 of the 1991 Act. In summary: (1) It must be different from all other denominations used by other members of the Union for the same, or a closely related, species; (2) It must not be liable to mislead or cause confusion concerning the characteristics, value or identity of the variety or identity of the breeder; in particular, (3) It must enable the variety to be identified; (4) No rights in the denomination shall hamper its free use as the variety denomination (even after expiry of the breeder's right); (5) Prior rights of third persons must not be affected and such rights can require a change of the variety denomination; (6) It may not consist solely of figures, unless this is an established practice.

The breeder must submit the same denomination to all members of the Union and, unless this is considered to be unsuitable within a particular territory, this same denomination will be registered by all the members of the Union. A trademark, trade name or other similar indication may be associated with the denomination for the purposes of marketing or selling, but the denomination must be easily recognizable.

UPOV has developed a document known as the "General Introduction to the Examination of Distinctness, Uniformity and Stability and the Development of Harmonized Descriptions of New Varieties of Plants", which sets out the principles, which are used in the examination of DUS. The identification of those principles ensures that examination of new plant varieties is conducted in a harmonized way throughout the members of the Union. This harmonization is important because it facilitates co-operation in DUS testing and also helps to provide effective protection through the development of harmonized, internationally recognized descriptions of protected varieties. In addition, UPOV has developed "Guidelines for the Conduct of Tests for Distinctness, Uniformity and Stability," or "Test Guidelines", for many individual species or other variety groupings. The purpose of these Test Guidelines is to elaborate certain of the principles contained in the General Introduction into detailed practical guidance for the harmonized examination of DUS and, in particular, to identify appropriate characteristics for the examination of DUS and production of harmonized variety descriptions.

## UPOV

The UPOV system of plant variety protection came into being with the adoption of the International Convention for the Protection of New Varieties of Plants (UPOV) at a Diplomatic Conference in Paris, on December 2, 1961. This was the point at which there was recognition of the intellectual property rights of plant breeders in their varieties on an international basis. The UPOV Convention was revised in 1972 and 1978; the most recent Act of the Convention dates from 1991. The UPOV Convention provides a *sui generis* form of intellectual property protection, which has been specifically adapted for the protection of plant varieties taking into account the particular features of plant breeding and the circumstances under which plant varieties are used. The Convention has been developed with the aim of encouraging breeders to develop new varieties of plants. UPOV mission statement is to provide and promote an effective system of plant variety protection, with the aim of encouraging the development of new varieties of plants for the benefit of the society.

### TRIPS Provisions

Under the TRIPS Agreement Members are bound to provide for the protection of plant varieties, either by patents or by an effective *sui generis* system or by any combination thereof, countries which at present do not protect plant varieties have some room to develop their own systems of *sui generis* protection. PVR is increasingly popular for this purpose—over 60 countries now provide PVR. The UPOV Convention, particularly as revised in 1978, can provide guidance on the content of such a regime, but countries, which have not adhered to UPOV, need not comply with that or other conventions in this field.

### Current Development

Business enterprises have been constructively involved in discussions leading to the International Treaty on Plant Genetic Resources for Food and Agriculture (PGRFA). This provides for genetic material of listed major crops to be exchanged freely, under provisions for sharing benefits arising from commercial exploitation of resulting products. Exchange will be subject to a standard Material Transfer Agreement (MTA), the details of which are to be determined. Business enterprises will help to negotiate a fair and practicable MTA.

## DATABASE RIGHTS

A database is defined a collection of independent works, data or other materials which are arranged in a systematic or methodical way and are individually accessible by electronic or other means. This is a wide definition which will cover traditional mailing lists and lists of customers as well as telephone directories, encyclopaedias and card indexes, whether held electronically or in paper form. Electronic databases are an integral part of a worldwide information market. The ever-increasing growth of information collected, processed and distributed by business reflects a valuable increase in investment in new products and services. Copyright protection does not protect, in certain cases, all kinds of databases such as non-original databases.

So far, in most countries databases are covered by copyright law to some degree, as being a work that shows originality in its selection, co-ordination and arrangement. However, the lawmakers of the European Union (EU) have decided that in order to provide greater protection to collections of information they should have a unified legal protection for databases. To do this they created a *sui generis* right called database right ("Database Directive"). It was created by Council Directive No. 96/9/EC of 11th March 1996 on the legal protection of databases. It aims at prohibiting unauthorized extraction or reutilization of substantial parts of a database that reflect a significant investment. This form of database protection should not affect the rights of existing rights holders, such as the creators of works incorporated in the contents of the database. Database rights lasts for 15 years under this regime, but can be extended if the database is updated. The policy disallows copying of substantial parts of a database (including frequent extraction of unsubstantial parts) and in that respect is similar to copyright.

In many other respects database right is similar to copyright: it is created automatically, vests in employers, does not have to be registered and is a right against use (not a monopoly).

The EU example has been implemented by all EU countries and a few other countries, such as Mexico and South Korea. Other jurisdictions currently offer or may be exploring different approaches to database protection. In the US, for example, compilations of data or facts are accorded a degree of protection if their arrangement meets minimum requirements of originality, or if the misappropriation of certain time-sensitive data constitutes unfair competition given the investment of the compiler and the unfair advantage to the user. Legislation has been introduced in the US to provide for EU-type *sui generis* protection, but has so far failed to gain sufficient support to become law.

Some have raised concerns that certain kinds of database protection may be so broad as to stifle the flow of and trade in information, but proponents believe that these fears can be addressed through legislation which provides appropriate access to non-original information while protecting and incentivizing the investment of data compilers and disseminators.

Without taking a position on the need for such protection, one should closely follow the development of the discussion of protection of databases at the international and national level to secure adequate legal protection of databases that at the same time safeguards the legitimate interests of users, compilers and disseminators.

When the WIPO Internet Treaties on Copyright, Performances and Phonograms were adopted in 1996, an international instrument on the protection of non-original databases was proposed as one of the pillars of a future international framework on content protection in the information society. While governments reached consensus over the WIPO Internet Treaties, the question of database protection constitutes "unfinished business". Since 1996, discussions on the possibility of an international agreement on the protection of databases have been ongoing within the WIPO Standing Committee on Copyright and Related Rights.

## SECURING INTELLECTUAL PROPERTY RIGHTS OVER TRADITIONAL KNOWLEDGE

Traditional knowledge (TK), indigenous knowledge (IK), and local knowledge generally refer to the matured long-standing traditions and practices of certain regional, indigenous, or local communities. Traditional knowledge also encompasses the wisdom, knowledge, and teachings of these communities. In many cases, traditional knowledge has been orally passed for generations from person to person. Such knowledge typically distinguishes one community from another. In a sense, it becomes their "identity." For some communities, traditional knowledge takes on a personal and spiritual meaning. Traditional knowledge can also reflect a community's interests. Some communities even depend on their traditional knowledge for survival. Subsequently, communities argue that traditional knowledge warrants respect and sensitivity.

*Ayurvedic Medicine*

*Yoga*

Commercial interest in plant and animal species in industrializing countries, and in traditional knowledge and remedies, has raised questions of ownership of such resources, previously assumed to be in the public domain. The existing system of intellectual property rights has been criticized for allowing individuals or entities to appropriate commercially valuable resources such as plant varieties, etc. At the same time, the holders of these resources have themselves started exploring the concept of communal intellectual property rights: to what extent can existing intellectual property rights provide an appropriate framework for the exploitation of traditional and biological resources? Is a new (*sui generis*) type of intellectual property right necessary? Or, is the most suitable solution to these issues found outside of the intellectual property system? Business enterprises are willingly participating in appropriate processes to define the relationship between traditional knowledge (TK) and intellectual property rights (IPRs). The form of any new *sui generis* right would be largely determined by its objectives, which are not yet generally agreed. Business enterprises are open to practical proposals for the protection of communal and indigenous intellectual property, and are engaging in constructive discussion. Any *sui generis* system for TK must be designed to coexist effectively with conventional IP rights such as patents. Moreover, the public domain should not be defined too narrowly or encroached upon without good reason.

Access and benefit-sharing (ABS) are twin principles of the Convention on Biological Diversity ("CBD"), which recognizes the sovereign right of the states over genetic resources. The CBD encourages bioprospectors to consult with concerned indigenous and local communities in any bio-prospecting and to agree terms with them for access to genetic resources. However, even when such consultations are pursued in good faith, new groups may subsequently emerge and challenge the authority of the groups initially consulted. More legal certainty is needed. Otherwise, the increased risk will result in lower benefits, and will discourage the access to resources that the CBD is intended to promote. Following the Convention on Biological Diversity, several national governments have passed, or are considering passing, legislation regulating access to biological resources. Governments should ensure that any such legislation having an impact on IPR is compatible with TRIPS Agreement.

Recently, various communities throughout the world have turned to intellectual property laws to preserve, protect, and promote their traditional knowledge. Certain communities have also sought to make equitable use of their traditional knowledge. Currently, only a few nations offer explicit *sui generis* protection for traditional knowledge. Two protective paradigms have been employed by these communities. The first protective paradigm seeks to prevent others from using or securing intellectual property rights over traditional knowledge. For example, some communities have created traditional knowledge databases to evidence their traditional knowledge as prior art in order to prevent perceived abuses such as biopiracy. Although traditional knowledge databases may pre-empt some from securing rights over traditional knowledge, databases do disclose such traditional knowledge to the public. This becomes a problem since many communities would rather keep such traditional knowledge within their community. A consequence of this defensive form of protectionism is the loss of an economic catalyst to discover new things. Other defensive efforts include pre-empting the registration of community names as trademarks and actions for misappropriation.

The second protective paradigm (often called "positivism") seeks to secure protective legal rights over traditional knowledge. This is achieved by either using the existing laws or using legislative means to enact new laws. Nevertheless, some countries, like the United States, may face constitutional problems with granting perpetual rights to these communities. There are also utilitarian concerns with granting legal rights to traditional knowledge. For instance, some forms of traditional knowledge (such as cures for disease) may be used to help others; and if exclusive rights were granted, some may go unhelped. Other concerns deal with the equitable sharing of benefits and resources. However, a number of countries are still undecided as to whether law should give traditional knowledge deference.

The World Intellectual Property Organization (WIPO) is currently working with different nations, organizations, and communities to address the policy/legal issues with traditional knowledge protectionism. It has concluded its issue-identification and assessment of the needs of the different stakeholders in the field of traditional knowledge, and is now actively engaged in exploring how the demands in this area should best be met—in particular through meetings of the Intergovernmental Committee on Intellectual Property and Genetic Resources, Traditional Knowledge and Folklore. Countries with traditional knowledge and genetic resources can help by classifying and documenting this, *e.g.*, in databases.

## INTELLECTUAL PROPERTY AND TRADITIONAL CULTURAL EXPRESSIONS/FOLKLORE

Indigenous and traditional communities often regard expressions of their traditional cultures/folklore as inseparable from systems of traditional knowledge (such as medical and environmental knowledge, and knowledge related to biological resources). In discussions about intellectual property protection, however, expressions of traditional cultures/folklore are generally discussed distinctly from traditional knowledge (or TK).

Although 'expressions of folklore' has been the term used most commonly in international discussions and is found in many national laws, some communities have expressed reservations about negative connotations of the word 'folklore'. International bodies like WIPO uses the terms 'traditional cultural expressions' (TCEs) and 'expressions of folklore' interchangeably. However, the choice of an appropriate term or terms, and the identification of the subject matter that it/they cover, is ultimately a matter for decision by policy-makers and relevant communities at the local and national levels.

Traditional cultural expressions, often the product of inter-generational and fluid social and communal creative processes, reflect and identify a community's history, cultural and social identity, and values. 'Traditional cultural expressions'/ 'expressions of folklore' means productions consisting of characteristic elements of the traditional artistic heritage developed and maintained by a community of a particular country or by individuals reflecting the traditional artistic expectations of such a community, in particular:

- Verbal expressions, such as folk tales, folk poetry and riddles, signs, words, symbols and indications;
- Musical expressions, such as folk songs and instrumental music;
- Expressions by actions, such as folk dances, plays and artistic forms or rituals; whether or not reduced to a material form; and,
- Tangible expressions, such as productions of folk art, in particular, drawings, paintings, carvings, sculptures, pottery, terracotta, mosaic, woodwork, metal ware, jewelry, basket weaving, needlework, textiles, carpets, costumes, crafts, musical instruments; architectural forms.

*Folk Painting*

Expressions of traditional culture or expressions of folklore may be either intangible, tangible or, most usually, combinations of the two—an example of such a 'mixed expression of folklore' would be a woven rug (a tangible expression) that expresses elements of a traditional story (an intangible expression).

*Folk Dance*

In general, it may be said that TCEs/folklore: (*i*) Are handed down from one generation to another, either orally or by imitation, (*ii*) Reflect a community's cultural and social identity, (*iii*) Consist of characteristic elements of a community's heritage, (*iv*) Are made by 'authors unknown' and/or by communities and/or by individuals communally recognized as having the right, responsibility or permission to do so, (*v*) Are often not created for commercial purposes, but as vehicles for religious and cultural expression, and (*vi*) Are constantly evolving, developing and being recreated within the community.

## PROTECTION OF TCEs/FOLKLORE

Indigenous and other traditional and cultural communities cite following examples when arguing that traditional creativity and cultural expressions require greater protection: Indigenous art has been copied onto carpets, T-shirts and greeting cards; traditional music has been fused with techno-house dance rhythms to produce best-selling 'world music' albums; hand-woven carpets and handicrafts are being copied and sold as 'authentic'; the process for making a traditional musical instrument have been patented; indigenous words and names have been trademarked and used commercially.

### Legal Options

Experience so far with TCE protection has shown that no single template or comprehensive 'one-size-fits-all' solution is likely to suit all the national priorities, legal and cultural environment, and the needs of traditional communities in all countries. Instead, effective protection may be found in a 'menu' of differentiated and multiple options for protection, perhaps underpinned by an internationally agreed set of common objectives and core principles.

The options include existing intellectual property systems (including unfair competition), adapted intellectual property rights (*sui generis* aspects of intellectual property systems), and new, stand-alone *sui generis* systems, as well as non-intellectual property options, such as trade practices and labeling laws, use of contracts, customary and indigenous laws and protocols, cultural heritage preservation laws and programmes, common law remedies such as unjust enrichment, rights of publicity, blasphemy, and criminal law.

Many countries and several regional organizations have elected to protect TCEs through *sui generis* measures. Most have done so within their copyright laws, following largely the Model Provisions, 1982. Others have elected to establish stand-alone IP-like laws and systems, examples of which are: (1) The Indigenous Peoples Rights Act of 1997 of the Philippines; (2) The Bangui Agreement on the Creation of an African Intellectual Property Organization (OAPI), as revised in 1999; (3) The Special Intellectual Property Regime Governing the Collective Rights of Indigenous Peoples for the Protection and Defense of their Cultural Identity and their Traditional Knowledge of Panama, 2000 and the related Executive Decree of 2001; and, (4) the Pacific Regional Framework for the Protection of Traditional Knowledge and Expressions of Culture, 2002.

## Relationship between TCEs and Intellectual Property

The artistic heritage of a community plays significant social, spiritual and cultural roles; it can also be as a source of creativity and innovation. The use of traditional cultural materials as a source of contemporary creativity can contribute towards the economic development of traditional communities through the establishment of community enterprises, local job creation, skills development, appropriate tourism, and foreign earnings from community products. Here intellectual property can play a role. By providing legal protection for tradition-based creativity, intellectual property protection can enable communities and their members to commercialize their tradition-based creations, should they wish to do so, and/or to exclude free-riding competitors.

The marketing of artisanal products also represents a way for communities to show and strengthen their cultural identity and contributes to cultural diversity. Here intellectual property can assist in certifying the origin of arts and crafts (through certification trademarks) or by combating the passing off of fake products as 'authentic' (through the law of unfair competition), for example. Communities have used their intellectual property to exercise control over how their cultural expressions are used, and to defend against insensitive and degrading use of traditional works.

Traditional cultural manifestations are also a source of inspiration and creativity for cultural industries, such as the entertainment, fashion, publishing, crafts and designs industries. Many businesses today, small, medium and large, in developed and developing countries, create wealth using the forms and materials of traditional cultures. For example, vibrant publishing, music and audio-visual industries in India and Nigeria draw upon local cultural materials.

There is already significant experience in developing and implementing intellectual property protection specifically for TCEs/Folklore at the international, regional and national levels. Copyright, for example, protects the products of creativity, in the form of original literary and artistic works, against certain uses such as reproduction, adaptation, public performance, broadcasting and other forms of communication to the public. It can also provide protection against demeaning or degrading use of a work, an issue that is often of concern in relation to traditional cultural materials. Not all aspects of intellectual property protection are focussed directly on innovation and creativity, particularly the law of distinctive marks, indications and signs (laws governing trademarks, geographical indications and national symbols) as well as the related area of the repression of unfair competition. These aim at the protection of established reputation, distinctiveness and goodwill, such as may be enjoyed by a traditional community in the production of handicrafts, artworks and other traditional products.

The elements and principles of the copyright system are particularly relevant to the protection of TCEs because many are literary and artistic productions and therefore already or potentially the subject matter of copyright protection. This is why many countries already protect folklore within copyright law. Rights related to copyright, particularly the rights of performers, are also directly useful.

The other main branch of intellectual property law, industrial property, has also been used to protect TCEs, especially trademarks (such as collective marks) and geographical indications, industrial designs (including textile designs), and the suppression of unfair competition. A contemporary interpretation, adaptation, collection or arrangement of old and pre-existing traditional materials can often be sufficiently original to qualify as a protected copyright work. Also, under Article 15.4 of the Berne Convention, anonymous and unpublished works (like much folklore) can be protected. Similarly, traditional designers working within their cultural heritage can register their new designs. Some indigenous and traditional words and symbols can be protected as trademarks.

In addition, the protection already available, internationally, under the WIPO Performances and Phonograms Treaty (WPPT) may be of great value. Folklore is often accessed and appropriated by third parties through its most recent traditional performance, for instance, when a performance of a traditional chant is recorded, the recording is what enables others to get access to that chant, so it is vital to determine how the recording is used and claims as to authenticity and/or origin. For example, a cheaply made souvenir item may carry a label falsely indicating that it is 'authentic', 'indigenous made', or originates from a particular community. Unfair competition law, as well as trade practices and labeling laws, are helpful here, as has been shown in several instances in practice. In addition, indigenous peoples have registered certification trademarks to help safeguard the authenticity and quality of their arts and crafts. In Australia, certification marks have been registered by the National Indigenous Arts Advocacy Association (NIAAA), and in New Zealand the Maori Arts Board, Te Waka Toi, is making use of trademark protection through the development of the Toi Iho™ Maori Made Mark. TCEs often have a strong link with a specific locality. This means that geographical indications can also protect TCEs, in particular when they are in the form of tangible products such as handicrafts that have qualities derived from their geographical origin, for instance, the Olinalá craft products from that region in Mexico. While the protected geographical indication is usually the name of the location itself, certain TCEs could be directly protected as geographical indications, such as indigenous and traditional names, signs and symbols.

Indigenous peoples and traditional communities are concerned that unauthorized commercial enterprises take their words, names, designs, symbols and other distinctive signs, and use and register them as trademarks. This practice can be challenged under general trademark principles. But some authorities, such as in the Andean Community, New Zealand and the USA, have amended their laws to strengthen defensive protection, explicitly enabling the barring of unauthorized registration of indigenous signs and symbols as trademarks.

**Role of WIPO**

The World Intellectual Property Organization (WIPO), which first began examining the relationship between intellectual property and the protection, promotion and preservation of traditional cultural expressions or 'expressions of folklore' several decades ago, has an active programme of policy development, legislative assistance and capacity-building in this area. UNESCO undertakes extensive work on the preservation of cultural heritage. WIPO and UNESCO co-operate on the protection of traditional cultural expressions. WIPO's work is, in line with its mandate, principally concerned with the 'protection' of TCEs in the intellectual property sense. In 1982, an expert group convened by WIPO and UNESCO developed a *sui generis* model for the IP-type protection of TCEs: the WIPO-UNESCO Model Provisions, 1982. This is called the WIPO-UNESCO Model Provisions for National Laws, 1982. They establish two main categories of acts against which TCEs are protected, namely 'illicit exploitation' and 'other prejudicial actions'. The Model Provisions have influenced the national laws of many countries. In 1984, WIPO and UNESCO jointly convened a group of experts on the international protection of expressions of folklore by intellectual property. In December 1996, WIPO Member States adopted the WIPO Performances and Phonograms Treaty (WPPT), which provides protection also for a performer of an expression of folklore. In April 1997, the 'UNESCO-WIPO World Forum on the Protection of Folklore' was held in Phuket,

Thailand. In 1999 WIPO and UNESCO jointly organized regional consultations on folklore. In late 2000, the WIPO Intergovernmental Committee on Intellectual Property and Genetic Resources, Traditional Knowledge and Folklore (the Committee) was established. The Committee has made substantial progress in addressing both policy and practical linkages between the intellectual property system and the concerns of practitioners and custodians of traditional cultures. Under the guidance of the Committee, the Secretariat of WIPO had issued a detailed questionnaire on national experiences, and undertaken a series of comprehensive analytical studies based on the responses to the questionnaire and other consultations and research. The studies have formed the basis for ongoing international policy debate and assisted in the development of practical tools. Drawing on this diverse experience, the Committee is moving towards an international understanding of the shared objectives and principles that should guide the protection of TCEs. As part of its broader programme on TCEs, WIPO also organizes workshops and seminars, expert and fact-finding missions, commission's case-studies, and carries out and provides legislative drafting, advice, education and training.

11

# INTELLECTUAL PROPERTY ON INTERNET

The Internet, which can be described as a network of networks, continues its remarkable expansion. It has millions of users today. An ever-increasing number of people throughout the world are being connected to the Internet in almost all countries. The World Wide Web, a key component of the Internet, has enabled all forms of expression—text, sound and images—to be shared on the Internet. Consequently, the purpose for which Internet is now used covers the full range of human activities: research, education, social communication, entertainment, and commerce. Intellectual property has gained importance in this digital environment as, increasingly, business assets are reflected in intellectual as opposed to physical property. However, this presents unique challenges and also unique opportunities in respect of the IP system, as ever adaptable, intellectual property has now migrated to the Internet and is being modified to suit the online environment. The challenges for the IP system could adversely affect invention, innovation and creative productivity, if intellectual property rights are not effectively protected through necessary legislative measures, as also the political will to enforce the needed protection. Information made available to the global information network is readily accessible simultaneously in every country of the world; hence, the challenges to present intellectual property system, in which rights are enforced on a territorial basis. Moreover, the online distribution of content presents significant opportunities and challenges to copyright owners, users and intermediaries such as search engines. It also raises crucial questions in areas such as ownership, licensing and management of IP as well as regarding the tools used to manage creative content and identify users and owners.

## IPR ISSUES

Digital technologies and Internet, in particular, have far-reaching impact on intellectual property and the international IP system. Digital technology enables anyone to make perfect copies. This can be done with speed, accuracy and in volumes that were not conceivable even a decade ago. Each copy in turn can be further reproduced and disseminated without any loss of quality. Works can be made available to the public in large numbers almost instantaneously. Previously, a user had difficulty in modifying the work created by someone else. Digital technology makes it possible for the users to alter the works with ease. In the digital domain, 'perfect' multiple copies can be generated by the same technology, which is employed for making use of the digital product. Hence, it has become more difficult for copyright owners to exercise control over replication of their works and to obtain compensation for such replication. Another challenge is because of the fact that digital works can be transmitted and used by multiple users, compared to the paper versions of the same works. A pirated version of a digital work can be loaded into a large computer system with multiple user networks, each of which can have virtually simultaneous use of the same copy.

Works in digital form are amenable to easy and quick modifications by users. Through digital sampling techniques, sound recordings can be mixed and combined with others to produce a new sound recording, different from original works. Photographs and video recordings in digital form can be manipulated to add, delete and combine elements from different works. Computer programs can, by processing through some re-engineering tools, be transmuted into unrecognizable forms. The user can sell all these products as new works.

In multimedia works it is possible to combine text, sound, still and moving images, into a single medium. Works protected by copyright will become less differentiated by type and more equivalent to one another because they will now be in the same medium. This equivalence of works in digital form will make it easier to create a difficult-to-classify work by combining what has previously been thought of as separate categories of works for copyright purposes. Therefore, another emerging challenge will be that of categorization.

According to the Gieschen Consultancy's 2006 Mid-Year Report, based on statistics compiled by the Business Action to Stop Counterfeiting and Piracy (BASCAP), some 14 per cent of counterfeit and piracy investigations now involve transactions carried out over the Internet. The absence of territorial limits on the Internet, along with the scope it offers for anonymity, has opened the door to infringements of intellectual property (IP) rights that are new in both nature and scale. Tangible counterfeit or pirated goods of almost every category are traded or exploited online, be it through legitimate business platforms such as online auction-houses, or through websites, which trumpet their illicit character. Massive amounts of copyright-protected content in digital form, including software, music, films, electronic games and text, are also distributed online without the copyright owners' consent via dedicated websites or file sharing networks.

The enforcement of IP rights with regard to such activities raises a number of legal questions. From an international perspective, the most comprehensive set of rules relating to the enforcement of IP rights is contained in the 1994 Agreement on Trade-related Aspects of Intellectual Property Rights (TRIPS Agreement). While a number of standards set out by this instrument apply equally to the off-line and the on-line dimension of IP enforcement, infringements carried out over the Internet pose some very specific obstacles to effective enforcement which are not addressed in the TRIPS Agreement or in any other global treaty.

## COPYRIGHT

In the field of copyright, vast numbers of works of literature, film and art, and notably computer programs, have already transferred to the digital environment. Digital technology enables the transmission and use of all of the copyrighted materials in digital form over interactive networks of the computers. Textual works such as books and newspapers are ideally suited to digitization. There has been real success in the online availability of science, technology and medical publications. Demand has also grown for the online collections of libraries. Online newspaper publishing is also prolific. Recently, numerous journalists and aspiring writers have engaged in online publishing to post 'blogs', web logs, or journals, that allow individuals to make their views available to the public without the need for intermediation by large publishing houses or distributors. In the field of fine art, indigenous craft and artifacts, numerous museums and art galleries have digitized their collections and made them available for viewing on the Internet. While the transmission of text, sound, images and computer programs over the Internet is already common place, this is also becoming true for transmission of audio-visual works such as feature films, as the technical constraints of narrow bandwidth begin to disappear. Materials protected by copyright and related rights, spanning the range of information and entertainment products, constitute much of the valuable subject matter of e-commerce. In fact, most of the copyright has to do with commerce. The focus on information remains the key to the e-commerce economy.

Digitization allows the conversion of materials into binary form, which can be transmitted across the Internet, and then re-distributed, copied and stored, in perfect digital form. Due to these capabilities of digital network technologies, Internet has been described as the world's biggest copy machine. It is a haven for unauthorized copies of the copyrighted work. The unfathomable size of the data travelling across networks and stored at interconnected sites and terminals makes detection of copyright violation a daunting task. The difficulties include identifying the culprit in the chain of dissemination of infringing material, deciding the appropriate jurisdiction and applicable laws. On the Internet, one can make an unlimited number of copies within a very short period of time and these copies can be transmitted to locations around the world in a matter of minutes. Thus, due to information technology the act of copying, modifying, and distributing of copyrighted materials on the Net become very simple, and difficult to trace by the authorities.

The enforcement of copyrights and its administration in this vast boundary-less environment requires re-thinking of copyright laws and policies. Right–holders need greater power to detect and stop the dissemination of unauthorized digital copies because it is now incredibly fast and easy to distribute copyrighted material on the Internet and to remove all traces of its existence on network computer terminals. Right-holders should feel secure in their ability to sell and license their property over the Internet, so that they will exploit this market fully and make more valuable works available through this medium. This would fuel the predicted increase in the volume of e-commerce trade in copyrighted works and performances.

Also being debated is the issue of liability of the service provider in infringement of copyrights. An Internet service provider (ISP) is the intermediary, who provides access to the websites to Internet users. As most of the copyright infringement takes place without the knowledge of ISP, he cannot be held responsible for that act. However, he may be held liable for copyright infringement if he allowed the same directly or indirectly with his knowledge and it is proved.

Besides unauthorized copying, other copyright violations that occur over the Internet occur via hyperlinks, deep linking, framing, and inlining. These e-commerce tools help in retrieving information, but when they interfere with the flow of commerce or when they support misrepresentation, then they infringe on copyrights.

### Hyperlink

Hyperlink is an element in an electronic document that links the user to another place in the same document or to an entirely different document. Although it is not a violation of copyright law to create a hyperlink, it is a violation of the law to create a link that contributes to unauthorized copying of a copyrighted work, if the linking party knew or had reason to know of the unauthorized copying and encouraged it.

### Deep Linking

Unlike hyperlinks, deep linking allows visitors to bypass information and advertisements at the home page and go directly to an internal page. As a result, sites can lose income because their revenues are often tied to the number of viewers, who pass through their home page. Some businesses also dislike the practice because bypassing the home page may mistakenly create the impression in a user's mind that the two linked sites are associated or endorse each other. As deep linking connects a user directly to secondary material on another site, bypassing that site's home or front page, this may amount to an infringement of copyright in the secondary material.

### Inlining

Inlining is the act of displaying a graphic file from another company's Website. It creates a reference to content from another Website such that the secondary material appears to be content originating from the first site. For example, inlining occurs if a user at site A can, without leaving site A, view a cartoon featured on site B. Such links, also called embedded links, do not require a copy to be made of the linked material, but may violate the author's right to display or communicate their work to the public.

All these copyright issues have been examined for several years through public and private processes, at the World Intellectual Property Organization (WIPO), and other international organizations. Significant progress has been made; there is now international consensus on some issues. In 1996, two treaties, commonly referred to as the Internet treaties, were accepted at WIPO: the WIPO Copyright Treaty (WCT) and the WIPO Performances and Phonograms Treaty (WPPT).

### WIPO Internet Treaties

Among other things, WIPO Internet treaties and their imperative statements require that right holders enjoy exclusive control over on-demand electronic disseminations of their works, and confirm that the reproduction right is fully applicable in the digital environment. They also require Member Countries to protect the technologies used to prevent infringement and the rights management information that right holders may choose to provide in digital form.

The most important issue addressed by these treaties is the definition of reproduction in the context of electronic transmission and storage. The treaties state that, “The reproduction right—and the exceptions permitted their under (copyrights originally enacted for non-digital form of literary or artistic work), fully apply in digital environment, in particular to the use of works in digital form. It is understood that the storage of a protected work in digital form in an electronic medium constitutes an act of copying within the meaning of reproduction.”

The WCT and WPPT also clarify the extent of right-holders control when works, performances, and phonograms are made available to the public for downloading or access on the Internet. WCT (Article 8) and WPPT (Article 14) clarify as follows, “Producers of phonograms shall enjoy the exclusive right of authorizing and making available to the public of their phonograms, by wiring or wireless means, in such a way that members of the public may access them from a place and at a time individually chosen by them.”

On the Internet, material is transmitted interactively on demand from individual users, at a time and place of their choice. The WIPO Internet treaties require that an exclusive right be granted to control such acts of ‘making available,’ while leaving it to individual countries to decide how to categorize this right under national law.

The moral rights in the digital environment are recognized by the WPPT in Article 5(1) as, “Independently of a performer’s economic rights, and even after the transfer of those rights, the performer shall, as regards his live aural performances or performances fixed in phonograms, have the right to claim to be identified as the performer of his performances, except where omission is dictated by the manner of the use of the performance, and to object to any distortion, mutilation or other modification of his performances that would be prejudicial to his reputation.”

An ideal scenario will be with a technology sophisticated enough to deter the ordinary consumer from seeking to circumvent the copyright laws, while granting legal redress against those, who represent a greater threat from hackers and those engaged in circumvention. It would fulfill the need of rights-holders to rely on technological measures to protect their works against infringement on Internet. The technological systems of protection include: anti-copy devices, access control, electronic envelopes, proprietary viewer software, encryption, passwords, watermarking, fingerprinting, metering and monitoring of usage, and remuneration systems.

According to WCT and WPPT treaties, Member States are to provide two types of technological adjuncts to the protection of copyrights in order to ensure that material can be transmitted safely on the Internet. The first technological adjunct is 'anti-circumvention' provision, and is addressed in the WCT (Article 11) and the WPPT (Article 18) as, "Contracting parties shall provide adequate legal protection and effective legal remedies against the circumvention of effective technological measures that are used by authors in connection with the exercise of their rights under this Treaty or the Berne Convention and that restrict acts, in respect of their works, which are not authorized by the authors concerned or permitted by law."

Another system could be based on electronic data attached to the works and objects of related rights. The data might identify the author or performer, the rights-holder, and the work or object itself, and may further describe the terms and conditions for its use. Several secure initiatives, sometime referred to as 'rights management systems,' have been proposed and several systems are in advanced testing.

As a second technological adjunct, the treaties protect 'rights management information', providing legal support to rights management systems, under the WCT (Article 12) and WPPT (Article 19). Here rights management information means information, which identifies work and the author of the work. Article 12 of the WCT obliges contracting States to provide adequate and effective legal remedies against any person knowingly performing any of the following acts knowing, or with respect to civil remedies having reasonable grounds to know, that it will induce, enable, facilitate or conceal an infringement of any covered by this treaty; to remove or alter any electronic rights management information without authority; and to distribute, import for distribution, broadcast or communicate to the public, without authority, works or copies of works knowing that electronic rights management information has been removed or altered without authority.

The music industry, for example, has developed copy proof compact disc (CD) technology that prevents CDs from being played on computer disc drives. Copy proofing employs various technologies either by including errors in the data encoded on the CD, which allows the disc to be played on a standard CD player, but not on a CD-ROM, or by masking audio files as data files so that the CD-ROM drive cannot recognize the music, etc.

The new treaties continue to provide flexibility to individual counties to develop exceptions and limitations appropriate to their particular circumstances. National copyright laws in most countries incorporate exceptions for copying for personal use, research, education, newspaper reporting, etc., based on principles of 'fair dealing'. The scope and flexibility of these exceptions differ in different countries. Since the digital technology enables unauthorized creation of unlimited, perfect and costless copies as well as their distribution, the copyright industries are concerned about the impact of this on their business and profitability. They are responding by using digital technology, in the form of encryption technologies and anti-circumvention measures, supplemented by contract law and *sui generis* form of data protection. It is a major challenge to see as to how the appropriate 'fair use' exceptions can be preserved in the digital context, especially for poorer developing nations.

## TRADEMARKS

Intellectual property, through the trademark system, also facilitates the identification of goods and services and allows consumers to distinguish those produced by a certain enterprise. Trademarks carry at least as much significance on the Internet as in the off-line world. They are of essential importance in electronic commerce. On-line enterprises are focussing on building recognition and goodwill, so as to inspire confidence in them and in their brands, and to remain competitive. Consumers, operating in virtual markets where face-to-face interactions are infrequent and there is little or no opportunity to inspect goods or services before purchase. In such a situation, consumers prefer enterprises that they recognize and that have brands that inspire confidence. They increasingly rely upon strong brand awareness and brand performance for the confidence to engage in e-commerce. So, in the virtual markets of the cyber world, there is an ever-greater need for trademarks. While trademarks are of greater importance in this virtual environment, they are also more vulnerable to infringement, dilution and anti-competitive practices.

The laws protecting trademarks apply on a territorial basis and are not tailored for the borderless world of e-commerce. However, there is a general international consensus that trademark protection under law should extend to the Internet, and that its scope should be neither less nor more extensive than the protection granted in the physical world. While existing national or regional trademark law systems apply, together with the relevant international treaties, these provisions are of a general nature, applying on a territorial basis, and are not made for the Internet. The challenges of this new medium of commerce are not limited to trademarks; they exist with regard to all kinds of distinctive signs online, including trade names and geographical indications.

## ISSUES AND CHALLENGES

Trademarks owners face new challenges with respect to use of their marks in the digital environment. For example, trademarks and logos may be used in a site or domain in connection with objectionable sites, or by trade competitors to divert search engine traffic, or dilute or tarnish a brand. More than 70 per cent of domain names associated with top brands are not registered by the true brand owner, prompting right holders to defensively register their marks as domain names, and take action to protect their mark.

### *Domain Names*

Domain names are a simple form of Internet addresses, designed to serve the function of enabling users to locate sites on the Internet in an easy manner. Because of the role played by the

Internet domain name system, identity on the Internet also goes beyond the trademark system. Domain names are user-friendly addresses that correspond to the unique Internet Protocol numbers that connect our computers to the Internet and enable the network routing system to direct data requests to the correct addressee. Domain names were originally intended to perform a purely technical function in a user-friendly way, but because they are intuitive and easy to remember they now perform a function as business or personal identifiers. Most businesses, whether e-commerce or not, advertise their domain name to signal a Web presence. In this way, although, as such, not an form of intellectual property, domain names now perform an identifying functions similar to that of a trademark. Because of the way in which people and search engines operate, most businesses use their trademark or trade name as their domain name, and this has caused conflict with the advent of predatory practices, known as 'cyber squatting'. Cyber squatting is the abusive or bad faith registration of an Internet domain name that is similar to a name in which another person has intellectual property rights, or some other legitimate claim. The growing number of cyber squatting disputes reflects the premium businesses are placing on domain names and their potential for facilitating electronic commerce.

In traditional commerce, trademarks are used to identify goods and services, while on the Internet; domain names are being used as business identifiers. The use of the domain name system has grown rapidly over the last few years. Precisely because domain names are easy to remember and use, the domain name system (DNS)—the central system for routing traffic on the Internet—has assumed a key role in electronic commerce. On the one hand, it facilitates the ability of consumers to navigate the Internet to find the websites they are looking for, and, on the other hand, it facilitates businesses' ability to promote an easy-to-remember name or word which may, at the same time, serve to identify and distinguish the business itself, or its goods or services, and to specify its corresponding online, Internet location.

Domain names have now acquired increasing significance as business identifiers. However, they are also posing certain challenges to the IP system. The conflict between domain names and standard intellectual property rights raise challenging policy questions. One system—the DNS—is largely privately administered. It gives rise to registrations that result in a global presence. The other system—the standard intellectual property rights system—is publicly administered on a territorial basis. It gives rise to rights that are exercisable only within the territory concerned. This conflict has given rise to a number of predatory and parasitical practices that have been adopted by some parties to exploit the lack of connection between the purposes for which the DNS was designed and those for which intellectual property exists. There have been many cases, where deliberate registration as domain names of well-known trademarks has been done. The idea is to sell the domain names to the owners of those marks, or simply to take unfair advantage of the reputation attached to those marks. Cyber squatting is universally condemned as an indefensible activity. Keeping this problem in view, the US government sought international support to request the World Intellectual Property Organization (WIPO) to initiate balanced and transparent processes to develop recommendations for a uniform approach to resolving trademark/domain name disputes involving cyber piracy. WIPO prepared and published a report containing recommendations dealing with domain name issues. Based on the report's recommendations, the Internet Corporation for Assigned Names and Numbers (ICANN), the organization responsible for management of domains, adopted the Uniform Domain Name Dispute Resolution Policy (UDRP). Under the UDRP, WIPO is the leading ICANN-accredited domain name dispute resolution service provider. Based in Geneva, Switzerland, the WIPO Arbitration and Mediation Center was established in 1994 to offer Alternative Dispute Resolution (ADR) options. WIPO is committed to promoting a reliable environment in cyber space and preventing abuse of domain names. The number of Internet domain name cyber squatting disputes filed by WIPO's Arbitration and Mediation Center increased by 25 per cent in 2006. 'Trademarks and Domain Names' has already been referred to in Chapter 6.

Some Internet practices that may raise trademark issues, such as 'hyper linking' and 'meta tagging', are important to facilitate users' navigation of the Web. Nevertheless, they raise concerns for trademark owners since they create association and links, thereby increasing the risk of confusion, dilution or other forms of unfair exploitation of trademarks. Such emerging practices are: (1) Use of trademarks as metatags, (2) Sale of trademarks as keywords, (3) Pop-up advertisements, (4) Mouse-trapping, and (5) Linking and framing.

### Metatag

A metatag is a key embedded in a website's Hyperlink Markup Language (HTML) code as a means for Internet search engines to categorize the contents of the website. These metatags are not visible on the website, but consumers looking for the products of the trademark owner might wrongly be directed by the search engines to someone else's website. Trademark owners have challenged the unauthorized use of their trademark as a metatag. Some courts have regarded this as a trademark infringement, stating that such use might suggest sponsorship or authorization by the trademark owner.

### Sale of Trademarks as Keywords

Some of the search engines 'sell' keywords to advertisers, who want to target their products to a particular group of Internet users. Thus, whenever the keyword is entered into the search engine, an advertisement appears along with any search results. This has been challenged by trademarks owners who are concerned that such advertisements might divert customers from their own website, or from the websites of their preferred or authorized web retailers. However, the legal treatment of such cases is still developing.

### Pop-up Advertisements

The use of a graphic trademark when linked to the trademark owner's site is sometimes a risky proposition. Unlike the use of a simple word link, a consumer is more likely to be confused into believing that the linked site is associated with or endorses the site that own the graphic trademark. The pop-up advertisement is a window, not initiated by the user that appears on top of the content page when a site is loaded. A user who clicks on the pop-up graphic will be redirected to the advertiser's website, otherwise, and unless closed by the user, the pop-up window will close automatically after a short period of time. Pop-up ads are used as marketing tools designed to track users' online activity and then deliver targeted advertising based on their preferences.

### Mouse-trapping

'Mouse-trapping' is an aggressive marketing technique that forces users to remain on a specific website, sometimes while disabling their browser functions or flooding them with pop-up ads. Whenever the user tries to leave the site by using the 'back', 'forward' or 'close' buttons, a new window is automatically opened that prevents the browser from leaving the site. To exist the loop, the user is forced to end the task or reboot his computer. In United States, the defendants are barred from diverting or obstructing consumers on the Internet and from launching websites or web-pages that belonged to unrelated third parties.

### Linking and Framing

Linking technologies enable Internet users to access content stored in the files of millions of individual computers and enable users to use links to retrieve information from files on the same or other websites. However, linking can also raise concerns of trademark infringement if it explicitly or implicitly suggests an unwarranted association web page is affiliated, approved, or sponsored by the trademark owner.

Framing involves displaying another company's web page within a bordered area of website. Framing may trigger a dispute under copyright and trademark law theories because a framed site arguably alters the appearance of the content and creates the impression that its owner endorses or voluntarily chooses to associate with the framer. It raises concerns of trademark infringement because of its potential to mislead or confuse viewers as to the origin of the site and the goods and services it displays. In contrast to linking, users viewing framed material usually remain on the original site and view content from both sites, possibly without being aware that the material has been called up from another site, raising the potential from trademark liability.

## TERRITORIALITY

When a trademark is used on the Internet it is immediately visible to a global audience and may be considered to have global effect. This particular feature of the Internet makes it difficult for businesses to foresee in which countries their business activities might become legally relevant. Due to the particularities of Internet technology, it is often difficult to fit the 'use' of a trademark on the Internet into traditional legal concepts of use in the physical world.

In some countries, where trademark protection depends on prior use of the mark in that country, the question arises whether use on the Internet can satisfy such a use requirement and, if so, what kind of use qualify as 'genuine use.' This is important because, in most countries, a trademark registration is subject to cancellation if the trademark has not been used within a certain period of time. It seems that use of a trademark on the Internet may qualify as 'genuine use' for the purposes of use requirements. The trademark owner will have to show that its trademark was actually present in that market, for example by providing actual sales or other commercially motivated relationships with customers in a country.

The finding of an infringement over the Internet would require a 'link' between the uses of the sign on the Internet and the country in which the trademark enjoys protection. While factors for establishing such a link with a particular country need to be considered, different countries may adopt different standards. If available, remedies are generally limited to the territory for which the owner holds an exclusive right. If it were possible to agree on a set of criteria at the international level, it would be easier for businesses to foresee in which countries their activities on the Internet might become legally relevant. Meanwhile, the practice of placing a territorial disclaimer on the website could serve the purpose of avoiding litigation. These disclaimers can include statements to deny any relationship with the other trademark holder or it can deny the availability of services in a particular country.

Infringement of trademark on the Internet can be done in many ways. Past cases provide precedence for justice, but seeing the problem posed by the global nature of Internet technology suggests a reconsideration of policies.

## PATENTS

The patent system has also migrated to the Internet, as businesses have sought to recoup research and development costs in digital technologies by patenting their online business methods. Patents related to e-commerce have been granted to certain inventions concerning: (1) Financial services, (2) Electronic sales and advertising methods, (3) Business methods, including those involving processes to be performed on the Internet, and (4) Telephone exchange and billing methods. Every big industry is moving to use the Web. They all realized that they have to use patents as a defense mechanism and to boost their portfolio. However, the new technologies pose challenges to the conventional legal scheme for the patent system.

### Business Method Patents

In the past, patents were granted to industrial processes and products and the 'information innovations' were excluded from the purview of patent law. Business models, which are improved ways for calculating, organizing information and managing, were unpatentable in the past. However, in countries like the US, the viewpoint of legislature has changed in recent years, and now information innovations are patentable, provided they meet the requirements for patentability.

The Japanese Patent Office defines 'business method inventions' broadly as "inventions, which are concerned with methods or systems of doing business using computers or the Internet". In fact, the technology-intensive nature of e-commerce means that many of its constituent processes may be patentable subject matter so long as the legal criteria for patentability are met. Some controversy has developed over patents granted with respect to business methods, originally by the United States Patent

Office and increasingly in other jurisdictions such as Australia, Canada, Japan and South Korea. A case involving State Street Bank, raised awareness of the patentability of business methods, as the United States Courts of Appeals held that methods of doing business should be subject to the same legal requirements for patentability as applied to any other processes, that is, they should be new, useful and non-obvious. Patents have since been granted for electronic shopping carts, online credit card payment systems, and for a system to manage personal privacy in a computer network. The European Patent Office has taken a more restrictive approach, requiring that the subject matter of a patentable invention have a 'technical character' or involves 'technical teaching'. 'Business Method Patents' has already been referred to in Chapter 4.

**Prior Art Effect**

The process of granting patents is embroiled in debate. One of the issues being contested is the identification of prior art in electronic form. Patents are granted only to inventions that are novel, involve an inventive step and are useful or industrially applicable. To determine if the requirements of novelty and inventive step are met, the claimed invention is compared with the existing state-of-the-art. The existing state-of-the-art is sometimes referred to as the 'prior art'. Prior art in electronic form, which exists in cyber space only ('cyber art'), raises questions as to its availability as 'prior art' and, thus, whether it can be applied against an invention for which a patent is sought in determining novelty or inventive step. The questions include whether that kind of information has become 'prior art' even if it was disclosed on the Internet for only a limited period.

Although similar questions have been addressed with respect to prior art published on paper, publication on the Internet may have different implications. Authenticity, veracity and integrity are the critical issues for prior art in cyberspace, since cyber art is considered to be more vulnerable to alteration and modification. The determination of the timing of the disclosure and the accessibility of the cyber art to the public, given the network's capacity for instantaneous dissemination on the international scale, are other concerns. Furthermore, national laws may extend the concept of the prior art to include prior uses. Under such national laws, the concept of 'use' may be revisited in a computer environment. In addition, the above-mentioned questions are applicable in the context of a grace period for public disclosure of an invention before filing a patent application.

Some patent offices have established examination guidelines for computer-related inventions. However, there is a little international consensus in this area.

### Enforcement of Rights

As in other fields of intellectual property, jurisdictional questions and enforcement rights are also relevant to patent protection. The Internet raises complex issues in this regard, as patent protection is provided on a country-to-country basis, and the patent law of each country has application only within its borders. For example, where patented software is sold and delivered over the Internet internationally, any infringement action would require a consideration of the jurisdictional and choice of law issues. Moreover, the first practical issue may be that of detection, since unauthorized importation of such software by means of the Internet, unlike the importation of tangible goods, cannot be detected and stopped by customs authorities. Besides, the questions of infringement and jurisdiction would be more difficult where a patented invention involves activities in several countries by several individuals. In the normal course, a patent confers on its owner the right to prevent others from 'using' the patented product or process. But what constitutes 'using' a patented product or process is increasingly complicated in the case of Internet-related e-commerce patents.

This clearly indicates the need for international harmonization of the formal requirements concerning patent applications and patents. WIPO has been addressing a number of issues in this area. For example, the Standing Committee on the Law of Patents (SCP) studied the desirability and feasibility of harmonizing rules concerning the patent law implications of the disclosure of technical information on the Internet, such as its impact on patentability.

# GLOSSARY

## A

**Abandonment:** Allowing an application or patent to lapse by failure to take an action prescribed by law in order to maintain it, *e.g.*, filing some required documents or payment on a fee due within the prescribed period of time.

**Acceptance:** When official examination of a patent specification is successfully completed the application is 'accepted'. Then depending upon the practice in a country, the application is laid open for possible opposition by the third parties or the patent is granted.

**Amendment:** The term signifies any change in an application or patent. Usually the change will be either in the text of the claims or in the description. Generally, the amendment is carried out in response to objections from the patent office or from the third parties in opposition. An applicant or patentee in suitable circumstances amends the application or patent.

**Anticipation:** Unpatentability of the invention due to existence of prior art is called anticipation.

**Anton Piller Order:** It is a court order that provides for the right to search premises without prior warning. This is used in order to prevent the destruction of incriminating evidence, particularly in cases of alleged copyrights or patent infringements. It is used in British derived legal systems.

**Appeal:** Taking the case to the higher court to find out whether the judgment by lower court was correct.

**Appellant:** One who appeals to higher court.

**Appellate Board:** Higher authority or court.

**Appellations of Origin:** It is a sign used on products to indicate their specific quality that is entirely due to the geographical environment in which they are produced.

**Applicant:** The person in whose name the patent application is filed. On issue of the patent, the person becomes the patentee. The application can either be alone or jointly with other persons.

**ARIPO:** The African Regional Industrial Property Organization (ARIPO) is made up of contracting States of the Harare Protocol of 1882. It has 14 African States as members. This system is less centralized. One has to file the application with the industrial property office of one of the member countries of the Harare Protocol. The grant of patent is valid in all the States.

**Artistic Work:** Under copyright law, paintings, drawings, sculptures, products of artistic craftsmanship, architectural works of art and engravings are regarded as artistic works.

**Assignee:** Person to whom a patent right has been transferred by the patent owner is known as assignee. Person may include government and business entities.

**Assigner:** While transferring the legal rights in the intellectual property, the owner transferor is known as the assigner.

**Assignment:** The transfer of ownership from one party to another is called the assignment. The term can apply to the process of transferring rights and also to the document of transfer, *i.e.*, the assignment deed.

**Attorneys:** Counsellors at courts, who are officers of courts.

## B

**Bayh-Dole Act:** The Bayh-Dole Act or University and Small Business Patent Procedures Act is a piece of United States legislation from 1980. Among other things, it gave US universities, small businesses and non-profit organizations intellectual property control of their inventions that resulted from federal government-funded research. The Act, sponsored by two senators, Birch Bayh of Indiana and Robert Dole of Kansas, was enacted by the United States Congress on December 12, 1980. The Bayh-Dole Act is a significant 20th century piece of legislation in the field of intellectual property in the US. Perhaps the most important contribution of Bayh-Dole is that it reversed the presumption of title. Bayh-Dole permits a university, small business, or non-profit institution to elect to pursue ownership of an invention before the government.

**Benefit Sharing:** Fair and equitable sharing of the benefits arising out of the utilization of genetic resources, including by appropriate access to genetic resources and by appropriate transfer of relevant technologies, taking into account all rights over those resources and technologies, and by appropriate funding.

**Berne Convention:** The Berne Convention for the Protection of Literary and Artistic Works (1886) is the main international copyright treaty. The Convention sets out and defines minimum standards of protection of the economic and moral rights of authors of literary and artistic works. The Berne Convention establishes, amongst other things, the rule of "national treatment", meaning that in every country, foreign authors enjoy the same right as national authors. The Convention is currently in force in 162 countries. The Convention is administered by WIPO.

**Biopiracy:** The appropriation of the knowledge and genetic resources of farming and indigenous communities by individuals or institutions seeking exclusive monopoly control (usually patent or plant breeders' right) over these resources and knowledge is called biopiracy.

**Biotechnology:** Any technological application that uses biological systems, living organisms, or derivates thereof, to make or modify products or processes for specific purposes is known as biotechnology.

**Bolar Provision:** Some countries permit the manufacturers of generic pharmaceuticals to use the technology of a patented pharmaceutical to perform work that would assist in the marketing or regulatory approval of the generic product, while the patent is in force. This "Bolar" provision then allows the generic producer to market and manufacture their goods as soon as the patent expires. Bolar provision conforms to the TRIPS Agreement. This is also known as the 'Bolar exemption'. It is a policy that allows generic manufacturers to prepare production and regulatory procedures before patents expire, so that products are ready for sale as soon as the patent ends, rather than having to go through the lengthy preparatory process only after the patent period is over.

**Brand:** Although the term "brand" is sometimes used as a synonym for a "trademark", in commercial circles the term "brand" is frequently used in a much wider sense to refer to a combination of tangible and intangible elements, such as a trademark, design, logo and trade dress, and the concept, image and reputation which those elements transmit with respect to specified products and/or services.

**Broadcast:** Communication to the public by any means of wireless diffusion, whether in any one or more of the forms of signs, sounds or visual images or by wire including a re-broadcast.

**Brussels Convention:** Brussels Convention Relating to the Distribution of Programme-Carrying Signals Transmitted by Satellite provides for the obligation of each contracting State to take adequate measures to prevent the unauthorized distribution on or from its territory of any programme-carrying signal transmitted by satellite. The distribution is unauthorized if it has not been authorized by the organization—typically a broadcasting organization—which has decided what the programme consists of. The obligation exists in respect of organizations that are nationals of a contracting State.

**Budapest Treaty:** The Budapest Treaty on the International Recognition of the Deposit of Micro-organisms for the Purposes of Patent Procedure was brought into force in 1980. The Treaty provides that the Member's Countries should recognize for their own patent procedures a deposit made in a recognized depositary institution. The main feature of the Budapest Treaty is that a Contracting State, which allows or requires the deposit of micro-organisms for the purposes of patent procedure must recognize, for such purposes, the deposit of a micro-organism with any "international depositary authority", irrespective of whether such authority is on or outside the territory of the said State. This eliminates the need to deposit in each country in which protection is sought.

## C

**Cartagena Agreement:** The Cartagena Agreement Legislation on Industrial Property has been formulated for Latin American countries and is in force in Bolivia, Colombia, Equador, Peru, and Venezuela. It is in force since May 1987. The objective of the Agreement is to provide common treatment by member states to foreign capital, trademarks, patents, licensing agreements and royalties.

**Case Law:** Generally, the patent statutes describe in written form the principles of the patent law. At times principles are also derived from the decisions of courts of law in particular cases. These cases are called as case law.

**CASRIP:** The Centre for Advanced Study and Research on Intellectual Property (CASRIP) is a part of the School of Law, University of Washington, Seattle, USA.

**CBD:** Signed by 150 government leaders at the 1992 Rio Earth Summit, the Convention on Biological Diversity (CBD) is dedicated to promoting sustainable development. Conceived as a practical tool for translating the principles of Agenda 21 into reality, the Convention recognizes that biological diversity is about more than plants, animals and micro-organisms and their ecosystems—it is about people and our need for food security, medicines, fresh air and water, shelter, and a clean and healthy environment in which we live. Ratified by 187 countries, the Convention on Biological Diversity (CBD) represents the first united effort by governments to address the rate at which the world's natural resources are being degraded and destroyed. The objectives of the Convention are the conservation of biodiversity, the sustainable use of its components, and the fair and equitable sharing of benefits arising from the use of genetic resources. To promote the conservation of biological diversity, the sustainable use of its provisions on the respect and recognition of TK are a key element of the CBD.

**Certification Marks:** Certification marks are given for compliance with defined standards, but are not confined to any membership. They may be used by anyone whose products meet certain established standards.

**Claim:** The claims of an application or patent define the invention or the scope of protection sought or obtained. These form a part of the patent specification as a whole. Claims are process, product or other forms. Claim defines the monopoly claimed in the patent and is used to decide infringement. What is not claimed is open to others.

**Collective Mark:** Collective marks are owned by an association whose members use them to identify them with a level of quality and other requirements set by the association.

**Community Trademark:** A trademark registration granted by the European Community Trademark Office and enforceable throughout EC member nations.

**Compulsory Licence:** A licence to exploit a patented invention granted by the state upon request to a third party for instance in order to remedy an abuse of rights by the patentee.

**Complete Specification:** Generally follows the provisional specification. It is a detailed specification: disclosure of the invention, its novelty with respect to prior art, demonstration of the invention through worked examples, results, diagrams, etc. The invention must be within the scope of what is described in the provisional specification. Improvements or modifications devised in the course of developments of the invention can be included in the complete specification. In certain cases, the improvements or modifications developed during the course of research may be made the subject matter of separate applications accompanied by provisional specifications. If all such improvements or modifications collectively constitute 'one invention' the applicant may combine all of them under a single complete specification and obtain a single patent for them to avoid multiplicity of patents for protecting various improvements or modifications individually.

If the complete specification is not filed within the stipulated period after the provisional specification, the application will be treated as deemed to have been abandoned and no further action can be taken thereon by the patent office. The contents of such an abandoned application will never be published by the patent office and will, therefore, remain confidential.

**Computer Program:** Computer program is defined as a set of works expressed in words, codes, schemes or any other form including a machine-readable medium capable of causing computer to perform a particular task or achieve a particular result.

**Computer Software:** Computer software is a computer program which carries out certain logical operations (algorithm) not only to solve complex mathematical problems but also to do things swiftly which a human being may take long to do and may make mistakes in doing so (like train or air reservations) and run machines on command from the computer.

**Conception:** It means the mental act creating the invention and is established when the first documentary record is made of the idea, even before any laboratory experiments have been carried out.

**Concept Patent:** In some countries, even idea can be patented. It need not have gone to the completion stage. In such case one can get a provisional patent, the term of which expires after some time, by which time the inventor is supposed to develop the idea and may file a final patent. In this field, even hours matter.

**Contributory Infringement:** Indirect infringement of intellectual property rights in which one person contributes to the direct act of infringement of another. Contributory infringement of a trademark, for example, occurs when a manufacturer of goods aids or encourages its distributors to pass of its goods as those of another manufacturer.

**Convention Country:** The country, which gives the applicants of patents of a particular country similar privileges (for instance priority rights) as are granted to its own citizens in respect of grant of patents and the protection of patent rights is qualified to be declared as a convention country.

**Convention on Cybercrime:** Drafted by the Council of Europe, the Convention on Cybercrime (2001) sets out a common criminal policy aimed at the protection of society against cybercrime. It is the first international treaty on crimes committed via the Internet and other computer networks, dealing particularly with infringements of copyright, computer-related fraud, child pornography and violations of network security.

**Copyright:** It is a legal right, which gives the creators of a wide range of material, such as literature, art, music, sound recordings, films and broadcasts, economic rights enabling them to control the use of their material in a number of ways, such as by making copies, issuing copies to public, performing in public, broadcasting and use online. Copyright does not protect ideas or such things as names or titles.

**Copyright Directive:** The Copyright Directive (2001) of the European Community on the harmonization of certain aspects of copyright and related rights in the information society harmonizes rights in certain key areas, primarily to meet the challenge of the Internet and e-commerce, and digital technology in general. It also deals with exceptions to these rights and legal protection for technological aspects of rights management systems.

**Copyright Management System:** Digital technology that controls access to electronic information, in order to protect the intellectual property rights of content owners, is called copyright management system. A variety of electronic copyright management systems are being developed, including marking technologies—water-marking, fingerprinting, and data hiding— that ensure the user's legal authorization, serial copy management systems embedded in digital recorders that determine whether a digital audio-tape is copyright protected, and new secure marketing and distribution strategies.

**Counterfeiting:** The act of producing or selling a product containing an intentional and calculated reproduction of a genuine trademark. A 'counterfeit mark' is identical or substantially indistinguishable from a genuine mark. Often, counterfeit goods are made to imitate a popular product in construction and appearance so as to deceive customers into thinking that they are purchasing the genuine merchandise.

**Creativity:** Creativity is capacity to have new thoughts and to create new things, new expressions. It is about new ways of looking at problems. It ensures a better and more prosperous future for mankind. Our societies are based on creativity. Our existence is powered by creativity. The world is what it is today because people have been creative.

**Cross Licensing:** Mutual exchange of licences between patent holders is called cross licensing. In a case where the patent owner wishes to practice his own invention but cannot do so without infringing on the other's patent, the parties can enter into cross licensing. That means one agrees to license to practice ones invention provided the other party also does the same to the first party.

**Cyber squatting:** It refers to the unfair competition for websites. The typical cyber squatter is one who knowingly reserves with a registrar a domain name consisting of the trademark or name of a company for the purpose of selling the right to that domain name back to the legitimate owner.

## D

**Database:** Database is a collection of independent works, data or other materials arranged in a systematic or methodical way and capable of being individually accessed by electronic or other means. It also includes collection of literary, musical or audio-visual works or other materials such as texts, sounds, numbers, facts or data representing any other matter or substance. Databases may also contain collections of expressions of folklore. Any recording of an audio-visual, cinematography, literary or musical works as such are excluded from the definition of database.

**Date of Patent:** Date of filing the complete specification is called the date of patent.

**Defendant:** The person(s) being sued for infringement constitutes the 'defendant'.

**'Delta Period' Provision:** The term of utility patent, which was 17 years from the date of issue, is extended to 20 years from the earliest claimed US filing date. In reconnecting the possible extended life of patents that were in force specific provision has been made, referred to as 'delta period'.

**Dependent Claim:** A claim in a patent that refers back to a previous claim and defines an invention that is narrower in scope than that in the previous claim. A dependent claim is written so as to be more restricted than the technology defined in the previous claim.

**Derivative Work:** A work based upon one or more pre-existing works, such as a translation, musical arrangement, dramatization, etc., in which a work may be recast, transformed, or adapted. A work consisting of editorial revisions, annotations, elaborations, or other modifications, which, as a whole, represent an original work of authorship, is a derivative work.

**Descriptive Mark:** A word, picture, or other symbol that describes something about the goods or services in connection with which it is used, such as their purpose, their size and colour, the class of users, the end effect on users. A descriptive term is not considered to be inherently distinctive; to establish validity for registration or protection in court, it needs proof of acquired distinctiveness, known as 'secondary meaning'.

**Design:** An industrial design is the ornamental or aesthetic aspect of an article. A design refers to the appearance of the whole or a part of a product resulting from the features of, in particular, the lines, contours, colours, shape, texture and/or materials of the product itself and/or its ornamentation.

**Digital Agenda:** With the dramatic rise in Internet use, especially for e-commerce and information and knowledge exchange, the intellectual property system becomes crucial for the orderly development of the digital society. In turn, the Internet poses many opportunities as well as complex challenges for the intellectual property community. Under its Digital Agenda: Electronic Commerce—a work programme for the Organization over the coming years, WIPO is responding to the confluence of the Internet, digital technologies and the intellectual property system. The Organization is formulating, through international discussions and negotiations, appropriate responses that will encourage dissemination and use of intellectual property such as music, films, trade identifiers and knowledge on the Internet, as well as ensure protection of the rights of their creators and owners.

**Dilution:** A type of infringement of a trademark in which the defendant's use, while not causing likelihood of confusion, tarnishes the image or blurs the distinctiveness of the owner's mark.

**Disclosure of Origin:** Disclosure of origin is a requirement on patent applicants to disclose in patent applications the geographical origin of biological material on which the invention is based.

**Disclosure Requirement:** According to the national legislation of most of the countries, a patent application must disclose the invention in a manner sufficiently clear and complete for the invention to be carried out by a person skilled in the specific technical field.

**Discovery:** A discovery relates to things which already exist in the nature and should not belong to any particular individual whereas invention is man-made. A discovery can be as simple as the observation of a previously unnoticed phenomenon while an invention is a human-devised machine, tool, or apparatus that did not previously exist. Discoveries can only come from the greatest mind.

**Doctrine of Equivalents:** An accused product or process will infringe, though it is outside the literal terms of claims, if it does the same work in substantially the same way to accomplish substantially the same result as the patented product or process. Such cases are called limiting equivalents or doctrine of equivalents.

**Doctrine of Fair Use:** Fair use is a principle in copyright law, which allows people to freely use segments or parts copyrighted materials for purposes of commentary and criticism, etc.

**Doctrine of First Sale or Doctrine of Exhaustion:** It allows the purchaser of a legally acquired copy of a protected work to transfer it without the permission of the right holder—in other words, the rights of a copyright holder on that particular copy ends once the copy is sold.

**Doha Declaration:** Doha Declaration on TRIPS and Public Health was agreed at the Doha WTO Ministerial Meeting in 2001. It states that the TRIPS Agreement should be interpreted and implemented in a way that supports public health. It clarifies some flexibilities allowed by the Agreement for that purpose.

**Domain Name:** Internet domain names are the human-friendly forms of Internet addresses, and are commonly used to find websites. A domain name also forms the basis of other methods or applications on the Internet, such as file transfer or e-mail addresses.

## E

**EMR:** One of the provisions of TRIPS Agreement provides that where a Member does not make available on the date of entry into force of the WTO Agreement, namely 1st January 1995, patent protection for pharmaceutical and agricultural chemical products commensurate with its TRIPS obligations, that Member(s) would have to provide exclusive marketing rights (EMR) for five years to a company (mainly a foreign one) that brings a new product to market. However, a patent application should have filed in these countries after 1st January 1995, a patent should have been obtained from another country (which provides product patents in pharmaceuticals, chemicals or agricultural products) after 1st January 1995, and the product should have been registered after 1st January 1995 in the country which has to provide EMR.

**Encryption:** Encryption is a technology for IP protection. It ensures that unintended recipients do not understand the communication. Businesses that need confidentiality or want to restrict access to material, or consumers and citizens, who want to protect their privacy, also use this technology.

**EPC:** The European Patent Convention (EPC) came into force in 7th October 1977. European Patent Offices administer it. The advantage of filing applications under EPC is to reduce the cost of obtaining patent protection by avoiding separate filing, separate searching to determine the novelty of the invention and multiple examination of the application. Such a system makes the entire process simpler, cheaper and quicker.

**Equitable Benefit Sharing:** The idea of an equitable balancing of interests is common to many legal systems. In intellectual property law, this is often phrased in terms of a balancing of the interests of right holders and the general public. The fair and equitable sharing of benefits from the use of genetic resources is one of the objectives of the CBD, and the CBD also encourages equitable sharing of benefits from the use of certain forms of traditional knowledge (TK). Thus, the principle of equitable benefit sharing is found in a number of national laws governing access and use of TK, especially when TK is associated with genetic resources. According to this principle, the TK holders would receive an equitable share of the benefits that arise from the use of the TK, which may be expressed in terms of a compensatory payment, or other non-monetary benefits. An entitlement to equitable benefit sharing may be particularly appropriate in situations where exclusive property rights are considered inappropriate.

**Evergreening:** Evergreening is a strategy adopted by the original patent holder to protect his patent from being copied by others. It occurs when the brand-name manufacturer literally 'stockpiles' patent protection by obtaining separate 20-year patents on multiple attributes of single product. These patents can cover everything from the aspects of the manufacturing process to tablet colour, or even a chemical produced by the body when the drug is ingested and metabolized by the patent.

**Examiner:** An examiner is a patent office employee, who studies application to verify patentability.

**Examination:** A full examination of the patent application, undertaken by a patent examiner, to determine whether the application complies with all the legal requirements for patentability set out in the legislation. The examination takes into account any documents found during the search.

**Exclusive Licence:** The exclusive licence means permission granted to transferee exclusively and licencer has no authority to grant another permission to third person.

**Exhaustion of Rights:** It is a principle whereby the right holders' intellectual property rights in respect of a product are considered exhausted (*i.e.*, he no longer can exercise any rights) when that product has been put on the market by the intellectual property holder, or by an authorized party.

# F

**Fair Use or Fair Dealing:** It is an exception to copyright allowing third parties to use the copyrighted material in certain circumstances. National copyright laws in most countries incorporate exceptions for copying for personal use, research, education, archival copying, library use and news reporting, based on principles of 'fair dealing' or 'fair use'.

**Farmers' Rights:** Rights arising from the past, present and future contributions of farmers in conserving, improving, and making available plant genetic resources.

**Final Injection:** After the trial of the suit, the court to stop the 'defendant' from continuing the act(s) of infringement may pass orders, which is known as final injection.

**'First to Invent' Principle:** Unlike most other countries in the world, the US Patent Office awards a patent to the person, who is the 'first to invent'. In other words, in the US, the first person who conceived the invention, and successfully reduced it to practice, is awarded a patent not the first person to file a patent application on the invention. To benefit from this, inventors must keep sufficient corroborated records to establish a date of conception and reduction to practice.

**Folklore:** Folklore is an art form comprising various types of stories, proverbs, sayings, spells, songs, incantations, and other formulas, which employs spoken language as it medium.

**Foreign Patent:** A patent is enforceable only within the territories of the patent granting country. In order to get protection in a foreign country, individual patent in each foreign country is to be obtained. This is called a foreign patent.

# G

**GAAP Act:** The GAAP Act (The Greater Access to Affordable Pharmaceuticals Act) closes loopholes in the Drug Price Competition and Patent Restoration Act of 1984 (Hatch-Waxman Act) that have allowed brand name drug companies to keep generic drugs off the market.

**Generic Medicine or Drug:** A generic drug is the chemical equivalent of a patented drug.

**Generic Name:** A word used by most people to name a class or category of product or service, such as personal computer or cellular phone. No one may have trademark rights to a generic name.

**Genetic Material:** Any material of plant, animal, microbial or other origin containing functional units of heredity is called genetic material.

**Genetic Resources:** Genetic resources are genetic material of actual or potential value.

**Geneva Convention (Phonograms):** The Geneva Convention for the Protection of Producers of Phonograms against Unauthorized Duplication of their Phonograms was concluded in 1971. The Geneva Convention obliges each Contracting State to protect a producer of phonograms, who is a national of another Contracting State against the making of duplicates without the consent of the producer, against the importation of such duplicates, where the making or importation is for the purposes of distribution to the public, and against the distribution of such duplicates to the public.

**Geographical Indications:** A geographical indication is a sign used on goods that have a specific geographical origin and possesses qualities or reputation that is due to that place of origin.

**Goodwill:** The value of a business or of a line of goods and services, beyond its tangible assets, which reflects its commercial reputation. A business with a well established goodwill could have all its tangible assets destroyed yet still own its reputation—its goodwill. Since a trademark or service mark is the symbol of a business goodwill, trademark infringement is a form of theft of goodwill.

**Grace Period:** A grace period is a period of time immediately preceding the filing of a patent application during which certain types of public disclosure or use of one's invention will not destroy the possibility of protection. For example, disclosures made at officially recognized exhibitions or at scientific meetings and in learned society publications.

**Grant of Patent:** If a patent application is not opposed after advertisement in the Gazette within the prescribed period, the patent gets 'granted'. However, if there is opposition, the patent is granted to the applicant only if the decision is in his favour.

## H

**Hague Agreement:** The system of international registration of industrial designs is governed by the Hague Agreement Concerning the International Deposit of Industrial Designs which dates from 1925 and has been revised at various times, in particular in London (1934 Act) and the Hague (1960 Act). The Geneva Act of the Hague Agreement Concerning the International Registration of Industrial Designs was concluded in 1999. The Act is aimed at making the system more responsive to the needs of users and facilitating adherence by countries whose industrial designs systems do not permit them to accede to the 1960 Hague Act. The main advantage of the Agreement is that by a single international deposit of an industrial design, it can be protected in many member countries, thereby minimizing the cost of protection. In addition, data concerning international industrial design registrations is accessible on-line and may be searched by anybody free of charge.

**Hatch-Waxman Act:** It is one of the first legislative attempts by the US Congress to balance innovation, competition, and prescription drug affordability—the Drug Price Competition and Patent Restoration Act of 1984, often referred to as Hatch-Waxman or the Hatch-Waxman Act for its framers. The Act was designed to increase timely access to generic drugs while ensuring that drug manufacturers have adequate patent protection to justify their investment in research and development.

# I

**Idea:** Idea is starting point of all intellectual creations, the seeds from which all innovations and creative works grow. Ideas shape our world. They are the raw materials on which our future prosperity and heritage depend. From thoughts, which inspire the latest musical hits, to the genius which produces literary masterpieces grow from the seeds of ideas.

**IIPD:** The Institute of Intellectual Property Development (IIPD) aims at disseminating information on all matters connected with providing training in the field of intellectual property research and management, giving advice and assistance to people in management, education, business and any other profession related to intellectual property development. The leaders of industry and scientific establishment actively support this IPR Institute.

**Importation:** When a product is imported into the country for which a patent (product or process) has been granted in the country. For example, if a patent is granted in India for a product or a process to manufacture the product and if the same product is imported into India, it would be importation. Importation would not be considered as having 'worked' the patent in India.

**Industrial Property:** Intellectual property is usually divided into two broad areas, namely industrial property and copyright. Industrial property consists mainly of patents, industrial designs, and trademarks.

**Industrial Property Licence:** The industrial property licence is a permission granted to do certain acts covered by the exclusive rights conferred by the law as regards a patent, an industrial design, a utility model, a plant variety, a trademark or a service mark.

**Infringement:** Infringement is unauthorized making, using or selling of anything protected by claims of a valid patent.

**Innovation:** Innovation is a process, which begins from the conception of an idea to the launching of a new or improved product/process in the market place.

**Innovation Patent:** The introduction of new second-tier patent protection right to be known as an 'innovation patent' replacing the existing petty patent system and intended to provide accelerated rights for incremental or lower level inventors at a lower cost than is available under the existing petty or standard patent systems has been agreed by the Australian government. It is proposed to grant innovation patent following simple formalities check.

**Intellectual Property:** In simple terms intellectual property is creation of human intellect, which has some commercial potential. It is the original creative works that have economic value and which results from human ingenuity, creativity and inventiveness. It is owned by an individual or an organization, which can then choose to share it freely or to control its use in certain ways.

**Intellectual Property Rights:** The rights, which protect intellectual creations through a system of national and international rules, are called intellectual property rights. Intellectual property rights aim at protecting the creative, insightful, unique and inventive creations of the human mind. It is a general term covering patents, copyrights, trademarks, industrial designs, geographical indications, layout designs of integrated circuits, and protection of undisclosed information.

**Interlocutory Injection:** As a part of an infringement proceeding the plaintiff may pray for 'interim relief' to restrain the defendant from continuing the act of infringement till the case is completely heard and disposed of. This is called an interlocutory injection.

**Invention:** A new and useful article, method or substance produced by manufacture. Inventions in the context of patents are successful solutions to technical problems.

**Inventive Step:** It is that feature of the invention, which relates to a solution of a problem, which has eluded earlier attempts. Earlier work may have suggested directions, but the present work has transcended the idea stage and the solution is arrived at through extensive experimentation, the results of which lead to the solution to the problem.

**Inventor:** Inventor is a person who first made the invention and applied for the patent. The inventor for the purposes of the patent law is the actual deviser of what is being claimed. Frequently, there may be more than one inventor because two or more persons may have been involved to arrive at the conception or realization of the final process or product. This does not mean that every person who has worked on the project is to be named as co-inventor. The co-inventorship should be restricted to those, who have made key contributions either in the research strategy or in the actual experimental invention. Those who have merely carried out experiments under the complete directions of others should not be included.

## J

**Jurisdiction:** Administration of justice or extent of authority over territory is called jurisdiction.

## K

**Knock Off:** An identical copy of a work or product that is protected by patent, trademark, trade dress or copyright is known as knock off.

**Know-how:** Know-how is practical information that may give a person or company a competitive advantage. Know-how covers every information that is necessary to set up a production plant or to commercialize the invention. Such information includes, for example, minute details (such as optimum conditions) of the production methods applicable to the invention or, in the case of mechanical inventions, the details of the engineering designs, drawings, etc. It is this know-how, which is traded while transferring technology from a laboratory to an enterprise or from an enterprise to another. Know-how is usually kept commercially confidential and separately disclosed only under the terms of licensing agreement executed between the seller and the buyer of the technology. It is this know-how, which imparts commercial value to an invention disclosed in a patent.

## L

**Lapsed Patent:** A patent is considered 'lapsed' when the renewal fee is not paid within the prescribed time.

**Licence:** It is a legal permit given by a patentee to other(s) to make, use or exercise the invention. The legal document needs to be registered with the patent office.

**Licence of Right:** A patent may be endorsed with the words 'licence of right' three years after it is sealed. In such cases any person may obtain, as a matter of right, a licence without having to establish a case for compulsory licence.

**Lisbon Agreement:** The Lisbon Agreement for the Protection of Appellations of Origin and their International Registration was concluded in 1958. The aim of the Agreement is to provide for the protection of appellations of origin, that is, the "geographical name of a country, region, or locality, which serves to designate a product originating therein, the quality and characteristics of which are due exclusively or essentially to the geographic environment, including natural and human factors".

**Locarno Agreement:** The Locarno Agreement Establishing an International Classification for Industrial Designs concluded in 1968 establishes an international classification for industrial designs, referred to as the Locarno Classification. The Locarno Classification has been revised several times by the Committee of Experts. The present (eighth) edition of the Classification incorporates all the revisions made in and before November 2002. In this most recent edition, the list of classes and subclasses consist of 32 classes and 223 subclasses. The alphabetical list of goods, which contains 6,831 entries, is presented in two parts: the first part lists all the goods in a single alphabetical list, irrespective of the class to which each of them belongs; the second part lists, separately for each subclass, in alphabetical order, the goods that belong to that subclass. The explanatory notes are incorporated in the list of classes and subclasses.

**Logo:** Logo is a graphic representation or symbol of a company name or trademark, usually designed for ready recognition. The term has no legal significance in the law of trademark.

## M

**Madrid Agreement and Madrid Protocol:** The Madrid System for the International Registration of Marks allows registration of trade and service marks with effect for several countries through a single international registration procedure administered by WIPO. In addition, data concerning international trademark registrations is accessible on-line and may be searched by anybody free of charge. The Madrid System for the International Registration of Marks (the Madrid System) is governed by two treaties: the Madrid Agreement Concerning the International Registration of Marks (Madrid Agreement) and the Protocol Relating to the Madrid Agreement Concerning the International Registration of Marks (Madrid Protocol). The Madrid Agreement was concluded in 1891, and the Madrid Protocol was concluded in 1989 in order to introduce certain new features into the Madrid System. These address the difficulties that prevent certain countries from adhering to the Madrid Agreement by rendering the system more flexible and more compatible with the domestic legislation of these countries.

**Madrid Agreement (Indications of Source):** The Madrid Agreement for the Repression of False or Deceptive Indications of Source on Goods was concluded in 1891. Under the Agreement, all goods bearing a false or deceptive indication of source, by which one of the Contracting States, or a place situated therein, is directly or indirectly indicated as being the country or place of origin, must be seized on importation, or such importation must be prohibited, or other actions and sanctions must be applied in connection with such importation.

**'Mail Box' Provision:** One of the provisions of TRIPS Agreement provides that where a Member does not make available on the date of entry into force of the WTO Agreement, namely, 1st January 1995, patent protection for pharmaceutical and agricultural chemical products commensurate with its TRIPS obligations, that Member(s) shall: "Notwithstanding the provisions of Part 17 (Transitional Arrangements) provide as from the date of entry into force of the Agreement establishing the WTO a means by which applications for patents for such inventions can be filed." That is those countries are obliged to accept patent applications in these areas from above-mentioned date. Such provision of the Agreement is called 'Mail Box' provision.

**Misappropriation:** Misappropriation is a common law form of unfair competition in which an individual or firm copies or appropriates some creation of another that is not protected by patent, copyright or trademark law or any other traditional theory of exclusive rights.

**Moral Rights:** Moral right is the right of the author to be credited as the author of a particular work and also the right to object to derogatory treatment of that work.

**Mosaicing of Publications:** An invention may be a judicious combination of various components or features, where each of the aspects is probably known. Mosaicing is a process by which an attempt is made to combine bits and pieces of the information from diverse sources to show that the alleged invention in a patent is not novel but is obvious to any unimaginative person.

**Most-Favoured-Nation Treatment:** The Most-Favoured-Nation (MFN) treatment principle prevents a Member from discriminating with regard to intellectual property among national of other Members. Thus, Article 4 of the TRIPS Agreement stipulates that a Member, which has granted any advantage, favour, privilege or immunity to the national of any other country, shall accord the same to the nationals of all Members, immediately and unconditionally. Certain specific exemptions from this obligation are set out in Article 4.

# N

**Nairobi Treaty:** The Nairobi Treaty on the Protection of the Olympic symbol was concluded in 1981. All Contracting States are obliged to protect the Olympic symbol (the five interlaced rings) against use for commercial purposes (in advertisements, on goods, as a mark, etc.) without the authorization of the International Olympic Committee.

**National Treatment:** Article 3 of the TRIPS Agreement requires each Member to "accord to the nationals of other Members treatment no less favourable than that it accords to its own national with regard the protection intellectual property". This treatment is called the principle of 'national treatment'.

**Nice Agreement:** The Nice Agreement Concerning the International Classification of Goods and Services for the Purposes of the Registration of Marks was concluded in 1957. The Nice Agreement establishes a classification of goods and services for the purposes of registering trademarks and service marks. The classification consists of a list of classes (based on types of products and services) of which there are 34 for goods and 11 for services and an alphabetical list of the goods and services.

**Non-exclusive Licence:** In the case of non-exclusive licence, the licencer retains the authority to grant permission to persons other than the first licencee.

**Non-obviousness Requirement:** An invention is considered to involve an inventive step (or to be non-obvious) when, taking into account the prior art, the invention would not have been obvious to a person skilled in the particular field of technology.

**Novelty Requirement:** An invention is new or novel if it does not form part of the 'prior art'. In general, prior art refers to all the relevant technical knowledge available to the public anywhere in the world prior to the first filing date of the relevant patent application. It includes, *inter alia*, patents, patent applications and non-patent literature of all kinds.

## O

**OAPI:** The African Regional Industrial Property Convention (OAPI) is based on the so-called Bangui Agreement, in which 14 African States, as members, created a common patent office. On filing an application a certificate is issued. If all the formal requirements are met and the invention disclosed is patentable, a patent will be granted which will cover all the 14-member countries.

**Obviousness:** Obviousness is a condition in which an invention cannot receive a valid patent because a person with ordinary skill in that technology can readily deduce it from publicly available information, *i.e.*, prior art.

**Off-patents:** These are the patents which have expired their terms and are open to be freely used by the public.

**Opposition:** After a patent application is examined by the Patent Office it is accepted if the Controller is satisfied that it has cleared all the tests of patentability under the Act. This is published and is open to 'interested persons' to challenge its grant. The opposition proceedings that may follow are held in the Patent Office by the Controller.

**Originality:** To obtain copyright, the work must be an independent creation, *i.e.*, it should not have been copied. This is called originality in the context of copyright.

## P

**Para IV Filing:** Para IV filing is one of the strategies that a generic drug manufacturer can employ to enter the US drug market. It means finding a flaw in an existing patent and making a filing under the Hatch-Waxman Act in the US to challenge the patent holder. Litigation is an inevitable part of making Para IV filing against the existing patent holder. On the basis of loopholes, the firm finds the patents, which are listed out in "Approved Drug Products" with Therapeutic Equivalent Evaluation, popularly known as the "Orange Book". A generic company is granted six months exclusivity to sell its version of a patented drug in the US if it defeats an original drug patent holder.

**Parallel Import:** Parallel imports occur when the actual goods that have been bought are resold in a jurisdiction other than that where the original product was sold.

**Paris Convention:** The Paris Convention for the Protection of Industrial Property applies to industrial property in the widest sense, including patents, marks, industrial designs, utility models (a kind of "small patent" provided for by the laws of some countries), trade names (designations under which an industrial or commercial activity is carried on), geographical indications (indications of source and appellations of origin), and the repression of unfair competition. The Convention signed originally by 11 countries in Paris on 20th March 1883. The Paris Convention for the Protection of Industrial Property is one of the pillars of the international intellectual property system.

**Passing Off:** Passing off is the use of trademark/trade name or other distinctive features attached to trade, which has acquired a distinctive identifiability. Passing off, traditionally a part of the trademark law, also finds applications in other branches wholly unconcern with trademark. Passing off occurs when there is a prospect of confusion of identity through the unauthorized use of similar marks or get-up, and such use damages, or is likely to damage, the goodwill and reputation of a business. It is a trademark infringement in which there is no proof of intent to deceive but likelihood of confusion can be proven.

**Patent:** Patent is an exclusive right granted by the State for an invention that is new, involves an inventive step and is capable of industrial application.

**Patent Agents:** Patent agents need certain qualifications to practise. They have to clear the examination for patent agents, which are conducted by the Patent Office.

**Patent Application:** Papers filed in the patent office requesting the grant of a patent is known as patent application. It includes a patent specification providing the full description of the patent and the claims and the prescribed fees. Before one gets a patent, a patent application is to be filed with the patent office, if the application is approved then a patent is issued. Sometimes the terms applications or specification are used synonymously.

**Patentee:** A patentee is the person for the time being entered in the Register of Patents maintained at the patent office and is the grantee or proprietor (by assignment) of the patent.

**Patent Information:** It relates to information concerning patented invention disclosed in a patent document.

**Patent Infringement:** Any unauthorized making, using, offering for sale or selling of a patented invention is called patent infringement.

**Patent Pending:** The status of a patent application after it has been received by patent office and acknowledged.

**Patent Rights:** Patent rights are granted by the State in consideration of the public disclosure of a new invention. The rights secured by patents can be utilized both as instruments of aggression to break open monopolies and as instruments of defense of monopoly privileges.

**Patent Search:** A search or study of patent material, generally, to obtain information concerning the existing development in a particular scientific or technological area: to check for prior development that might anticipate a prospective patent application or to make other uses of the technical information contained therein.

**Patent Specification:** An application for patent is accompanied with a patent specification. The patent specification is a key document in which the details of the invention to be protected are disclosed. The patent specification is a legal as well as scientific document susceptible to interpretation by courts of law. Therefore, disclosure in the specification should be made diligently. The specification can be either a provisional or complete specification.

**PCT:** The Patent Co-operation Treaty (PCT) was concluded in 1970. The PCT makes it possible to seek patent protection for an invention simultaneously in each of a large number of countries by filing an "international" patent application. Such an application may be filed by anyone, who is a national or resident of a Contracting State. The Treaty regulates the formal requirements with which any international application must comply. The most successful and widely used of treaties is the Patent Co-operation Treaty, which implements the concept of a single international patent application which has legal effect in the countries which are bound by the treaty and which are designated by the applicant. Once such an application is filed, an applicant receives valuable information about the potential patentability of his invention (through the international search report and the optional international preliminary examination report) and has more time than under the traditional patent system to decide in which of the designated countries to continue with the application. Thus, the PCT system consolidates and streamlines patenting procedures and reduces costs, providing applicants with a solid basis for important decision-making.

**Performance:** Performance is to recite, render, play, dance, or act a copyrighted work, including the radio or television broadcast of a performance and the reception of such broadcast. The right to perform a copyrighted work publicly is granted to all types of copyrighted works except for pictorial and sculptural works and sound recordings.

**Person Interested:** It includes a person engaged in, or in promoting, research in the same field as that to which the invention relates.

**'Person Skilled in the Art':** Most of the patent laws throughout the world provide that an invention shall be taken to involve an inventive step if it is not obvious to a 'person skilled in the art'. The relevant person (the man skilled in the art) must have skill in the art with which the invention described in the patent concerned. In some cases, the patent may include within it information derived from utilizing more than one aspect of science and technology and in such cases the notional skilled addressee, the person skilled in the art, will consist of a combination of scientists or technicians having those skills. Each case will depend upon the description in the patent.

**Petty Patents:** Petty patents or utility models often cover only mechanical inventions and differ from patents in that, a utility model application is not examined in regard to substance or non-obviousness (or inventive step) and the duration of protection is shorter. This system is an inexpensive and rapid supplement to a patent system, as well as means of removing lesser inventions from the patent system thereby revising the quality of the patents that are issued. Many countries including Japan, Italy, Philippines, Germany, Portugal and Spain have introduced legislation for grant of utility models.

**Phonograms Convention**
*See* **Geneva Convention (Phonograms)**

**Phonorecord:** Phonorecord is the material object that stores or fixes copyrightable sounds, such as audio-tapes, compact discs, computer chips that store sounds, and the likes, other than the sound track of a motion picture.

**PIC:** The Prior Informed Consent (PIC) is the consent given by a party to an activity after being fully informed of all material facts relating to that activity. The CBD requires that access to genetic resources shall be subject to the prior informed consent of the country providing the resources. According to the principle of prior informed consent (PIC), traditional knowledge (TK) holders should be fully consulted before their knowledge is accessed or used by third parties and an agreement should be reached on appropriate terms; they should also be fully informed about the consequences of the intended use. The agreed scope of use may be set out in contracts, licences or agreements, which would also specify how benefits arising from the use of the TK should be shared. The principle of PIC concerning access to genetic resources is one of the cornerstones of the CBD. Given the close relationship between genetic resources and some forms of TK, this same principle is also used in a number of national laws concerning access to and use of TK.

**Pipeline Protection:** With regard to pharmaceutical and agricultural chemical products, the TRIPS Agreement effectively provides for pipeline protection. Pipeline protection is given to those patents for which an application is pending in one member country and for which patent has been granted in another member country and marketing approval is obtained in the latter country.

**Plaintiff:** The patentee or his assignee can file a suit in the High Court for infringement of his patent. They constitute the 'plaintiff'.

**Plant Breeders' Rights:** Rights granted to breeders of new, distinct, uniform and stable plant varieties. They normally offer protection for at least twenty years. Most countries have exceptions for farmers to save and replant seeds on their holdings, and for further research and breeding.

**Plant Patent:** A distinct, new and unobvious variety of plant, including mutants, hybrids and newly-found seedlings, other than tuber—propagated plant or a plant found in an uncultivated state, is patentable in USA. US companies have made sweeping claims of ownership of all varieties of transgenic plants like cotton, soyabean and brassica family.

**PLT:** An international harmonization treaty on patent formalities, the Patent Law Treaty (PLT) was adopted in June 2000, to standardize divergent formal requirements applied in national and regional patent systems to patent applications and patents. Users of the patent system will thus be able to rely upon predictable and simple procedures for filing national and regional patent applications and for the maintaining of patents in all contracting parties. The PLT entered into force on April 28, 2005.

**Prior Art:** The availability of the knowledge at the time of patenting is called 'prior art'. It is the background of the invention and earlier descriptions in the scientific literature. This describes, in the form of a brief write-up, what is described or known before the invention. This refers to anything known in the public domain. This could be in the form of lectures, broadcasts, newspapers, reports, books, patent specifications, etc. Even public use is considered to be prior art. This is very important while determining the novelty of the invention.

**Priority:** When a patent application is filed at the patent office it gets a priority as of that date. Convention countries can claim the priority of the first filing of the patent in any of the member countries within 12 months. In all countries except the USA 'first to file' gets the priority.

**Priority Date:** The date from which a claim is applicable. In India, the date of filing the complete specification is the priority date. In countries like USA, the priority date is the date of the first conception of the invention.

**Product Claims:** There are two main types of product claims, the product *per se* claim and the product-by process claim. A *per se* claim is one that extends to the substance or micro-organism as such and is independent of any defined process of preparation or derivation. This is also referred to as the absolute product protection. A product-by process claim, on the other hand, defines a substance in terms of some particular method of production. Hence, it is more limited in scope as compared with the *per se* claim and is avoided by the choice of method or route to the procurement of the product different from that defined in the claim.

**Provisional Specification:** A patent application is filed to obtain priority. The applicant is expected to disclose the essential features with a description of the invention, its field of application and usefulness. A provisional specification discloses the nature of the invention and helps to establish the identity of the invention and registers the earliest authorship of an invention in the patent office, on first-come-first-served basis. It is a document of record and no amendment by addition of a new matter will be allowed. Although, a patent application accompanied with provisional specification does not confer any legal patent rights to the applicants, it is, however, a very important document as it establishes the earlier ownership of an invention by inventor's *vis-à-vis* later inventions on the same subject.

**Publication:** Publication refers to making a work available to the public by issuing of copies or by communicating the work to the public.

**Public Domain:** Public domain is the status of an invention, creative work, commercial symbol, or any other creation that is not protected by some form of intellectual property. Items that have been determined to be in the public domain are available for copying and use by anyone. The copying of such items is not only tolerated but also encouraged.

**Public Use:** A public use occurs when an invention is not prevented from observing the use. There are various exceptions and conditions pertaining to the prior public use.

## R

**Register of Patents:** This is a register maintained by the patent office. It has records of names, addresses, the invention, number of the patent, date of sealing, all details of assignments, transmission amendments, revocations, licences, and all other information on the propriety/validity of the patent.

**Register of Trademarks:** The Register of Trademarks is a record, which is maintained as a statutory requirement of the Trademark Registry. It contains the prescribed particulars of all registered trademarks including the name and addresses of their proprietors and their registered users, if any. Assignments and transmissions, disclaimers, conditions or limitations are also entered the register.

**Rental Rights:** According to TRIPS Agreement, in respect of at least computer programs and cinematographic works, a Member shall provide authors and their successors in title the right to authorize or to prohibit the commercial rental to the public of originals or copies of their copyright works. A Member shall be excepted from this obligation in respect of cinematographic works unless such rental has led to widespread copying of such works which is materially impairing the exclusive right of reproduction conferred in that Member on authors and their successors in title. In respect of computer programs, this obligation does not apply to rentals where the program itself is not the essential object of the rental.

**Reverse Doctrine of Equivalents:** Even where an accused product falls within the literal terms of a patent, if the accused product is so far changed in principle from the patented product, that it performs the same function in a substantially different way, infringement liability is unwarranted. Such cases fall under non-limiting equivalent or reverse doctrine of equivalents.

**Reverse Engineering:** It is the process of evaluating something to understand how it works in order to duplicate or enhance it. Particularly relevant in the copyright field where reverse engineering of software may be necessary to ensure interoperability with other programs. It is also relevant, for example, to semi-conductors and the production of generic medicines.

**Revocation:** A patent is granted by the Patent Office after examining it within the framework of the Patents Act. This, however, does not guarantee the validity of a patent. Its validity can be challenged under prescribed grounds. If the challenge is upheld in the High Court the patent becomes 'invalid' and is 'revoked'. The entire process is called revocation.

**Right of Publicity:** It is the inherent right of every human being to control the commercial use of his or her identity.

**Rights Management Information:** Rights management information means information, which identifies the work, the author and the owner of the work, or information about the terms and conditions for the use of the work. Such information may be attached to the copyrighted works electronically.

**Rome Convention:** The Rome Convention for the Protection of Performers, Producers of Phonograms and Broadcasting

Organizations, concluded in 1961, secure protection of performers on their performances, phonograms of producers of phonograms and broadcasts of broadcasting organizations. The Convention's membership is currently signed by 83 countries.

**Royalty:** The payment received by the licence seller of a patent from licence buyer is usually termed as a royalty. There are various ways in which the royalties may get paid, for example, as a lump sum payment, as a percentage of profit, as a percentage of sales volume, based on the number of un-expired patents covered by the licence, a minimum royalty or maximum royalty.

## S

**'Safe Harbour' Provisions:** The term of utility patent, which was 17 years from the date of issue, is extended to 20 years from the earliest claimed US filing date. In reconnecting the possible extended life of patents that were in force specific provision has been made, referred to as 'delta period'. Similarly, some adjustments were provided for the statutory patent infringement remedies on payment of an equitable remuneration to the patentee, often called the 'safe harbour' provision.

**Satellites Convention (Brussels):** The Convention Relating to the Distribution of Programme-carrying Signals Transmitted by Satellite, concluded in 1974, provides for the obligation of each Contracting State to take adequate measures to prevent the unauthorized distribution on or from its territory of any programme-carrying signal transmitted by satellite. The obligation exists in respect of organizations that are nationals of a Contracting State. The provisions of this Convention are not applicable, however, where the distribution of signals is made from a direct broadcasting satellite.

**Sealing of Patent:** This follows the grant of a patent. The patent is considered sealed when its details are entered in the Register of Patents administered by the Patent Office.

**Search:** A search of the prior art by a patent examiner, which brings to the patent applicant's attention documents which are thought by the patent examiner to establish whether the invention in the patent application is novel and inventive.

Primary search material is the disclosures in other patent applications, but all forms of prior art in principle should be covered.

**Service Mark:** A service mark is very similar in nature to a trademark. Both are distinctive signs; trademarks distinguish the goods of one enterprise from those of others, while service marks fulfill the same function in relation to services.

**Sound Recording:** Sound recording is a category of copyrightable work consisting of the sounds that are recorded on a phonorecord.

**State-of-the-Art:** The 'State-of-the-Art' comprises any information/ knowledge existing on a subject in the patent literature, academic literature or trade literature.

**Strasbourg Agreement:** The Strasbourg Agreement Concerning the International Patent Classification was concluded in 1971 and establishes the International Patent Classification (IPC). The International Patent Classification divides technology into eight sections with approximately 70,000 sub-divisions. Each sub-division has a symbol, which is allotted, by the national or regional industrial property office that publishes the patent document.

**Substantial Similarity:** Substantial similarity refers to the degree of resemblance between a copyrighted work and a second work that is sufficient to constitute copyright infringement by the second work. Exact word-for-word or line-for-line identity is not necessary for copyright infringement. Rather, US courts have chosen the phrase "substantial similarity" to define the level of similarity that, together with proof of validity and copying, constitutes infringement.

**Suggestive Marks:** Suggestive mark is a word, picture, or some other symbol that suggests, but does not directly describe, something about a good or service in connection with which it is used as a mark.

***Sui generis* Intellectual Property Rights:** There are specialized varieties of so-called *sui generis* intellectual property rights, such as circuit design rights (called mask work rights in USA law, protected under the Integrated Circuit Topography Act in

Canadian law, and in European Community Law by Directive 87/54/EEC of 16th December 1986 on the legal protection of topographies of semi-conductor products), plant breeders' rights, plant variety rights, industrial design rights, supplementary protection certificates for pharmaceutical products and database rights (in European law).

**Surrogate Patent:** EMR is often called surrogate patent, because once a company gets an EMR, no one else can sell the product.

**Swiss Claims:** There are many substances or chemical compositions that have more than one therapeutic effect or medical use. Where subsequent research brings forth the 'second medical use' that was not anticipated, such 'second medical use' of the substance already known to have a medical use is also protected in several national jurisdictions. Such types of claims are known as 'Swiss claims'. Swiss claims can be defined as 'the claim for the use of a substance or composition that has already been used for medical purpose for a 'specified new medical purpose'."

# T

**Technical Information:** Technical information means all the physical matter in the form of drawings, blue prints, diagrams, catalogues, specifications, instructions and lists with respect to the application, design, operation or maintenance of facilities utilizing the said process.

**Technological Protection:** Technological protection refers to ways of introducing by technological means defenses against copying or unauthorized use. The most common examples are forms of encryption in the digital media, and introducing characteristics into plants that make harvested seeds less productive, or possibly sterile.

**Technology:** The technology means the systematic knowledge essentially required for the manufacture of a patent.

**Term of a Patent:** It is a period for which patent is 'entitled to be enforce' provided the renewal fees are paid within a prescribed time.

**TKDL:** The Traditional Knowledge Digital Library (TKDL) project, is an initiative of several Indian Government agencies, proposes to document the disclosed traditional medicinal knowledge available in public domain by sifting and collating information on TK from the existing disclosed literature covering Ayurveda. The TKDL compiles the information in digitized format in five international languages, which are English, German, French, Japanese and Spanish. An inter-disciplinary team of Ayurveda experts, a patent examiner, information technology experts, scientists and technical officers has worked for one and a half years for creating the TKDL of Ayurveda. TKDL seeks to give recognition and legitimacy to the existing TK and enable protection of such information from getting patented.

**TKRC:** Traditional Knowledge Resource Classification (TKRC) is an innovative structured classification system for the purpose of systematic arrangement, dissemination and retrieval. This has been developed for about 5,000 sub-groups against one group in international patent classification, *i.e.*, AK61K35/78 related to medicinal plants.

**Trade Dress:** Trade dress refers to characteristics of the visual appearance of a product or its packaging (or even the facade of a building such as a restaurant) that may be registered and protected from being used by competitors in the manner of a trademark. It is also called as product personality.

**Trademark:** A trademark is a sign capable of distinguishing the goods or services produced or provided by one enterprise from those of other enterprises.

**Trade Name:** Trade names or commercial names and designations are those that identify an enterprise.

**Trademark Law Treaty (TLT):** The Trademark Law Treaty (TLT) was concluded in 1994 and aims to approximate and streamline national and regional trademark registration procedures through the simplification and harmonization of certain features of those procedures, thus making trademark applications and the administration of trademark registrations in multiple jurisdictions less complex and more predictable.

**Trade Secret:** A trade secret is information of any type that is actually or potentially valuable to its owner and not generally known or readily ascertainable by the public, and which the owner has made a reasonable effort to keep secret.

**Traditional Knowledge:** Traditional knowledge (TK), indigenous knowledge (IK), and local knowledge generally refer to the matured long-standing traditions and practices of certain regional, indigenous, or local communities. Traditional knowledge also encompasses the wisdom, knowledge, and teachings of these communities.

**Transitional Arrangement:** The TRIPS Agreement provides that no Member would be obliged to apply the provisions of the Agreement before expiry of a period of one year following the entry into force of the Agreement establishing the WTO on 1st January 1995. Additional delays for the date of application of the provisions of the Agreement are permitted for developing and least-developed country Members. Such provision of the agreement is called the 'transitional agreement'.

**TRIPS Agreement:** The Agreement on Trade-related Aspects of Intellectual Property Rights (The TRIPS Agreement) aims at harmonizing international trade hand in hand with effective and adequate protection of intellectual property rights. The TRIPS Agreement was drafted to ensure the provision of proper standards and principles concerning the availability, scope and use of Trade-related Aspects of Intellectual Property Rights. At the same time, the Agreement provides means for the enforcement of such rights. The TRIPS Agreement is binding on all 149 members of the World Trade Organization. Under the TRIPS provisions, countries can adopt a variety of measures in formulating their legislation in accordance with the objectives and principles laid down in the Agreement.

## U

**Unfair Competition:** Unfair competition is a commercial conduct that the law views as unjust, giving a civil claim against a person, who has been injured by the conduct. Trademark infringement has long been considered to be unfair competition. Other recognized legal categories of unfair competition are false advertising, trade libel, infringement of a trade secret, infringement of the right of publicity, and misappropriation.

**Universal Copyright Convention:** International protection to literary and artistic works is regulated by two conventions, namely Berne Convention (1886) and Universal Copyright Convention (1952). UNESCO administers the Copyright Convention.

**Uruguay Round Negotiations:** In 1986 the Uruguay Round of Multilateral Trade Negotiations commenced. In the negotiations, for the first time, included not only the traditional goods sector but also three new areas, namely, investment, intellectual property rights (IPR) and services.

**Utility Requirement:** To be patentable, an invention must be capable of being used for an industrial or business purpose. An invention cannot be a mere theoretical phenomenon; it must be useful and provide some practical benefit. The term "industrial" is meant here in the broadest sense as anything distinct from purely intellectual or aesthetic activity, and includes, for example, agriculture. In some countries, instead of industrial applicability, the criterion is utility.

## V

**Vendible Product:** Vendible product as a result of manufacture implies trading or industrial character of the processes, which are intended to be comprehended.

**Vienna Agreement:** The Vienna Agreement Establishing an International Classification of the Figurative Elements of Marks was signed on 12th June 1973. The members of the Agreement have formed a special union and adopted a common classification for the figurative elements of marks. The classification has no effect in respect to the extent of protection afforded to the mark. The classification comprises 29 categories, 144 divisions and some 1,887 sections in which the figurative elements of marks are classified.

## W

**Watermarking:** It is a technology of IP protection. Watermarking is the process of modifying image data for inserting codes for carrying information.

**WCT:** The WIPO Copyright Treaty (WCT) was concluded in 1996. It extends copyright protection to two additional subject matters: (i) Computer programs, and (ii) Compilations of data or other material (databases) in any form, which by reason of the selection or arrangement of their contents constitute intellectual creations, and it grants new rights corresponding to the new forms of exploitation of works in the digital environment. WCT supplements the Berne Convention for the Protection of Literary and Artistic Works, adapting its provisions to the new requirements of the Information Society.

**Well-known Marks:** "Well-known marks" are marks that are considered to be well-known by the competent authority of the country where protection for the mark is sought.

**WIPO:** The World Intellectual Property Organization (WIPO) is an international organization dedicated to helping to ensure that the rights of creators and owners of intellectual property are protected worldwide and that inventors and authors are, thus, recognized and rewarded for their ingenuity. This international protection acts as a spur to human creativity, pushing forward the boundaries of science and technology and enriching the world of literature and the arts. By providing a stable environment for the marketing of intellectual property products, it also oils the wheels of international trade.

**WIPO's Arbitration and Mediation Center:** WIPO's Arbitration and Mediation Center helps to meet those needs for companies and individuals anywhere in the world. The Center maintains an extensive list of specialized mediators or arbitrators from over 100 countries, who conduct dispute resolution procedures according to rules made available by WIPO.

**WIPO Convention**

The Convention Establishing the World Intellectual Property Organization was signed at Stockholm on July 14, 1967, and entered into force in 1970. WIPO is responsible for the promotion of the protection of intellectual property throughout the world through co-operation among States, and for the administration of various multilateral treaties dealing with the legal and administrative aspects of intellectual property.

**WIPOnet:** Given the strategic importance of information technology in making the international intellectual property system more efficient, WIPO is carrying out a major project to develop and establish WIPOnet—a global intellectual property information network.

WIPOnet will promote international co-operation by facilitating the digital exchange of intellectual property information between intellectual property offices of its member States. It will also provide the means to undertake operations related to intellectual property rights management, in particular, those related to the international treaties, such as the Patent Co-operation Treaty (PCT). In doing so, WIPOnet will promote the progressive development and application of global standards and guidelines, and enhance the worldwide use of strategic information for more effective protection and enforcement of intellectual property rights. WIPOnet is of particular relevance to developing countries, as it would facilitate the electronic integration of developing countries in the international digital environment, thus narrowing the information gap that exists between the developed and developing countries. To further this objective, developing country intellectual property offices will be provided Internet connectivity and basic equipment under the WIPOnet project.

**WIPO-UNESCO Model Provisions for National Laws, 1982:** In 1982, Model Provisions for National Laws on the Protection of Expressions of Folklore against Illicit Exploitation and Other Prejudicial Actions (the Model Provisions, 1982) were adopted under the auspices of WIPO and UNESCO. They establish two main categories of acts against which TCEs are protected, namely 'illicit exploitation' and 'other prejudicial actions'. The Model Provisions have influenced the national laws of many countries. Several States and other stakeholders have suggested that the Model Provisions require improvement and updating.

**WIPO Worldwide Academy:** WIPO believes that the human capital of developing countries is key to their realizing the full benefits of the national and international intellectual property systems. The WIPO Worldwide Academy helps to develop those human resources, setting up modern and tailor-made training programmes for policy advisers, development managers, and other target groups.

**Working of a Patent:** When a patent is exploited and put to use commercially.

**WPPT:** The WIPO Performances and Phonograms Treaty (WPPT) was concluded in 1996. The Treaty deals with intellectual property rights of two kinds of beneficiaries: (i) Performers (actors, singers, musicians, etc.), and (ii) Producers of phonograms (the persons or legal entities who or which take the initiative and have the responsibility for the fixation of the sounds). They are dealt with in the same instrument because most of the rights granted by the Treaty to performers are rights connected with their fixed, purely aural performances (which are the subject matter of phonograms).

**'Wrongful Obtaining':** A term used when the invention is obtained (fully or partially) by someone by wrong or unfair means from the inventors/assignees.

**WTO:** The World Trade Organization (WTO) was established with the successful conclusion of the Uruguay Round GATT Multilateral Trade Negotiations on April 15, 1994. One of the negotiated agreements is the Agreement on Trade-related Aspects of Intellectual Property Rights (TRIPS), which came into force on January 1, 1995. The TRIPS Agreement brought with it a new era in the protection and enforcement of intellectual property rights, enhancing the value of WIPO's program of work. On

January 1st, 1996, an Agreement between the World Intellectual Property Organization and the World Trade Organization entered into force. It provides for co-operation concerning the implementation of the TRIPS Agreement, such as notification of laws and regulations and legal-technical assistance and technical co-operation in favour of developing countries.

# MAJOR SOURCES

This list includes all the major sources from which many ideas have been borrowed in the course of writing this book. The author wishes to record his deep gratitude and heartfelt thanks to all those, whose painstaking work has been referred to in this publication.


1. Agreement on Trade-related Aspects of Intellectual Property Rights, GATT, 1994.
2. *Creative Expression—An Introduction to Copyright and Related Rights for Small and Medium-sized Enterprises*, WIPO Publication No. 918(E) (World Intellectual Property Organization, Geneva), 2006.
3. *Current and Emerging Intellectual Property Issues for Business—A Roadmap for Business and Policy-makers,* (International Chamber of Commerce, Paris), 2006.
4. Encarta Reference Library (Microsoft Corporation, Seattle) 2003.
5. Friedman, Thomas L, *The World is Flat: A Brief History of the Twenty-first Century* (Farrar, Straus and Giroux, New York), 2005.
6. Ganguli, Prabuddha, *Gearing Up for Patents—The Indian Scenario*, (Universities Press (India) Limited, Hyderabad), 1998.
7. IDEA—The Intellectual Property Law Review.
8. Idris—Kamil, *Intellectual Property—A Power Tool for Economic Growth*, WIPO Publication No. 888.1 (World Intellectual Property Organization, Geneva), 2003.
9. *Integrating Intellectual Property Rights and Development Policy,* (Commission on Intellectual Property Rights, London), 2002.

10. *Intellectual Property for Business,* (Small and Medium-sized Enterprises Division, World Intellectual Property Organization, Geneva).

11. *Intellectual Property and Traditional Cultural Expressions/ Folklore*, WIPO Publication No. 913(E) (World Intellectual Property Organization, Geneva).

12. *Intellectual Property and Traditional Knowledge*, WIPO Publication No. 920(E) (World Intellectual Property Organization, Geneva).

13. *Intellectual Property on the Internet: A Survey of Issues,* (World Intellectual Property Organization, Geneva).

14. *Inventing the Future—An Introduction to Patents for Small and Medium-sized Enterprises*, WIPO Publication No. 917(E) (World Intellectual Property Organization, Geneva), 2005.

15. *Journal of Intellectual Property Rights.*

16. *Learn from the Past Create the Future: Inventions and Patents*, WIPO Publication No. 925(E) (World Intellectual Property Organization, Geneva), 2005.

17. *Looking Good—An Introduction to Industrial Designs for Small and Medium-sized Enterprises*, WIPO Publication No. 498(E) (World Intellectual Property Organization, Geneva), 2003.

18. Mashelkar, R.A. and Alikhan, Shahid, *Intellectual Property and Competitive Strategies in 21st Century* (Kluwer Law International), 2004.

19. *Making A Mark—An Introduction to Trademarks for Small and Medium-sized Enterprises*, WIPO Publication No. 900(E) (World Intellectual Property Organization, Geneva), 2003.

20. Sarkar, Pritiman, *Maharaja's New Clothes—A Patent Chronicle* (Publications & Information Directorate, CSIR, New Delhi), 1995.

21. Sople, Vinod V, *Managing Intellectual Property—The Strategic Imperative* (Prentice – Hall of India Private Limited, New Delhi) 2006.

22. Subbaram, N.R. and Thyagarajan, G., *Gearing up for the Efficient Management of Intellectual Property Rights in the 21st Century* (Committee on Science and Technology in Developing Countries, Chennai) 1998.
23. *WIPO Intellectual Property Handbook: Policy, Law and Use*, WIPO Publication No. 489 (World Intellectual Property Organization, Geneva).
24. *WIPO Magazine*.
25. *WIPO SMEs Newsletter*.
26. www.ideafinder.com/features/turningpoint/index.htm
27. www.learnntc.com/connect2learn/**creativity/creativity**.cfm

# INDEX

## C

## D

## E

## F

## N



## O



## P

## U